Temporality, Eternity, and Wisdom

Studies in Rhetoric/Communication
Thomas W. Benson, Series Editor

Temporality, Eternity, and Wisdom

The Rhetoric of Augustine's Confessions

Calvin L. Troup

University of South Carolina Press

© 1999 University of South Carolina

Published in Columbia, South Carolina, by the
University of South Carolina Press

Manufactured in the United States of America

03 02 01 00 99   5 4 3 2 1

    Library of Congress Cataloging-in-Publication Data

Troup, Calvin L., 1961–
  Temporality, eternity, and wisdom : the rhetoric of
Augustine's Confessions / Calvin L. Troup.
    p. cm.
    Includes bibliographical references and index.

    ISBN 1-57003-308-0 (hard : alk. paper)
    1. Augustine, Saint, Bishop of Hippo. Confessions. 2. Eternity.
3. Time. I. Title.
BR65.A62 T78 1999
270'.2'092—dc21   98-58083

To Amy Lynne

In the beginning was the Word, and the Word was with God, and the Word was God. He was in the beginning with God. All things were made through Him, and without Him nothing was made that was made. . . . And the Word became flesh and dwelt among us.

John 1:1–3, 14

Contents

Series Editor's Preface		ix
Preface		xi
Introduction		1
Chapter 1	The Integrity of Philosophy and Rhetoric	11
Chapter 2	Protocols for Reading the *Confessions*	36
Chapter 3	The Significance of Incarnational Wisdom in Time	82
Chapter 4	Rhetorical Interpretation	117
Chapter 5	The Wisdom of Incarnational Rhetoric	145
Notes		179
Bibliography		185
Index		193

Series Editor's Preface

Saint Aurelius Augustine (354–430 C.E.) was born and educated in North Africa. By 384 he was a professor of rhetoric in Milan. He converted to Christianity and returned to Africa, where in 395 he was appointed bishop of Hippo. Augustine's *De doctrina Christiana* is regarded as having adapted classical, pagan rhetoric to Christian uses, thus carrying them forward into the period that followed the collapse of the Roman empire. Every comprehensive account of the history of rhetorical theory includes a discussion of *De doctrina Christiana*.

Augustine's *Confessions* has been his most widely read book, the subject of centuries of admiration, interpretation, and intellectual controversy. In *Temporality, Eternity, and Wisdom,* Calvin Troup argues that any reader attempting to comprehend Augustine's *Confessions* should see it as a book that both preaches and performs Augustine's vision of a Christian rhetoric. Hence, this book is an effort to read the *Confessions* more fully as an autobiographical and religious text by seeing it as a rhetorical discourse and at the same time to contribute to our understanding of Augustine's rhetorical theory and practice. Troup argues that the *Confessions* has been relatively neglected as a source of rhetorical wisdom because rhetoricians have been drawn to the explicitly theoretical rhetoric expounded in *De doctrina Christiana*, because the *Confessions* seems to turn its back on rhetoric in its description of Augustine's resignation from his rhetorical "chair of lies" in Milan, and because of a century-long debate about the alleged Neoplatonism of the *Confessions*.

Troup reads the *Confessions* as enacting through its form a dynamic relation between speaker and listener that suggests a core insight of Augustinian theology and rhetoric—the Incarnation as "the eternal Word made flesh." With singular grace and good will, Troup illustrates Augustine's view that a rhetorical theory cannot properly exist apart from conscientious rhetorical practice. Troup's book is thus an important contribution both to the history of rhetorical theory and to the practice of rhetorical criticism. It is also a work that should attract the attention of any serious reader of the *Confessions*.

THOMAS W. BENSON

Preface

I initiated this project as a first step in a sustained rehabilitation of an important, but neglected, voice in the history of rhetoric and humane studies in the West. Aurelius Augustine, bishop of Hippo, lived on the cusp of the transition from what we have labeled "classical antiquity" to the Middle Ages. He has been included in most historical surveys of rhetoric, but ordinarily in a most cursory fashion.

One reason for treating Augustine this way may be that, despite the fact that his intellectual and spiritual pedigree are set in late antiquity, the general effects of his expansive body of writings have their greatest impact in the medieval period—a time thought until recently to be the darkest of times in Western intellectual history.

In the course of work on the project, I discovered a second, perhaps more probable, reason for the benign neglect of Augustine by rhetorical scholars. Although his life and work are permeated by rhetorical thought, principle, and practice, he nowhere treats rhetoric systematically, with the exception of the fourth book of *De doctrina Christiana*, which taken in isolation appears to be a mere Christianization of Cicero.

In short, Augustine's time and temper are both transitional and integrational, a rather poor match for the disciplines and divisions of late-twentieth-century academia. Augustine, through the *Confessions*, has taken me to places I wanted to go but could not get to alone. He has opened new insights into how rhetoric intersects with history, philosophy, society, and faith, and has presented a premodern paradigm for rhetoric as *the* intersection and integrator that enables him to negotiate our interdisciplinary boundaries so deftly.

If interdisciplinary study is not merely postmodernist fashion, but rather has become a necessity for negotiating the realities of postmodern life, I trust that Augustine might become as essential a guide to the reader of this book as he has proved to be for me, though perhaps in different ways. "For what harm comes to me . . . if I think differently than another thinks as to what he who wrote these words thought?"

A quiet conspiracy of providences initiated this project and has brought it to fruition. Many people have greatly aided my work. Truly, none but me are responsible for its faults, but many have contributed to whatever its merits may be. Carl Vaught's insight, sharp critical eye, and encouragement have proved invaluable combined with his thoroughgoing knowledge of Augustine and the *Confessions*. I am deeply grateful to Tom Benson, upon whose rhetorical and editorial sensibilities I have depended. I appreciate the discussion, commentary, and support from Stephen Browne, Herman Cohen, and Thomas Beebee, who have all advanced the project. Special thanks are also due to Greg Books, John and Colleen DeLong, Rosa Eberly, Janie Fritz, Enrico Pucci, Gordon Keddie, and David Spear, whose discussions, readings, thoughts, and patience have been a constant source of encouragement. My deepest gratitude belongs to Amy, my wife, and my daughters—Rebekah, Laura, Miriam, and Hannah—who have persevered with charity and brought me joy throughout the project.

Temporality, Eternity, and Wisdom

Introduction

How could the *Confessions* possibly promote rhetoric? In his account of resigning the chair of rhetoric in Milan, Augustine plainly states that he taught from a "chair of lies" [cathedra mendacii] and counted his professorship as a bondage from which he craved release (9.2.4, 9.4.7). Based on such statements in the narrative, the conventional wisdom about Augustine and rhetoric has been that he converts from rhetoric to Christianity and in the process leaves rhetoric qua rhetoric, adopting a philosophy and theology hostile to it (Hagendahl 556–57; Murphy, "Christianization," 26).

Common assent to Augustine's postconversion dexterity with language merely reinforces the image of an eloquent philosopher-theologian nimbly applying a style he rejects in principle but continues to practice. Even recent book-length treatments of the *Confessions* by a rhetorician and a literary critic take this stance.[1] Beyond the apparent abdication of rhetoric by Augustine himself in the *Confessions,* the renaissance of scholarly attention to the book in the past hundred years has neglected a positive, conscious role for rhetoric in the work.[2]

Yet I contend that the *Confessions* does promote rhetoric—directly, positively, and pervasively—contrary to a narrowly defined debate on the degree and character of Neoplatonic influence in the text that has dominated critical commentary.[3] This debate effectively disregards the symbolic action within the *Confessions*—its character as a dynamic discourse in which a speaker and listener can interact.

Instead, the vying Neoplatonic interpretations dissect the text, excising useful portions as representative of the whole. But such interpretations of the *Confessions* produce unsatisfactory readings. In one sense, they are not "readings" of the text at all. They analyze excerpts and dispense with the discourse as a whole, particularly portions that conflict with their hypotheses. Such interpretations explain away as much of the text as they explain; and as a consequence, they have difficulty accounting for the enduring ability of the text to engage contemporary readers with its richness, depth, and complexity.

My reading of the *Confessions* attempts to concentrate on its symbolic action—how the text works to engage people. Through the process, I argue that rhetoric is promoted in conjunction with Augustine's explicit commitment to the power of the Incarnation. I recognize that this reading cuts directly across the grain of the scholarly interpretive tradition surrounding the *Confessions*. It does so with respect to not only the positive role of rhetoric in Augustine's enterprise, but also the issue of the Incarnation.

Dynamics of the Incarnation in the Text

For Augustine, the Incarnation is the embodied Logos—the eternal Word made flesh (7.9.14). As this speaking Word functions theologically in prophetic fulfillment, so it resonates rhetorically, meeting and exceeding the standard of embodied speech required for Cicero's ideal orator (*De oratore*, 1.28). In the first chapter of the first book, Augustine announces that the process by which he received the faith—a faith that energizes these confessions and his life's work as a bishop—came to him "by the incarnation of your Son and through the ministry of your preacher" [per humanitatem filii tui, per ministerium praedicatoris tui] (1.1.1). The relation between incarnation and rhetoric, the temporal lifeblood of the proclamation of God's Word through preaching, are established from the start.

The Incarnation permeates the entire *Confessions*, inhabiting the narrative account as an obstacle to Augustine's progress in his philosophical travels with Cicero, the Manichaeans, the Skeptics, and the Platonists (Mallard 43–44, 112–15). Observing the placement of some of the explicit references to the Incarnation suggests the dynamic role it plays through the course of the text.

As he reflects on the influence of Cicero, Augustine praises his critiques of certain Greek philosophers and reports his proximity to Colossians 2:9, which he quotes in reference to Christ: "For in him dwells all the fulness of the Godhead corporeally" [quia in ipso inhabitat omnis plenitudo divinitatis corporaliter] (3.4.8). During a meditation upon his life as a Manichaean, Augustine contrasts his wanderings with the clear direction of the incarnate Word, who emerged in the flesh through "the virgin's womb" [virginalem uterum] and "ran forth and cried out by words and deeds" [sed cucurrit clamans dictis, factis] (4.12.19).

The Incarnation stands as the most pronounced obstacle to the Platonists—most pronounced because it was their *singular* problem as perceived by Augustine at the time. It points out for him the Platonists' one glaring inadequacy: they denied the actual embodiment of the Logos. Their Word was never made flesh (7.9.13–14). Augustine concludes his critique of the books of the Platonists by asserting both the deity of the Logos and "the Word made flesh."

By attributing full deity to Jesus, Augustine contradicts the Neoplatonists' view of Christ as great but a mere man (7.18.24). Yet he leaves little room for ambiguity about the full humanity of the Incarnation, professing that "he ate and drank, slept, walked about, was joyful, grew sad, and preached" [quia manducavit et bibit, dormivit, ambulavit, exhilaratus est, contristatus est, sermocinatus est] and notes later in the same passage, "I acknowledged that in Christ there was a complete man: not merely a man's body, nor an animating principle in the body but without a mind, but a true man" [totum hominem in Christo agnoscebam: non corpus tantum hominis aut cum corpore sine mente animum, sed ipsum hominem] (7.19.25).

From Augustine's account of his "putting on" the incarnate Christ at conversion, the Incarnation informs his narrative on memory, time, and eternity, and interpretation that constitutes the second half of the work (8.12.29). Augustine confirms that he recognized in the Incarnation a divine and embodied mediator, one who had died "a true death in the flesh" [vera morte carnis mortuus] (9.4.9). But the rhetorical significance of the Incarnation is found most pointedly in the union of embodiment with speech and other signifying acts.

The incarnation precedes, intercedes, and concludes the tenth book's meditation on memory and the eleventh book's meditation on time and eternity (10.4.6, 10.42.67–43.69, 11.8.10, 11.29.39). Using the example of book 10, Augustine first proclaims Christ's signifying in the flesh by both "word and deed" as necessary for belief, the prerequisite for his inquiry (10.4.6). Having discussed epistemology as a dialogue between the Word signifying externally and internally, he concludes the book by attacking the deceitful image of disembodiment, an enticement presented by fallen angels appealing to human pride (10.42.67–68). The incarnation shatters this deceit of disembodiment, a desire characteristic of the Neoplatonism of Augustine's day:

> We could think that your Word is far from union with men, and we could despair of ourselves, unless he had been "made flesh and dwelt amongst us." (10.43.69)
>
> potuimus putare verbum tuum remotum esse a coniunctione hominis et desperare de nobis, nisi caro fieret et habitaret in nobis. (10.43.69)

How the Incarnation and rhetoric interact—the embodied Word as speaking in the flesh to humanity—emerges through the story of Augustine's life and should enrich our understanding of both. To understand this relationship we must recognize the distinction between the dominant school of rhetoric in Augustine's day—the Second Sophistic—and a broader conception of rhetoric.

Redeeming Rhetoric from the Second Sophistic

The Second Sophistic rewarded delivery, style, and ornamentation with little or no attention to substance. It dominated fourth-century Roman schools of rhetoric, which were *the* system of higher education and the last step in preparation for imperial service. Although students read Cicero and Quintilian, Roman rhetoric had long since abandoned a significant deliberative or forensic role. In practice, rhetoric had become a form of public entertainment and high civic culture for the empire. The ethical and inventional elements in the rhetorics of republican Rome and its Greek predecessors had disintegrated.[4]

Therefore, when Augustine gives up his "chair of lies," he means nothing more than that he abandons the Second Sophistic, for to him rhetoric and the Second Sophistic are synonymous. He does not accept a chair of theology in its place. Augustine's move is from the "chair of lies" to a "chair of truth," in which rhetoric still plays a crucial role, a redeemed and esteemed role, and a role which is taught explicitly and implicitly. That is, Augustine's bishopric was rhetorical *and* theological *and* philosophical. As W. R. Johnson says,

> It is no wonder that we find philosophy and theology in him even as we find rhetoric and politics in him. He is a philosopher and a journalist, a theologian and a bureaucrat, more than these, none of these, and all of these because he had been gathered into the unity for which he prayed. (229)

Implications of the Incarnation for Rhetoric

The Word incarnate is the unity Augustine seeks in the *Confessions*. It is no accident that he initiates the text by presenting the Incarnation and preaching as the grand conspiracy to produce belief—a decidedly rhetorical goal. Temporal discourse plays a crucial role in the production of belief and understanding. In other words, the process that dominates Augustine's experience and practice is rhetorical, and entirely consistent with the Incarnation. Both represent the integration of form and substance in embodied speech.

Unlike the Second Sophistic, which divorced rhetoric and philosophy, the *Confessions* presents them as united. It marries a penchant for practical viability with theoretical depth. On its surface the text presents scores of examples of rhetorical structure. For instance, the account of the "pear-stealing episode" in book 2 follows a conventional, deftly executed rhetorical pattern. Augustine also plumbs the depths of the inner workings of signs, beginning in his early discussion of the acquisition of language and reaching fruition in various meditations on the semiotic appeal of the Incarnation.

Through the Incarnation, Christ speaks simultaneously in word and deed, to senses and soul, enacting the semiotic combination necessary to energize Augustine's conversion to Christianity and transition to the "chair of truth." From its semiotic soundness, the Incarnation's rhetorical resonance comes forth from Augustine's conversion to guide him through the postconversion narrative and meditations. Therefore, Augustine's despair at finding no starting point to begin his quest for Wisdom is averted (*avertitur*) by the Word incarnate, he is converted (*convertitur*), and embraces the incarnate Word.

These turnings point to the completion of Augustine's definitive and conscious transition from the Neoplatonists to a community of distinctive Christian orthodoxy (Mallard 112, 130–31; D. O'Meara, *Neoplatonism,* 41; Starnes, *Conversion,* 101). Augustine no longer reacts against the Second Sophistic. The Incarnation enables him to advance to a positive rhetorical stance because it embodies Wisdom—a vision integrating rhetoric, philosophy, and moral purity Augustine appropriates from Cicero's *Hortensius* and seeks through his early adult life. He can now articulate a rhetoric, redeemed in conception and practice, that is essential to negotiating temporal life.

Through the incarnate Word, God inhabits the very temporal frame He created and produces belief in people through acts of human significance. Rhetoric thereby becomes a legitimate linchpin within the Christian orthodoxy of the *Confessions.* Augustine insists on a self-consciously performative and public pursuit of Wisdom that contemplation or mysticism alone can never achieve.

I am arguing that the performative dimension inherent in Augustine's *Confessions* is consciously rhetorical: a performance intended to produce belief modeled on the inherent integrity of the Incarnation. Like the incarnate Word, the preacher must not only speak the words of Scripture but embody the words spoken (13.21.30–31). The rhetorical embodiment in time drives the question that takes Augustine to the Garden in Milan: Where can I live life with integrity in time?

Augustine finds the other options he engages and examines to be finally unlivable. But the incarnate Word integrates time and eternity, local and universal, contingency and truth as Logos—the embodied Word both spoken and acted from eternity in time. It is this Logos that serves as the functional prerequisite for Augustine's pursuit of his vital question. Only the Incarnation provides an affirmative answer.

On Interpreting the Confessions

Here we arrive at a pivotal point for interpreting the *Confessions.* Regarding rhetoric, philosophy, and interpretation, the Incarnation contradicts

Neoplatonism. Just as the Neoplatonists of Augustine's day denied the Incarnation, today's dominant critical debate about the degree of Neoplatonic influence in the *Confessions* discounts the Incarnation as an issue in interpreting the text. Therefore, textual criticism within the terms of the debate produces inadequate readings, for they cannot account for the Incarnation or its grounded and time-bound rhetorical implications.

Readings that presume Neoplatonic ascendancy in the text before they engage it *must* discount the Incarnation, because any serious attempt to account for the embodied Logos as significant reveals their presumption and explodes the interpretation. The Neoplatonic interpretive paradigm, once imposed upon the *Confessions,* cannot allow the Incarnation to disrupt the tendency of that paradigm to produce readings of the text that promote the Neoplatonic impulse to escape the material world in pursuit of a purely intellectual, disembodied, and transcendent union with "the One."

The Neoplatonic impulse is profoundly anti-Incarnational and decidedly antirhetorical. It eschews the human body and the material world as the cause of evil; despises society, community, and human relations; and covets departure from time and space into a transcendent eternity. The incarnational impulse, by contrast, invests the human being—soul *and body*—with eternal significance in the temporal, social, and communal dimensions of experience.

In the Incarnation, Augustine encounters an intimate otherness and dynamic immutability that enacts what emerges through the *Confessions* as a paradigm with a pronounced rhetorical cast. The embodied Word satisfies Augustine's keen desire for the practical integration of rhetoric, philosophy, and semiotics and enables him to live within the extreme tensions—philosophical, social, spiritual, and practical—implicit in the Incarnation. His continuing questions and reflections on these tensions, tensions which many of us experience ourselves, makes the *Confessions* perennially engaging and worthy of our consideration.

It is my purpose to attend to how Augustine invites us to work through these questions, the assumptions about language that lead him to the pursuit of Wisdom, and where that pursuit takes us if we join him. The *Confessions* itself appeals to us to adopt and participate in its worldview. It is a public document, produced to do work in the world. The text goes beyond being a devotional meditation between Augustine and God, or an exercise in speculative philosophy and theology, although these are obvious elements.

Clearly, the argument I present in this inquiry into the *Confessions* does not conform to most critical commentary. For instance, one of the most renowned current scholars in the debate about the influence of Neoplatonism on Augustine, Robert J. O'Connell, dismisses the significance of the Incarnation in the *Confessions* (*Odyssey,* 24). Although most scholars are not so explicit, the Incarnation is rarely if ever made central in the interpretation of the *Confessions* and is often ignored entirely.

My argument constitutes a refusal to adopt the terms of the debate over the alleged influence of Neoplatonism. Instead, I attempt to show how a rhetorical approach to the text can enrich our engagement with Augustine's most widely read work and can rehabilitate our reception of a text that has recently started to resonate with a wider contemporary audience.

I am not alone in my desire to circumvent the dominant scholarly debate on the *Confessions* and pursue questions that begin with the text in its context allied to rhetoric. A few scholars working within Augustinian studies have challenged both the terms and the assumptions about Augustine and Neoplatonism that frame that debate (Starnes, *Conversion*, 284–85; O'Donnell, *Augustine*, 45–47, 92–96; Hartle 232). Meanwhile, scholars beyond the traditional bounds of Augustinian studies have inquired into Augustine from the perspective of semiotics, literary criticism, and rhetoric.

These studies consider Augustine's texts at close range to examine his meditations on and use of language. In the process, they have produced scholarship that contradicts conventional assumptions about his thought and practice, including groundbreaking semiotic thought and claims that Augustine attempts to sanctify rather than mortify rhetoric (Eco 33; Sutherland 142–45, 152). Yet most of these inquiries into Augustine's fascination with the function of discourse in human experience have focused on *De doctrina Christiana* and *De magistro*; few have addressed the *Confessions*.

A Strategy for Interpretation

My own inquiry begins from the position proposed by Colin Starnes, who suggests that "we must turn back to the *Confessions* to see whether the text itself—in which such startling and complete oppositions are found—does not also provide the principle in terms of which they may also be reconciled" (*Conversion*, 285). I choose this course as a strategy for circumventing the stagnant, polarized critical history and debate without ignoring it altogether. We need to focus on the *Confessions*, not the debate surrounding it. Nevertheless, we enter an existing dialogue and hope to make contributions that will enliven it and broaden its scope.

Returning to the text and granting it priority is a considered strategy of rhetorical scholarship chosen specifically for such a case as the *Confessions*. As Steven Mailloux has stated, in cases where the debate has constructed mutually exclusive critical positions, returning to the text and producing a rhetorical history effectively shows "that the traditional solutions to the problem are not—as the critical history would have it—mutually exclusive" (Mailloux 97).

I proceed on the following assumptions: (1) The text is the primary site for interpretive activity—that is, the text as a whole. The holistic nature of this critical stance specifically resists two recurrent problems in traditional interpretations of the *Confessions:* reading portions of the text in isolation from the whole, and interpreting the text in isolation from the immediate political, social, and intellectual conditions in which Augustine composed it. (2) The historical and biographical context are prerequisite to engaging the text on its own terms. In the case of the *Confessions,* the critical tradition has frequently ignored the everyday context of Augustine's life, resulting in anachronistic interpretations that lack textual support and sometimes contradict the text itself. (3) Upon engagement, the text—taken as a whole—discloses cues to guide its interpretation through the rhetorical transaction with the listener or reader.

My understanding of what occurs in rhetorical transactions has been shaped by Mikhail Bakhtin, especially where Bakhtin argues that earlier utterances always precede human communication, and that we communicate with the expectation that our messages will provoke responses:

> Any understanding of live speech, a live utterance, is inherently responsive, although the degree of this activity varies extremely. Any understanding is imbued with response and necessarily elicits it in one form or another: the listener becomes the speaker. . . . Sooner or later what is heard and actively understood will find its response in the subsequent speech or behavior of the listener. (*Speech,* 69)

Bakhtin's key term *utterance* is determined by oral communication. Like the speech-act theorist, and unlike the structuralist, he makes a careful distinction between mere linguistic units (words, phrases, and sentences) and units of speech communication (utterances). An utterance is defined by the change of speaking subjects, not by grammatical conventions (*Speech,* 71ff). By hearing an utterance as always being a part of a larger dialogue, the *Confessions* becomes an integral site of textual, intertextual, contextual, and extratextual discourses:

> The living utterance, having taken meaning and shape at a particular historical moment in a socially specific environment, cannot fail to brush up against thousands of living dialogic threads, woven by socio-ideological consciousness around the given object of an utterance; it cannot fail to become an active participant in social dialogue. After all, the utterance arises out of this dialogue as a continuation of it and as a rejoinder to it—it does not approach the object from the sidelines. (*Dialogic,* 276–77)

Utterance makes Bakhtin's approach particularly useful in this case, since his project encourages critics to "hear" and "see" written discourse as living, situated, human speech. Bakhtin and Walter Ong both make the point that *Augustine* operated in the midst of a culture that, although literate, was still dominated by orality (Ong 36; *Dialogic,* 135).[5]

Through the course of the study that follows, I first consider the changing role of rhetoric in the *Confessions.* Augustine is well schooled in the Roman rhetoric of the Second Sophistic. Through his experience as student and professor of rhetoric, he establishes an enduring association with Marcus Tullius Cicero, whose work he appropriates to establish his own views on the proper relation between rhetoric and philosophy. The first chapter concludes by framing Augustine's general views about the relation between rhetoric and philosophy at the time of the composition of the *Confessions.*

The second chapter offers contemporary readers a primer for engaging the *Confessions.* It attempts a provisional recreation of the historical situation and social conditions in which Augustine produced the text. The *Confessions* is placed in a larger discursive context to which Augustine responds, highlighting issues of orality and literacy in his age as crucial for contemporary readers. Recognition of explicit and implicit cues to readers are contingent on understanding discursive conventions, both in the larger culture and within Augustine's ecclesiastical community. These factors emerge through a discussion of Augustine's preconversion experience and conversion to Christianity—covering the narrative of books 1–9.

Augustine's encounter with the incarnate Word initiates his pursuit of wisdom, a pursuit first envisioned while reading Cicero's *Hortensius.* Chapter 3 engages Augustine's development of the incarnate Word as pervasive, making discourse integral to his discussion of memory and epistemology in book 10 and to his discussion of eternity, creation, and time in book 11. The dominance of discourse prompts us to examine Augustine's views about semiotics, Truth, and rhetoric in the *Confessions* from this vantage point.

Ordinarily, book 12 is labeled an "exegetical" book. Chapter 4 addresses Augustine's extended discussion of the interpretive issues that arise here, interwoven with his discussion of the first few verses of the first chapter of Genesis. Manifestations of his semiotic and rhetorical sensibilities become evident as he outlines his commitments to critical practice, which he finally enacts in book 13. Augustine directs this final book—his example of interpretive practice—to a public audience as an exhortation addressed to their specific historical situation.

From Augustine's applied semiotic and rhetorical commitments to his grounded, rhetorical approach to interpretive practice, chapter 5 juxtaposes the *Confessions* with some postmodern assumptions about subjectivity, temporality, relativism, and truth. Augustine corresponds in provocative ways with contemporary dialogue on these issues—ways that have motivated this inquiry as a means to contribute to our own discussions as well as our knowledge of Augustine.

I do not presume to provide an exhaustive account of the *Confessions*. To do so would ignore its depth, the richness of its discourse, and the limitations of the particular interpreter and interpretation in general. Furthermore, much surpassing scholarship on the *Confessions* precedes and has contributed to this comparatively meager offering, and much good work will doubtless be forthcoming. My prime ambition in this inquiry is to provide a charitable reading of the *Confessions* that might stimulate others to engage Augustine's text on its own terms, not only on its surface but also in its depths.

Augustine has long been recognized as a transitional historical figure between the ancient and the modern worlds. Beneath this current of recognition lies an unspoken assumption that the *Confessions* continues to be relevant. I agree that Augustine should be valued today, if for only one theme woven throughout the *Confessions:* his belief that the pursuit of authentic wisdom can occur only through the responsible integration of philosophy and rhetoric conditioned by humility, self-control, and charity. In one way this is a timeless theme; in another, it is radically temporal. Augustine invites us to live in this tension between time and eternity by embracing wisdom—the application of the Incarnation in our own present.

Chapter 1

The Integrity of Philosophy and Rhetoric

Augustine attacks rhetoric in the *Confessions,* unleashing a scathing critique on his former profession. The train of comments that runs from book 1 through book 9 "breathes a deep-seated hostility" and condemns rhetoric outright, according to Hagendahl, who calls the *Confessions* a "manifesto of fanatical religiosity" (715). Fanatical or not, through the words of the manifesto Augustine effectively dismantles the entire rhetorical system of the Late Roman Empire.

It was a system he knew as a student, teacher, and master (Murphy, "Christianization," 26). Augustine's first salvo against rhetoric comes in the account of his early life in the schools of Roman North Africa. He asserts that from the first his studies were calculated to enable him to "succeed in this world and excel in those arts of speech which would serve to bring honor among men and to gain deceitful riches" [ut in hoc saeculo florerem, et excellerem linguosis artibus, ad honorem hominum et falsas divitias famulantibus] (1.9.14). This initial statement charges rhetoric with the ignoble end of pursuing public praise for its own sake and promoting deceit as a means to that end. Rhetoric ignores substance, concerning itself with form alone. It operates from a posture that is oblivious to justice, morality, or truth. These three points remain the coordinates for Augustine's assault on rhetoric throughout the *Confessions.*

Rhetoric does not dominate the narrative, but it surfaces repeatedly as the touchstone of his preconversion education and professional career. Evidently, he was fully engaged as a student in what he now—as bishop of Hippo—regards critically.

> Moreover, my studies, which were called honorable, were directed to the practice of law, so that I might excel at it and become so much the more distinguished because so much the more crafty. So great is the blindness of men, who even glory in their blindness! I was already the leading student in the school of rhetoric, and in my pride I rejoiced and I was swollen up with vanity. (3.3.6)

> Habebant et illa studia, quae honesta vocabantur, ductum suum intuentem fora litigiosa, ut excellerem in eis, hoc laudabilior, quo fraudulentior. tanta est caecitas hominum de caecitate etiam gloriantium. et maior iam eram in schola rhetoris et gaudebam superbe et tumebam typho. (3.3.6)

As Augustine presents his transition from student of rhetoric to his career as a teacher of rhetoric he restates his objections more forcefully, implicating himself as a propagator of rhetoric.

> In those years I taught the art of rhetoric, and being vanquished by greed, I sold a skill at speech designed for victories in court. I preferred, as you, Lord, know, to have good students—such, that is, as are called good—and without deceit I taught them to be deceitful, not so that they would work against the life of an innocent man, but sometimes in behalf of a guilty client. From afar, O God, you saw me falling down on slippery ground, and you saw my faith shining amid such smoke, and this faith I who was their comrade showed forth in my teaching to men who loved vanity and sought for lies. (4.2.2)

> Docebam in illis annis artem rhetoricam, et victoriosam loquacitatem victus cupiditate vendebam. malebam tamen, domine, tu scis, bonos habere discipulos, sicut appellantur boni, et eos sine dolo docebam dolos, non quibus contra caput innocentis agerent, sed aliquando pro capite nocentis. et, deus, vidisti de longinquo lapsantem in lubrico, et in multo fumo scintillantem fidem meam, quam exhibebam in illo magisterio diligentibus vanitatem et quaerentibus mendacium, socius eorum. (4.2.2)

Although he may seem to be harder on rhetoric than on himself in this case, Augustine criticizes his own pursuit of rhetoric for "damnable and inflated purposes" [fine damnabili et ventoso per gaudia vanitatis humanae], his own lie-filled oration for the Emperor, and his teaching from a "chair of lies" [cathedra mendacii] (3.4.7, 6.6.9, 9.2.4). He also acknowledges that when he first listens to Ambrose preach, he attempts to judge the bishop's eloquence without reference to the content of the message (5.13.23–24). Including his own actions, Augustine castigates rhetoric as a system by which men seek personal fame and fortune through public eloquence, employing whatever means necessary—including skillful deceit (1.9, 1.14.26, 4.2.2, 9.2.2, 9.12.32). This kind of rhetoric Augustine holds in contempt: it is the rhetoric of the lie.

In the light of the *Confessions*, James J. Murphy's claim that Augustine was the major proponent of rhetoric responsible for its preservation in medieval times appears to be far-fetched (*Rhetoric*, 56–57). But Murphy is not alone in his claim. George F. Riley says that "Rhetoric after Augustine remained respectable for fourteen centuries" (112). This paradox demands a closer examination of the rhetoric Augustine condemns.

Rhetoric of the Second Sophistic

Rhetoric was *the* system of education in the Roman Empire (G. Riley 45–46). As noted by Augustine, rhetorical studies were "directed to the practice of law." Rhetoric trained young men for imperial service, whether in the courts or government offices of various sorts (Clarke 143). Orators often had status and salaries commensurate with the most popular entertainers:

> it was announced that a rhetorician of repute was to deliver a panegyric or some other discourse in the theatre, intense excitement was caused, and eager crowds filled the benches; after a speech which repels the modern mind by its turgid flattery and strained employment of an outworn mythology he would be escorted to his home in triumph. (McCabe 18)

Since before Cicero, rhetoric was the pinnacle of Roman education, and the entire system channeled promising students in that direction (Brown, *Augustine*, 36). By the fourth century, when Augustine was in the system, Rome had developed a burdensome bureaucracy, much of which would be fed by a stream of talent from the schools of rhetoric: "It had its planned economy, its state factories, compulsory syndicalism, hereditary social classes, crushing taxation, a ruthless judicial system, and of course . . . a secret police" (Marrou 7).

Augustine ascended through Carthage—the best school of rhetoric in all of Roman North Africa—and then taught for a short time in his hometown of Thagaste. He returned to Carthage as an instructor before moving on to Rome, and finally to the chair of rhetoric in the imperial capital of Milan (Clarke 142, 145). He followed what might be considered the perfect "career path" into government service, which was ultimately interrupted by his conversion (Brown, *Augustine*, 69–72; Clarke 142). For the son of a poor North African, who had to depend on a patron to pay much of his way through school, rhetoric was perhaps the only way out of brutal labor and poverty (Marrou 12; Brown, *Augustine*, 21; G. Riley 54).

The form of rhetoric taught in the Roman schools of rhetoric, and the rhetoric described by Augustine in the *Confessions,* is called the Second Sophistic. While admitting that the practitioners of the Second Sophistic sometimes focused only upon "style, ornament, and the cleverness of the orator," George A. Kennedy elegantly defends the Second Sophistic as being far from the degenerate rhetoric represented by Augustine (38–40).[1]

Kennedy points to just the ability to raise people like Augustine from modest circumstances to productive roles within Roman society as a great attribute of the Second Sophistic. He tends to focus, however, on the most famous and exemplary Sophists—the type of rhetorician Augustine had become—and only on the external civil effect of sophistic. Augustine, on the other hand, saw the system's effect on himself and his numerous friends, acquaintances, and students who had likewise been trained in it.

Trained indeed. For the rhetorical schools of fourth-century Rome had become standardized and tied to a narrow canon of acceptable texts and practices. As Charles Sears Baldwin notes, "Greco-Roman rhetoric was as pervasive as Roman law and almost as constant," and rhetoric and sophistic were synonymous at the time (9). Critics of the Second Sophistic have cited the narrowness of sophistic training as stultifying to the intellect and moral sensibilities of Roman students.

Of greatest account in this regard was the sophistic practice of declamation, which called on students to speak to either side of a given case according to the circumstances, which M. L. Clarke claims, "could hardly fail to blur the distinction between true and false" (161). What resulted was the sophistical emphasis on delivery and pleasing use of language to the exclusion of substantial meaning (Keenan 74). Clarke explains:

> From an early age the Roman was taught to find the materials for his compositions and practice speeches according to certain rules. He was taught the topics to be drawn upon and the arguments to be used. He was not taught to think for himself; all his material was drawn from outside himself, from the theme with which he was presented and from the traditional topics of the schools. Rhetoric would thus encourage a certain conventionality of thought. (160)

Clarke concludes that the intellectual regimen of the schools of rhetoric destroyed curiosity (160). One indication that curiosity and creative thought were compromised is the fact that the canons of rhetoric fell into disuse after Quintilian, effectively eliminating the creativity demanded by rhetorical invention (Baldwin 39). The result was a rhetoric in which "the speech was a work of art in itself. . . . Whether the words made sense or nonsense, were true or false, was indifferent" (Clarke 162).

Yet this indifference was a cultured indifference, and it may have been less an apathy toward truth in a given case than a certain cultural agnosticism about whether truth existed at all. A Roman governor, having been trained in sophistic rhetoric, might well ask "What is truth?" The question could be posed, but never naively, and the inquisitor might well scorn any response. As McCabe notes, "The Romans had the disadvantage of approaching the higher problems only after a prolonged Greek effort seemed to have proved their insolubility. It was a sceptic who brought philosophy to Rome" (18).

In fact, Romans probably were as skeptical about philosophy in general as they were of truth; the Romans had long since dichotomized rhetoric and philosophy, exalting the former and virtually ignoring the latter (Brown, *Augustine,* 36; Hagendahl 588). Teachers of rhetoric might dabble in philosophy occasionally or introduce students to bits and pieces of philosophical discourse when it was convenient, but philosophy was no part of the standard rhetorical training (McCabe 54–55). Whereas in later ages the liberal arts, including philosophy, might be opposed to science, in the Roman world philosophy played the counterpart to the liberal arts, and few attempted to traverse the distance between the two (Marrou 17–18).

Accentuating the divide, rhetoric was a distinctly public and civil pursuit, whereas philosophy was a private issue. Philosophy and religion were understood to be related integrally at the time. Peter Brown says in his biography of Augustine that for centuries,

> The idea of philosophy had been surrounded with a religious aura. It involved far more than an intellectual discipline. It was a love of "Wisdom." "Wisdom" would console and purify its devotees; it demanded, in return, self-sacrifice and moral readjustment. (40)

Cicero's *Hortensius* is exemplary in this regard. This treatise, which Augustine regarded as his first encounter with philosophy and the catalyst to his own pursuit of wisdom, inveighs against the desires of the flesh as a hindrance to true happiness (*Confessions,* 3.4; Hagendahl 496). James Shiel uses Augustine as an example of how thoroughly integrated religion and philosophy were at the time:

> An indication of the religious motive permeating Greek philosophy is the fact that right at the end of antiquity it was an "exhortation to the philosophic life," written by Cicero in imitation of a previous one by Aristotle, the *Protreptikos,* which first turned Saint Augustine's thought towards Christianity. (23)

It may seem somewhat ironic that Cicero, the greatest of all Roman orators, might stimulate Augustine to reject rhetoric and embrace philosophy. But this is exactly what happened. The way in which it happened will resolve the irony—clarifying what Augustine rejects when he abandons rhetoric and what he embraces when he pursues philosophy.

Rejecting the Second Sophistic

When Augustine abandons rhetoric in the *Confessions*, he abandons something that is at once greater than and less than we might assume. On the one hand, by rejecting rhetoric in the Late Roman context, Augustine forsakes the Roman educational establishment in its entirety. He jettisons a central institution of Roman society and a linchpin of Roman culture. On the other hand, his abandonment of rhetoric viewed in terms of the history of rhetoric and philosophy merely means dispensing with one particular conception. It is not necessarily the comprehensive attack on everything educational and intellectual that Hagendahl perceived.

What Augustine *does* reject, forsake, abandon, and condemn is the rhetoric of the Second Sophistic (G. Riley 111; Murphy, "Christianization," 28–29). Murphy ably proposes that Augustine's rejection of the Second Sophistic does not demand the rejection of *all* rhetorical theory:

> No student of rhetorical history would deny that the period from the death of Cicero to the fall of Rome was marked by rhetorical excesses. Yet it should not be overlooked that the Second Sophistic was an oratorical, not a theoretical phenomenon. That is, the rhetoric itself—the theory of speaking—remained unchanged from the days of Cicero and Cato the Younger. It was only the speaking that changed. (*Rhetoric*, 25)

Murphy's point is crucial to understanding what Augustine rejects, and what he retains, from his experience as a student and teacher of rhetoric and as an accomplished Sophist in fourth-century Rome. He rejects the rhetoric of the lie—the Second Sophistic. He retains Cicero, the theoretical basis from which he transforms and promotes rhetoric once again.

Cicero, Rhetoric, and Philosophy

Cicero provides stimulation, continuity, and language that aid Augustine's transition from the Second Sophistic to the pursuit of wisdom. The significance of Cicero rests not in the details of his rhetorical theory, but in the fundamentals of his thought for Augustine. Two closely related elements make Cicero's work crucial for Augustine: (1) the integration of philosophy and rhetoric in the education of orators, and (2) philosophical eclecticism.

The radical nature of Cicero's well-known insistence that the ideal orator be trained in rhetoric *and* philosophy does not appear radical apart from the Roman dichotomy between philosophy and the liberal arts. Cicero's works stand against the prevailing practice of the fourth-century Roman schools, which recognized philosophy as nothing more than an auxiliary distraction from the serious business of education. Nevertheless, Cicero's works were cherished as an important part of the Roman rhetorical curriculum, despite the fact that they were never implemented and explicitly contradicted the institutional practice of the day (Murphy, "Christianization," 25).

Cicero's challenge to the polarization of philosophy and rhetoric appears prominently in each of his three most commonly used texts on rhetoric: *De inventione* (1.1.1), *De oratore* (1.4.20–22), *Orator* (3.13–15). In the first he calls for the integration of wisdom and eloquence; in the second and third he calls for the training of the ideal orator in eloquence and philosophy, understood in these cases to be a broad knowledge of all the liberal arts (Clarke 55; DiLorenzo 259). The orator's comprehensive knowledge is actualized in the speech such that the style and substance, the wisdom and the utterance, cannot be separated without doing violence to both and destroying the message (DiLorenzo 258; Baldwin 60).

The second element, eclecticism, is that characteristic of Cicero's philosophy by which scholars can claim him as a Stoic, Sophist, Platonist, Skeptic, or another sort of philosopher. For example, Cicero's approach to philosophy allows William Sattler to write an article, "Some Platonic Influences in the Rhetorical Works of Cicero," to follow through on his thesis showing Platonic influence, but to conclude by saying of Cicero that, "The actual body of his rhetorical teachings stem largely from Isocrates, Aristotle, and Stoic writings" (169). Riley calls Cicero "an avowed eclectic" and notes that Cicero never sought a philosophical system—instead he viewed philosophy as an ongoing quest for wisdom (88). Apparently the quest for wisdom was a lifelong journey that Cicero never abandoned (Brown, *Augustine,* 80). His philosophical quest committed him not to a system but to philosophy as a guide for wise human action (prudence) (G. Riley 170).

The two elements identified—integration of rhetoric and philosophy and philosophical eclecticism—converge in praxis through *ornatus,* the name for rhetorical ornamentation used in *De oratore.* Raymond DiLorenzo's brilliant article on ornatus speaks directly to the point:

> *Ornatus* partakes of the nature of wisdom. . . . Wisdom is knowledge embodied in speech which, by attracting others at the level of their senses, enters into them at the level of their convictions and becomes the impetus of their actions. (258)

In effect, Cicero insists that philosophy and rhetoric must be taught together because they are one in practice—the expression of wisdom. How and why these Ciceronean doctrines are crucial to Augustine can be best shown by establishing the association between Cicero and Augustine.

Cicero and Augustine

Augustine maintains a lifelong "association" with Cicero. Many scholars favor a different term: "influence." A ready catalyst for intellectual debate, influence is easy to assert but difficult to substantiate. In the case of Augustine and his work, influences have come to dominate the discourse to such an extent that one might wonder if Augustine ever had an original thought, despite protestations that he was an intellectual giant (Matthews 245).

Association, on the other hand, is proposed here as an alternative term on the assumption that Augustine had at least as many original thoughts as most people, and indeed, far more. Oddly, influence and permanency seem to be related closely, often occurring in tandem. By contrast, we will look to the association between Augustine and Cicero through Augustine's education, Cicero's philosophy, and a dynamic and continuing dialogue—attempting to heed Ernest L. Fortin's warning:

> [Augustine] himself certainly made no great effort to conceal his indebtedness to . . . Cicero. But it would be a grave misconception to think that one can give an adequate account of his thought merely by listing the parallels between the two authors. One is reminded of Lord Acton's remark (to Mary Gladstone) that a disposition to detect resemblances is one of the greatest sources of error. (99)

Education with Cicero

Augustine first encounters Cicero at school. Eventually, his interest expands far beyond the confines of the classroom, but as long as he remains a student and instructor of rhetoric, the words of Cicero are his close companions. Roman schools still used Cicero despite the decline of Ciceronean practice ages before Augustine started primary school in Thagaste (G. Riley 26).

Augustine reads Cicero's rhetoric texts—*De inventione*, *De oratore*, and *Orator*—probably while in Madaura (Reeves 141; Hagendahl 553–54). In Carthage he reads the *Tusculanae disputationes* and *De officiis* as part of his advanced studies (Bourke 19). He begins reading Cicero and others outside of school in Carthage as well (J. O'Meara, *Young*, 94–95). During this time he encounters the *Hortensius* and Aristotle's *Ten Categories*. O'Meara classifies this early manifestation of intellectual curiosity as an act of subtle defiance against the conventionality of the Roman rhetorical school (*Young*, 94).

The transition from student to teacher solidifies Augustine's grasp of Cicero, whose texts he reportedly uses in Thagaste, Carthage, Rome, and Milan (G. Riley 68, 144–45; Brown, *Augustine*, 65). He teaches Cicero's dialogues in Carthage, appealing to Cicero as the philosopher of top rank in the Roman world (Testard in G. Riley 69, 93).

With his own schooling, teaching, and reading, Augustine is said to have known Cicero by heart (Brown, *Augustine*, 36). Although the claim that he actually memorized the entire Ciceronian corpus is suspect, he probably knew the key school texts by memory and maintained a high level of familiarity with Cicero's other available works (Hagendahl 15). Yet Augustine surpasses his day-to-day use of Cicero's text to achieve a dialogue with him. His association with Cicero began when he read the *Hortensius* out of school (Testard in G. Riley 145). It would continue throughout his life and set him apart during the death throes of the Roman Empire.

> Everywhere in the Roman world mounting pessimism and the lack of faith in man's ability to work out his future could be discerned. The old gods were powerless. Life was a matter of luck. Fate was inevitable. Cicero's eloquence protesting man's ability to contribute to his own fate became lost in the fatalism of Tacitus except for the few who would read and act on Ciceronian admonitions. (Briton et al. 65)

Augustine is one of the few. He reads much more Cicero than he can teach and pursues philosophy beyond the constraints of the schools. He will become a philosopher on his own initiative—and in that sense he is self-taught; but on the other hand he might fairly be represented as working in constant association with Marcus Tullius Cicero—the master of Roman philosophy (G. Riley 145).

Philosophy with Cicero

In the obvious philosophical turning point for Augustine—his reading of the *Hortensius*—Cicero introduced Augustine to an expansive intellectual world populated by orators, philosophers, and ideas he had never imagined and to a demanding but impressive moral regimen (Harnack 149). The immediate result was an appreciation for the true breadth and depth of Cicero's own work (Hagendahl 488).

Augustine does not receive from Cicero a closed philosophical system like ones he later encounters in the Manichaeans and the Neoplatonists. Instead, Cicero—a "second-hand popularizer" to some—trained Augustine in the *study* of philosophy as only an eclectic could (Marrou 19). Secondhand or not, Augustine wholeheartedly avails himself of Cicero's guidance to the extent that at his retreat at Cassiciacum and later in his first monastery at Thagaste, Cicero still plays a significant role in the discussions (Hagendahl 555). Hagendahl, after a review of the stenographic records from the debates at Cassiciacum, claims that the debaters used copies of Cicero's *Hortensius* and the *Academica* (493).

Cicero opened the world of philosophy to Augustine through the translation and interpretation of Greek philosophers, for Augustine did not read Greek, at least until late in his life (G. Riley 77). He became Augustine's dominant source, introducing various schools of philosophy that he esteemed (Matthews 237). Among them, Augustine becomes familiar with Isocrates, Aristotle, Plutarch, and Socrates (Keenan 17, 76; Mourant 4). Cicero had translated Plato's *Timaeus*, which may have been the only Platonic dialogue available to Augustine in Latin (Hagendahl 525). Through the *Tusculanae disputationes*, Augustine encounters Pythagorus, Democritus, Plato, Aristotle, Crantor, Epicurus, Dinomachus, the Stoics, and the Peripatetics, at least (Hagendahl 510). The works in which Augustine shows the greatest philosophical interest are exactly those that were most neglected by his fellow rhetoricians: the dialogues *Hortensius*, *Academica*, and *De republica* (Hagendahl 588).

B. B. Warfield summarized the initial relationship between Augustine and Cicero well:

> If Augustine can be said to have had a philosophical master before he fell under the influence of the Neo-Platonists, that master must be discerned in Cicero. And from Cicero he derived rather a burning zeal in the pursuit of truth than a definite body of philosophical tenets or even a philosophical point of view. (136)

However, Warfield makes a commonplace assumption about the association between Augustine and Cicero. He suggests that Augustine encounters a weak philosophy in Cicero's *Hortensius* that diminishes rapidly when he embraces Neoplatonism and Christianity (G. Riley 72). But Cicero's presence at Cassiciacum and Thagaste suggests that Augustine never discards one master in exchange for the other. With the quest for wisdom in the *Hortensius* comes Cicero's eclectic approach to philosophy and his rhetoric, which demands the integration of philosophy and eloquence in the person of the orator.

Intellectual Dialogue with Cicero

Adolf Harnack, working from the same assumptions as Warfield, suggests that Cicero's residual effect extends—perhaps unconsciously—beyond that point when Cicero's moralism inspires Augustine in the direction of philosophy. He says, "Augustine remained, as the earliest books he wrote as a Catholic Christian prove, far more powerfully and permanently influenced than he is willing to allow" (149–50). Harnack seems to have missed the fact that Cicero's "influence" on Augustine extends through his entire corpus and gains intensity in Augustine's later works (Hagendahl 484, 584). Hagendahl states, "Cicero holds his predominant position right to the end: his rhetorical treatises are the basis for the instructions to the clergy in *doct. Christ.* IV . . . and he is the only profane author of whom reminiscences, although scant, are to be found in the last work, *c. iulian.op.imperf.*" (722).

The evidence in Augustine's own works contradicts the notion that the *Hortensius* episode in the *Confessions* exhausts Cicero's association with Augustine. The *Hortensius* itself serves more than a momentary purpose in Augustine's experience. Augustine includes fragments of the *Hortensius* in *Contra academicos III, De beata vita, Soliloques, De civitate Dei, Contra Julianum,* and *De trinitate* (Outler 65n 4).

On a larger scale, Hagendahl presents 134 pages of direct testimonies in Augustine's work from Cicero according to the following standard:

> To the classical scholar it goes without saying that literary influence can be established for certain only on the basis of textual correspondence between two texts, and not, as is often the case, merely because of a more or less obvious correspondence in thought or subject matter. (11)

Hagendahl concludes from his massive philological study, *Augustine and the Latin Classics*, that Cicero is by far most mentioned: "Among the profane Latin authors in Augustine's works Cicero takes first place, far ahead of Virgil and Varro" (569). Augustine mentions Cicero most frequently among pagan authors in his correspondence as well (Keenan 77). In Hagendahl's study, the numbers hold relatively steady, with a dip immediately after Augustine's ordination, followed by an increase toward the end of his life (569–77).

Of course, numbers may deceive; and they reveal nothing about how a writer refers to or quotes a source. This is particularly telling in the case of Augustine and Cicero. The quality of Augustine's discourse suggests that he engages Cicero's ideas directly, considering them carefully. In his writing, Augustine consistently shows: (1) high respect for Cicero's work, which is demonstrated by, (2) direct engagement with Cicero on a variety of topics in many major works, which suggests that, (3) Augustine uses Cicero as an interlocutor in his consideration of key questions—occasionally embracing, sometimes rejecting, and often revising or expanding on Cicero's discourse.

Augustine expresses his respect for Cicero directly in *City of God*, calling him "one of the most learned men, and certainly the most eloquent" (22.6). *City of God*—one of Augustine's later works—produced a flurry of Ciceronean quotations (Hagendahl 573). Using Cicero's own standards, Augustine frames him as the ideal orator—learned and eloquent (see also *Orator* 3–4). However, the respect Augustine reserves for Cicero is not manifested primarily in praise, but in scholarly dialogue. Augustine knows Cicero's work intimately. Peter Brown says of Augustine's knowledge of Cicero in the *City of God*, "The old bishop would flaunt, by innumerable direct citations, his own mastery of all the writings of Cicero" (*Augustine*, 300).

Looking specifically at the *City of God*, notable examples emerge of Cicero's value in dialogue for Augustine, and Augustine's varied responses to Cicero's ideas. Augustine brings Cicero into his discussion of Plato's view of poetry (2.14). He agrees with Cicero's view of the danger of poetry, and, having drawn on Cicero, diminishes the image of Plato. This passage is particularly important because in it Augustine privileges Cicero's view over Plato's, even though the two views are somewhat similar.

Like Augustine's statement in the *Confessions* about the single problem with the *Hortensius*, Augustine heartily approves of Cicero's statement in *De republica* on the lost morality of Rome in book 2.21. Augustine argues that had the work been written in the Christian era, the statement would be imputed to Christian sources.

Augustine rejects Cicero's view of foreknowledge (5.9). Cicero argues against all foreknowledge, including the foreknowledge of God. Augustine agrees that Cicero's statements on divination are accurate but says Cicero has only argued persuasively about the self-refuting cases. Augustine maintains that Cicero's argument cannot be maintained in reference to God.

Augustine mentions Cicero's *Consolations* as an example of the inadequacy of even Cicero's most eloquent lamentation over the death of his daughter in the absence of faith in God (19.4). But in the very next section, Cicero's *In verrem* (2.1.15) is quoted, where, according to Augustine, Cicero genuinely moves the heart. Augustine uses the passage as a direct and positive comparison with a quote from the Gospel of Matthew.

Later, again affirming the wisdom of Cicero, Augustine appropriates a quotation in *De republica* where Scipio is addressing Roman ideals of justice (19.21). Augustine uses Cicero's standard to argue that a Roman republic never existed, because justice was a condition for the republic and by Cicero's own definition there was never true justice in Rome.

Finally, Augustine sometimes includes Cicero in theological issues (22.20). He quotes Cicero's *Tusculum Disputations* (1.27) where Cicero says God is immaterial as part of the Augustinian case for the resurrection of the body, and a universal understanding of the immaterial nature of God, even without scriptural revelation.

Obviously, these passages do not begin to exhaust the dialogue between Augustine and Cicero in the *City of God*, let alone Augustine's corpus. However, they do represent Augustine's varied and respectful treatment of Cicero. In the *City of God*, "The hardest words Augustine ever said about Cicero are balanced by words of respect and esteem"

(Hagendahl 583). Despite the rhetorical excesses of the day, Augustine's respect for Cicero has been recognized as genuine. Riley notes:

> Cicero awakened Augustine to a sense of criticism, creativity, and originality long before Augustine's reading of the Neo-Platonists. Again, in examining the works of Augustine one finds that as he grew older in life the barrier between him and Cicero, from a philosophical point of view, widened, but at the same time his respect for Cicero grew. (195)

Cicero is not the only pagan voice Augustine airs in his own work. One might argue that as the classical master of the Latin language and Roman rhetoric, Augustine must use Cicero for the sake of his own reputation and expediency. Indeed, Augustine's mastery of Cicero serves him well. However, the way he deploys Cicero in discourse, the overwhelming reliance on him compared to other pagan sources, and the abiding respect reserved for Cicero indicate a dynamic, enduring association through the course of Augustine's life.

Augustine's Philosophical Praxis

Augustine frustrates philosophers. At best he is an enigma; at worst he is a rhetor, religious fanatic, or both. He is not systematic enough; he cannot see an idea through to its proper philosophical conclusion (Brown, *Augustine,* 123). What he has gained through his prolonged interaction and mastery of Cicero is not what most commentators expect to see when they look for philosophy—it is more a method and less a system. Unlike Plotinus, who attracted disciples and adherents, in Augustine we see Cicero cultivating a colleague—an independent practitioner—rather than a follower.

A Representative Critique

Commentators on Augustine generally acknowledge some association with Cicero. But they see in the relation an Augustinian lapse from the philosophical aspiration they have assigned to Cicero and rhetoric. Hagendahl's statements on the matter are representative:

> In one respect an unbroken line runs through the whole of his literary work. Like all Fathers before him—and to a higher degree than Jerome—Augustine was impregnated with the intellectual training received in the pagan school. He remains all his life—as Alfaric and Marrou have emphasized—what he was from the beginning, a grammarian, a rhetor, and a dialectician of the traditional type. (724)

Hagendahl identifies the enduring Ciceronean connection in Augustine but wrongly attributes it to his rhetorical training in the schools. As noted earlier, although Cicero was read in the schools, he was not practiced there. Augustine was far from a passive receiver of Cicero's philosophical method. He had to pursue it entirely on his own.

Next, Hagendahl mistakenly equates Augustine's rejection of the Second Sophistic with a devaluation of all rhetorical training:

> However much the mature man may look down on his former profession as "vanity fair," he finds oratorical training, even if not necessarily acquired in the school of rhetoric, indispensable to the Christian preacher, and reverts to Cicero and the best tradition of ancient theory when he instructs the clergy how to deliver a sermon. (725)

In the Late Roman Empire, *where* one received oratorical training would be paramount to Augustine. The oratorical training in the schools of rhetoric would vary diametrically from Augustine's own instructional agenda. His reply to Dioscorus's school questions addresses this issue directly (Meer 253).[2] Finally, Hagendahl reveals his own standards for a satisfactory philosophy:

> While turning from one theory of life to another Augustine remained fundamentally the same in one respect. The search for truth had for him nothing in common with the unprejudiced and disinterested pursuit of science: the motive posed and the end in view were knowledge of himself and personal happiness. (725)

Again, Hagendahl identifies a continuity in Augustine that emerges from his agreement with Cicero on the goal of wisdom as the happy life, *de beata vita* (Bourke 203). In the meantime he introduces an anachronistic test to Augustine's philosophy without regard for the equally "prejudiced" and "interested" philosophies of late antiquity.

Cicero on Rhetorical Retainer

That Augustine approximates Cicero's philosophical/rhetorical approach has already been suggested. To develop the hypothesis more directly, Cicero's main philosophical coordinates—integration of rhetoric and philosophy and an eclectic approach to philosophy—must be compared with Augustine's practice. That Augustine obtained an enduring love for wisdom, initiated by *Hortensius*, seems to be accepted universally.

But Augustine was no Ciceronean. Proponents and detractors agree on his philosophical independence. Paul Henry, commenting on the relationship between Augustine and Aristotle's theory of personality, cites the case as "one of the clearest instances of Augustine's independence of mind in the midst of contemporary and current modes of thought, and of a certain natural nonconformism" (2). Others, viewing the same phenomenon, recognize Augustine as a self-taught philosopher, exposed to a number of philosophies but ascribing allegiance to none (Brown, *Augustine,* 93; Meer 561; G. Riley 137–38). Henri Marrou heralds Augustine's self-taught status to account for his creative originality—his limited access to Greek philosophy forcing him to exercise his brilliance in original ways (15).

The critical space constructed by Augustine's philosophical posture enables him to consider and reformulate ideas most effectively for his own purposes. For example, Brown claims that Augustine is able to make the works of Plotinus and Porphyry "his own to such an extent . . . that he felt he could elaborate their thought in very different terms." This not as sheer exploitation, but because of his unequaled ability to "master the Neo-Platonic authors with an originality and independence of mind" (*Augustine* 95).

That Augustine exercises such intellectual creativity in a philosophical context dominated by Neoplatonism makes those views dubious which represent him as a mere historical composite of the Late Roman Empire (Marrou 28; Campenhausen 185). The agility with which Augustine comprehends and assesses ideas are certainly historically situated, but he hones a unique philosophical regimen with Cicero as his accomplice (G. Riley 143).

In *De doctrina Christiana,* Augustine describes his method of appropriating aspects of varying philosophies as taking "Gold from the Egyptians," a scriptural analogy he shares with Ambrose and other church Fathers (2.40.60; Brown, *Augustine,* 84). In the words of Hans von Campenhausen:

> Augustine knew neither the medieval grading nor the modern separation of theology and philosophy. To him there is but one truth. . . . If this Christian truth is to be understood, intellectually adopted, and confirmed, he has no hesitation in turning, consciously or unconsciously, back on the modes of thinking and logical laws, to the conceptions, expressions and traditions he had learned from Cicero, Aristotle, and the "Platonists," which have there proved to be right. (224–25)

Not only does Augustine explicate this "Gold from the Egyptians" method in the treatise, but he also incorporates Cicero's ideal synthesis of philosophy and rhetoric in oratory (G. Riley 147).

The relationship between *De doctrina Christiana* and Cicero's rhetorical texts, particularly the *De oratore* and *Orator,* has been so well documented and widely accepted that it will not be rehearsed again here (Baldwin 55; Clarke 151; Murphy, *Rhetoric,* 61–62; Meer 411; Hagendahl 554). More important to this discussion are the divergences—beyond the clear echo of Cicero's "wisdom and eloquence" that recur in *De doctrina Christiana,* book 4. By using Cicero and altering his rhetoric in the same stroke, Augustine aligns himself with Cicero's philosophical method and puts it into practice on the old master.

Briefly, Augustine takes full advantage of Ciceronean terms throughout *De doctrina Christiana*, reforming and fashioning a distinctively Christian rhetoric (Baldwin 54; Milovanovic-Barham 12). In the midst of intense ecclesiastical controversy over the role of rhetoric in the ascendant Christian culture, Augustine invokes Cicero's *paiedeia*, appealing equally to Christians and pagans at the turn of the fifth century (Murphy, *Rhetoric*, 65; Kevane 175; Press, *"Doctrina,"* 114–15). He does the same with the term *doctrina*.

> Augustine's use of *doctrina* in the DDC is a rhetorical *coup*. He took advantage of the variety of its meanings and the variations in how it would be understood from different cultural standpoints to argue simultaneously for his side and speak to both sides of the dispute between Christianity and "pagan" culture. (Press, *"Doctrina,"* 108)

Far from being a simple "Christianization," Augustine more than reworks Cicero's rhetoric; he adopts Cicero's classical framework but remodels and invests it with a Christian sense (Milovanovic-Barham 3, 10; Fortin 87). As W. R. Johnson says, "What Augustine did that no one else did or tried to do was to give theoretical warrant for the transformation of pagan literacy to Christian literacy" (222). Central to the transformation was the shift from Cicero's predominantly forensic inventional strategies to an invention dominated by textual interpretation (Murphy, *Rhetoric*, 61–62; Press, "Subject," 120–21).

Augustine's rhetoric in *De doctrina Christiana* presents a radical reorientation of the wisdom from which the orator must draw the substance of his speech, but his insistence that rhetoric is a synthesis of wisdom and eloquence remains constant. Going beyond Cicero, Augustine both dispenses with distinctions *between* the liberal arts and includes philosophy *within* the liberal arts for the first time (G. Riley 116, 134, 137–38). No wonder W. R. Johnson exclaims about how difficult it gets "to distinguish the philosophy from the theology, the theology from the Isocratean rhetoric, the rhetoric from the Ciceronean humanism, and the humanism from the mysticism that informs all of Augustine's thinking and writing, suffering and doing" (228).

The harmony Augustine's thought and discourse exemplify cannot be discussed in a merely cursory fashion. However, we may begin to consider it here by recognizing it as an extension and transformation of Augustine's association with Cicero. Augustine extends from their shared interest in philosophy. For Augustine, "wisdom, the object of philosophy, is always identified with happiness" (Gilson 3). Like Cicero, he wants a goodness that produces enduring human happiness—that is, blessedness. Wisdom is also the object of rhetoric, since for both Cicero and Augustine, wisdom is philosophy expressed with eloquence—an intensely practical, rhetorical pursuit (Gilson 3).

The transformations from Cicero, as exemplified briefly in *De doctrina Christiana*, are also promoted by Augustine's association with Cicero, especially Cicero's philosophy. Augustine's creativity, originality, and appropriation of knowledge from diverse sources illustrates the crucial point that Augustine is not and never was a systematic philosopher (Gilson x; Oates 1:ix–x).

> Saint Augustine's thought cannot strictly be called a "system." It is rather a world view or a "universe view," one which comprehends God and all of reality in their manifold and complex interconnections. In contrast there have been many philosophers who have constructed "systems" from the time of the earliest Greeks . . . through Hegel. (Oates 1:ix–x)

Augustine arrives at an "open view" rather than a "closed system." Whitney J. Oates rightly indicates that the openness makes Augustine vulnerable to the attacks of strict rationalists, since his perspective admits revelation and faith along with reason and perceives human knowledge to be ultimately incomplete (1:ix–xi). But in exchange for the rationalism of a "closed system," Augustine opens himself to "all aspects of reality" and can affirm that "life runs beyond logic" (x).

Augustine the Orator

Augustine never reverts to rhetoric out of a lack of philosophical erudition or due to some permanent, but suppressed, influence from Cicero. Instead, like Cicero, he operates self-consciously and elegantly with an open philosophical approach that integrates wisdom and eloquence in rhetoric, even when that means a radical change from Cicero's own rhetorical texts. Furthermore, the *De doctrina Christiana,* written during the time when Cicero was cited explicitly the least, demonstrates that Augustine never abandons rhetoric qua rhetoric in practice, but rejects only the rhetorical abuses of the Second Sophistic (Hagendahl 575).

The entirety of Augustine's practice as bishop-orator in Hippo and throughout Roman North Africa could be offered as evidence that Augustine was as consistent in practice as he was in thought. Frederik van der Meer, in his exhaustive chronicle of Augustine's bishopric in Hippo, including sermons, letters, major and minor treatises, presents this summary:

> Whoever begins to read the *sermones* of the Bishop of Hippo knows after the first few pages that the theory in the last part of *Christian*

> *Knowledge* had been lived and experienced long before it was written down. The portrait that is there drawn, in a few rapid strokes, of the servant of the word might well be an involuntary self-portrait of Augustine himself, for all that is written there applies to him. Augustine follows his own precept. He preaches in truly popular fashion and is always clear, he is careful not to be solemn for too long or to sound perpetual notes of triumph, and like the Bishop of Meaux, he ignores all difficulties with a contemptuous eagle eye. With a facility that is quite inimitable he masters his three categories and mingles them one with another; improvises sudden transitions, or neglects to make any transition at all. (413)

In his own time, reacting as Cicero did to Sophistic excesses, and conscientiously practicing a rhetoric that attempted to integrate style and substance, based on a love of wisdom and the end of achieving a happy life, Augustine attempts to become an ideal orator. Rhetoric and philosophy never constitute an either/or proposition. They continue their interplay as counterparts that, taken together, produce wisdom.

Confessions *Revisited*

The first three books of *De doctrina Christiana* were written a year before Augustine began work on the *Confessions* (Brown, *Augustine*, 184; Miethe xxi). Kenneth Burke makes the interesting suggestion that *De doctrina Christiana*, like the *Confessions,*

> concerns the development from the selling of words to the preaching of the Word. But in the work on Christian rhetoric, he is partly asking how to adapt for ecclesiastical purposes the verbal skill of the pagans, and partly attempting to show that Christianity already had an eloquent body of letters, whereas the autobiography places the emphasis on the break rather than the bridge between the two realms. (49)

Without contesting Burke's summary judgment of the two works, the connection he makes gives some impetus to applying a second, better-tuned ear to the *Confessions*. If we attend to the text, remembering that Augustine rejects the Second Sophistic and not rhetoric, what emerges? One approach might be to reinterpret the condemnations of rhetoric as teaching by contrast, so that the listener might construct a positive image of what is approved by reversing the consistently negative diet of commentary. But in this case, Augustine teaches positive tenets that coincide neatly with *De doctrina Christiana*, although sometimes through negative illustrations.

As the *Confessions* progresses, a significant reversal in expression takes place, while the reaction against the Second Sophistic subsides and Augustine gains insight into truth. Yet even in the first book positive instruction on rhetoric emerges. The first evident, if subtle, suggestion comes in the form of a question:

> Was there no other subject on which to exercise my talents and my tongue? Your praises, Lord, your praises, set forth in your Scriptures, would have held up my heart's young vine, so that it would not have been snatched away by empty trifles, the filthy prey of flying creatures. In more ways than one is sacrifice offered to the transgressor angels. (1.17.27)

> itane aliud non erat, ubi exerceretur ingenium et lingua mea? laudes tuae, domine, laudes tuae per scripturas tuas suspederent palmitem cordis mei, et non raperetur per inania nugarum turpis praeda volatilibus. non enirm uno modo sacrificatur transgressoribus agelis. (1.17.27)

The answer supplied reinforces speaking ability as a God-given gift and does not censor training, even declamation, but only the subject of the exercise. The ethical emphasis continues in 1.18.29, where a barb directed at preoccupation with pronunciation is followed by the ethical injunction, "No knowledge of letters is more interior to us than that written in conscience" [et certe non est interior litterarum scientia quam scripta conscientia]. Again wisdom is clearly emphasized in a rhetorical context.

The famous passage on Augustine's discovery of the *Hortensius* represents the first clear injunction that even the most eloquent orator speaks best when listeners can recognize that they have been moved by the message itself, and not by the style of the messenger alone.

> In the ordinary course of study I came upon a book by a certain Cicero, whose tongue almost all men admire but not his heart. This work contains his exhortation to philosophy and is called *Hortensius*. This book changed my affections. . . . Nor did it impress me by its way of speaking but rather by what it spoke. (3.4.7)

> et usitato iam discendi ordine perveneram in librum cuiusdam Ciceronis, cuius linguam fere omnes mirantur, pectus non ita. sed liber ille ipsius exhortationem continet ad philosophiam et vocatur Hortensius. ille vero liber mutavit affectum meum. . . . neque mihi locutionem, sed quod loquebatur persuaserat. (3.4.7)

Augustine can hardly be suggesting here that *Hortensius* is one of Cicero's more humble efforts at eloquence. Cicero's eloquence is a given;

what awakened Augustine was the book's wisdom. Augustine knew the next speaker mentioned, Hierius, only by reputation, yet he dedicated his first treatise, *De pulchro et apto* (not extant), to this speaker. Of Hierius he says, "They marveled that a Syrian, first educated in Greek eloquence, should later become so wonderful a master of Latin and so deeply learned in all matters that pertain to philosophy" [laudibus stupente, quod ex homine Syro, docto prius graecae facundiae, post in latina etiam dictor mirabilis extitisset, et esset scientissimus rerum ad studium sapientiae pertinentium] (4.9.21). The marvels correlate well with Augustine's own experience as an outsider to Italian culture, since Hierius was a Syrian. But even more impressive was his skill at language combined with philosophy.

The relative neutrality of eloquence is addressed somewhat abstractly in book 5 through a series of oppositions that accept some level of eloquence as a constant, leaving the value of the rhetoric to be determined by its association either with wisdom or foolishness:

> Already, therefore, I had learned from you that nothing should be held true merely because it is eloquently expressed, nor false because its signs sound harsh upon the lips. Again, I learned that a thing is not true because rudely uttered, nor is it false because its utterance is splendid. I learned that wisdom is like wholesome food and folly like unwholesome food: they can be set forth in language ornate or plain, just as both kinds of food can be served on rich dishes or peasant ware. (5.6.10)

> iam ergo abs te didiceram, nec eo debere videri aliquid verum dici, quia eloquenter dicitur, nec eo falsum, quia incomposite sonant signa labiorum; rursus nec ideo verum, quia inpolite enuntiatur, ned ideo falsum, quia splendidus sermo est: sed perinde esse sapientam et stultitiam, sicut sunt cibi utiles et inutiles; verbis autem ornatis et inornatis, sicut vasis urbanis et rusticanis utrosque cibos posse ministrari. (5.6.10)

The most explicit indicators in the *Confessions* that a rhetoric other than the Second Sophistic should be practiced come through the description of Ambrose's eloquence and its effect on Augustine. Augustine relates his initial observations of Ambrose the bishop:

> I came to Milan, and to Ambrose, its bishop, a man famed throughout the world as one of its very best men, and your devout worshipper. By his eloquent sermons in those days he zealously provided your people with the fat of your wheat, the gladness of your oil, and the sobering intoxication of your wine. (5.13.23)

> et veni Mediolanium ad Ambrosium episcopum, in optimis notum orbi terrae, pium cultorem tuum, cuius tunc eloquia strenue ministrabant adipem frumenti tui, et laetitiam olei, et sobriam vini ebrietatem, populo tuo. (5.13.23)

Augustine represents Ambrose first as devout, then as eloquent, and finally as the provider of substance to his congregation. Ambrose parallels and extends upon the earlier images of Cicero and Hierius as the positive example Augustine knew personally and whose rhetoric he observed firsthand. Augustine further relates Ambrose's rhetoric—his wisdom and eloquence—as an indivisible, irresistible force for good, even against resistance.

> Although I was not anxious to learn what he said, but merely to hear how he said it—for such bootless concern remained with me, although I had no hope that any way lay open for a man to come to you—yet at the same time with the words, which I loved, there also entered into my mind the things themselves, to which I was indifferent. Nor was I able to separate them one from another, and when I opened up my heart to receive the eloquence with which he spoke, there likewise entered, although only by degrees, the truths that he spoke. (5.16.24)

> Cum enim non satagerem discere quae dicebat, sed tantum quaemadmodum dicebat audire—ea mihi quippe, desperanti ad te viam patere homini, inanis cura remanserat—veniebant in animum meum simul cum verbis, quae diligebam, res etiam, quas neglegebam. neque enim ea dirimere poteram. et dum cor aperirem ad excipiendum, quam diserte diceret, pariter intrabat et quam vera diceret, gradatim quidem. (5.16.24)

Finally, Augustine provides a catalog of the things he remembers of the liberal arts, without praise or blame, including the main categories of rhetorical education at the time:

> Here also are all those things learned from the liberal studies which have not yet slipped away, and are put back as it were into an interior place that is yet not a place. Of these things it is not images that I carry about, but the things themselves. For what literature is, what skill in disputation is, how many kinds of questions there are, and whatever else of such subjects I know, all this is in my memory in such wise that I have not retained the image while leaving the reality outside. (10.9.16)

> hic sunt et illa omnia quae de doctinis liberalibus percepta nondum exciderunt, quasi remoto interiore loco; nec eorum imagines, sed res

> ipsas gero. nam quid sit litteratura, quid peritia disputandi, quot genera quaestionum, quidquid horum scio, sic est in memoria mea, ut non retenta imagine rem foris reliquerim, aut sonuerit aut praeterierit. (10.9.16)

This cursory reading of the most obvious, positive statements about rhetoric in the *Confessions* acquit the text of any charges that it is an unremitting attack on rhetoric. In fact, it appears to be much more discriminating and precise. True, Augustine excoriates the Second Sophistic, but not without providing an alternative framework for the advance of a new rhetoric that corresponds quite closely to the later work in book 4 of *De doctrina Christiana*. The correspondence would be even more distinct if the negative images were considered.

Summary: *Rhetoric and the* Confessions

When we examine texts of Augustine, W. R. Johnson suggests that "it makes more sense to place him with the great humanist rhetoricians (for example, Isocrates, Cicero, Petrarch, Erasmus, Voltaire, and Russell) than it does to place him with the great Western philosophers (for example, Aristotle, Epicurus, Plotinus, Aquinas, Spinoza, and Kant)" (217). Rhetoricians have acknowledged this for nearly a century regarding Augustine's *De doctrina Christiana,* and extensive theoretical work has been done on the text, especially book 4.

The suggested correspondence between *De doctrina Christiana* and the *Confessions* could be pursued, but already a clear connection between these two books has been established in the *Confessions'* remarks about rhetoric. Moreover, *De doctrina Christiana* is far from a well-developed rhetoric. It is so brief as to draw the charge of impoverishing traditional rhetoric (Hagendahl 567).

However, a more interesting avenue exists. Johnson has said: "The young Augustine thought of himself as a Platonist, but even before he read the *Hortensius* his mind had been deeply stamped by the doctrines of Isocrates as Cicero had elaborated them" (226). He further argues that although Cicero and Augustine were both sincere students of Plato,

> [w]hen Augustine assumed his duties at Hippo, he had Plato in his mind and in his heart, but he had Isocrates in his blood. The *Confessions*, the *Civitas*, the pamphlets . . . are all tinged with memories of the calm joy of Cassiciacum. But what we hear in these books constantly and what Christian Europe learned from them was the message of the need for the unity and harmony of the human race: *consociatio hominum et communitas*. (227)

With Johnson, we read as dubious any charge that the *Confessions* condemns rhetoric outright. Textual evidence and an enduring association between Cicero and Augustine suggest a reformation of Augustine's rhetoric and philosophy from his days as a Roman Sophist. The Cicero-Augustine association, like Johnson's claims, fly directly in the face of most scholarship that has been devoted to the *Confessions* in the past century (Starnes, *Conversion*, 277–89). While rhetoricians have written books and articles on the Ciceronean influence in *De doctrina Christiana*, Augustinian scholars have settled into a debate on the various timbres of Neoplatonic influence in the *Confessions*. The debate itself has become a topic of scholarly commentary.

Philosophers, historians, and theologians have been debating whether Augustine's conversion was to Neoplatonism or Christianity for more than a century (Starnes, *Conversion*, 277). The historical debate revolves around Augustine's *Confessions* and has overshadowed consideration of the text. Scholars generally agree that Augustine studied certain elements of Neoplatonism found in the works of Plotinus and Porphyry (J. O'Meara, "Neoplatonism," 35). At issue is the question of when and to what extent Augustine converted to Christianity. Two general positions emerge: (1) Augustine was primarily a Neoplatonist functioning within the doctrinal constraints of the Christian Church; (2) he was a Christian who harmonized Neoplatonism and Christian doctrine on an intellectual plane. The historical accuracy of the *Confessions* and particularly Augustine's account of his conversion supposedly hang in the balance.

Adolph Harnack and Gaston Boissier initiated the debate in 1888 with complementary articles questioning the historical authenticity of Augustine's *Confessions* by contrasting it with his *Dialogues*. The *Dialogues* were written immediately after Augustine's conversion as recorded in the *Confessions*, which were dictated about twelve years later (Starnes, *Conversion*, 277). The effect of the position taken by Harnack and Boissier reverses Augustine's claim of radical Christian conversion and asserts that it is instead a natural progression:

> In wide circles the "Confessions" are viewed as the portrait of a Prodigal Son, of a man who, after a wild and wasteful career, suddenly comes to himself and repents, or else as the picture of a heathen who, after a life of vice, is suddenly overcome by the truth of the Christian religion. No view can be more mistaken. . . .
>
> In his external life this change presents itself as a breach with his past; and it is in this view that he has himself depicted it. To him there is here nothing but a contrast between the past and the present. But in his inner life, in spite of his own representations, everything appears to us a quite intelligible development. (Harnack 138–40)

In 1918, Prosper Alfaric takes up the mantle of this historicist position about the *Confessions*. Alfaric suggests that at the time of Augustine's conversion he was a disciple of Plotinus and converted to Neoplatonism, not Christianity (Starnes, *Conversion*, 279).

Reaction to the historicist position came primarily from a theological perspective. Etienne Gilson and Charles Boyer responded to Alfaric in 1919 and 1920 respectively, claiming that Augustine's Christianity preceded his encounter with Neoplatonism and that Augustine's Neoplatonism was sanctioned by the church and secondary to church doctrine.

Pierre Courcelle moderated and forcefully restated the response to the historicist view by arguing that Augustine encountered Christianity and Neoplatonism as an already integrated package within the church. In the preaching of Ambrose at Milan, Augustine heard the assimilation (Starnes, *Conversion*, 280–81).

Since Courcelle the debate has continued—almost exclusively among Augustinian scholars. John J. O'Meara and A. Solignac both contend that Neoplatonism was the dominant force in Saint Augustine's thought. Robert J. O'Connell extends Courcelle's work to the point of "reconstructing Augustine's history on the assumption of the identity of Neo-Platonism and Christianity" (Starnes, *Conversion*, 287–88).

Mary T. Clark challenges O'Connell's thesis, and he immediately fires back (Clark, "Book Review"; O'Connell, "Reply"). She also writes on "Augustine the Christian Thinker" in *From Augustine to Eriugena: Essays on Neoplatonism and Christianity in Honor of John J. O'Meara*. Perhaps the most ambitious illustration of the Neoplatonic position is Henry Chadwick's "Neoplatonic" translation of the *Confessions*. In the introduction to the translation, Chadwick asserts that "From the first paragraph of the *Confessions* onwards, Augustine can express Neoplatonic themes in language which sounds like a pastiche of the psalter."

Could this debate—one which has dominated scholarly attention for a century—have missed what Johnson claims is the crux of the *Confessions*? Augustine operates within an open, eclectic philosophical environment—not committing to any one philosophical school. Brown claims that Porphyry was the "first systematic theologian in the history of thought" and then contrasts him to Augustine, the nonsystematic, "too flexible" thinker and writer (*Augustine*, 91, 123). Oates concurs, distinguishing between Augustine and the Neoplatonists, who thought they were completing Plato while producing a closed system that negates the dynamic dualism of Platonic thought (1:xi).

Working from assumptions that divide philosophy from rhetoric, theology from faith, and reason from revelation, we may have proceeded to systematize the *Confessions* too quickly. The volume of scholarship that attempts to systematize Augustine's work testifies to the fact that such theories abound. But the question remains: "What have these theories to do with Augustine?" In too many cases, as we shall see, to sustain systems and theories not evident in the *Confessions* the theories are declared to be obscured deliberately as esoteric teachings. Then, without textual evidence or contrary to it, a latent system emerges as Augustine's.

Recently, certain scholars have circumvented the debate over Augustine's relation to Neoplatonism and its imposition of various systems onto the *Confessions,* returning instead to the primary text. Ann Hartle, in her consideration of the *Confessions,* ignores the Neoplatonist debate and commits only an extended footnote which begins with this statement:

> It is here that my own position on the question of Augustine's Platonism begins to work out, not as a taking of one side in the debate or as the reconciliation of both sides, but as a rejection of the terms in which the debate is carried on. (232n. 8)

Likewise, Colin Starnes refuses to admit the terms of the debate on Augustine and Neoplatonism into his commentary on *Confessions,* books 1–9 (*Conversion,* xiii–iv). He presents a thorough review of the debate in an appendix. Starnes concludes that neither side in the debate can hope to account for the *Confessions* on its own terms. Both sides must import presuppositions alien to the text and exalt the few places where the text supports these presuppositions while suppressing or changing points in the text that challenge their paradigms and openly resist their readings (*Conversion,* 277–89).

James J. O'Donnell has published a three-volume commentary on the *Confessions* that does not submit to the terms of the debate as a controlling influence, which it has been for so many scholars of the *Confessions.* The rejection of the Neoplatonic terms of debate is a radical departure, and represented by only a few scholars. The debate still dominates scholarly discourse on the *Confessions.*

Rather than engage in that debate, we too will return to the *Confessions* itself to inquire directly into Augustine's work on its own terms and in its own context.

Chapter 2

Protocols for Reading the *Confessions*

The *Confessions* is a prayer. But it is not a private prayer, or even a literary device akin to a private prayer. In the *Confessions,* Aurelius Augustine, bishop of Hippo, publicly addresses God and expects listeners to join in the appeal. The bishop's voice resounds in an open, discursive cathedral to lead and instruct a community of fellow sinners. No less was expected of Augustine, and to this readers who engage the *Confessions* on its own terms must respond.

The question is: Can the reader of today hope to engage the text or respond to it? The distance between the Late Roman Empire and today challenges our ability to hear Augustine's *Confessions.* But the inevitable temporal distance through which we must strain to hear voices from the past has been further disrupted by critical commentary that isolates the text from the sociohistorical context in which it emerged.

The *Confessions,* particularly in the early parts of the narrative, grounds itself in the social practices of the Late Roman Empire—especially in North Africa. But even Pierre Courcelle, esteemed as the most prominent modern defender of the *Confessions'* historicity, neglects almost entirely the contents of books 1–5 (Starnes, *Conversion,* 26, 192, 194). As Colin Starnes points out:

> Well over half of the first nine books is largely ignored because it contains little that is specific to Augustine—and this is especially true of the first two books where Augustine sets the problem to which Christianity was to be the final solution. . . . The paucity of historical information peculiar to Augustine does not mean that their content is any the less historical or verifiable for being general. . . . These general points, and the conclusions he draws from them, are no less historical

than the later parts of the text where he discusses events that are unique to himself—and they must be taken into account if we are to understand what Augustine is attempting in the *Confessions*. (*Conversion,* 26)

Starnes's point raises a fundamental contrast between the information historicists concern themselves with and the approach we are maintaining toward the *Confessions*. Courcelle and others doing similar work view Augustine and his work as determined almost entirely by specific historical precedents, a person bound to produce certain texts—like the *Confessions*—because of his historical position. Our perspective also concerns itself with Augustine's historical situation, but it does so not to enable us to decide what he must do but to help us understand the choices he makes as he reads his own circumstances. We are as interested in what novel rhetorical resources Augustine applies in his situation as we are in possible models from the past he may have imitated. Rhetoric is an art practiced by free agents who observe and sometimes violate the constraints and conventions of the moment.

One literary critic has said of Plato's works, "The simplest student will be able to understand, if not all, yet a very great deal of what Plato said; but hardly anyone can understand some modern books on Platonism" (Lewis 200). Of course Augustine was not Plato, but the same statement could have been written about him as well as about modern books on the *Confessions*. For the general reader—a person who reads the *Confessions* as a classic of cultural, philosophical, or devotional literature—the work itself may yet resonate on its own. But for one who encounters the *Confessions* as a text to be read and understood within some larger intellectual milieu, books *about* the *Confessions* (like this one), must come into play.

It is my premise that the secondary literature, while not homogeneous, has only recently included voices that challenge what Kathleen E. Welch has termed the "Lure of the Informational" (23). Welch refers to a common impulse among critics to decontextualize classical discourse in the process of reducing it to informational meanings and formulas. This impulse has been dominant in critical literature on the *Confessions*. Although most scholars laud the *Confessions* as a rich and complex text, they have found the temptation irresistible to resolve its ambiguities, tensions, and paradoxes by reducing its meaning—whether psychological, philosophical, theological, religious, or formal—to summary propositions, usually *about* Augustine or his philosophy.[1]

All this is not to suggest that previous commentators have ignored historical facts about Augustine's life in the Late Roman Empire. Unlike some other periods of classical antiquity, documentation abounds for the period in which the *Confessions* was composed, and commentators often rely on such facts to support their interpretations. It is their approach to interpretation—the lure of the informational—that drives the wedge between the text and the context. The historical approach to discursive production, performance, and theory in which the text emerged are generally neglected. Peter Brown warns of just this problem:

> Our appreciation of the *Confessions* has suffered from the fact that they have become a classic. We tend to accept or dismiss them according to our own standards, as if Augustine were still our contemporary. (*Augustine*, 165)

Too many commentators have committed exactly this error. Instead of reading the *Confessions* as dynamic human discourse—produced and received under conditions unique to its own historical context—critics tend to read the text as they would read contemporary discourse, then work to classify it as another isolated fact in a static historical time period, perhaps as an influential relic of church history, a seminal work on psychology, or a foundational exemplar of Christian Neoplatonism.

To do so, the critic must import critical coordinates from outside the text, often characterized as "dominant influences" upon the author, and then announce a summary interpretation, categorizing either the text or Augustine. Ordinarily such criticism, by positing a single propositional statement of its contents, practices a form/content dichotomy that judges form as irrelevant ornamentation that affects meaning only inasmuch as it helps or hinders the discovery of the "real" meaning of the text: its abstracted propositional content. In extreme cases, critics become duty bound to demonstrate how the very absence of internal textual evidence confirms the veracity of the meaning they have assigned. In other cases, the "real" meaning has some textual support but seems to be resisted by other portions of the text. In both cases, critics advance claims that the "real" meaning is brilliantly obscured or occulted by the author. The logic of such occulted meanings is as unassailable as a conspiracy theory. However, this same logic ignores the texture of the discourse and violates the integrity of form and content through which the text's meaning is constructed.

Assertions that the *Confessions* is "about" Christian Neoplatonism and that the "historical accuracy" of Augustine's conversion narrative is suspect exemplify such criticism. These issues have spawned an esoteric scholarly debate that has raged since 1888 (Starnes, *Conversion*, 277–85). The problem with this sort of approach is that neither side in the debate can account for the text as a whole. Therefore, they are of limited value for even the most serious readers of the *Confessions*. As Colin Starnes has noted:

> Each side in this debate has a possible interpretation because both sides are indeed found in the *Confessions*. The difficulty comes from

the partiality of each view which is claimed to be an adequate interpretation of the whole. On this basis no ultimate reconciliation or resolution is possible. The division can only harden into a stalemate where neither side can incorporate what is correct in the other and the student is left between mutually exclusive positions, neither of which is entirely satisfactory. (*Conversion*, 285)

The combatants Starnes identifies have polarized their discussion, but they continue to share a critical conviction that what the *Confessions* are about can be summarized simply and that criticism ought to aspire to such a summary. They put themselves in the position of needing to explain away a great deal because their interpretive approach is not equal to the discourse they claim to explain. And so they take a critical posture that categorically knows the text better than it knows itself—even if it means violating the integrity of the text to do so.[2]

The effect of such criticism is felt in the reception of the text, not in the text itself. For one text can never domesticate another—the reader actualizes each. In other words, critical discourse may domesticate a reader, but not another text. Texts continually invite new readings. And an undomesticated reader may hear all sorts of affirmations in a text that a commentator is obliged to deny by an imported critical method.

By contrast, the critical approach I am employing is an effort to help enrich undomesticated readings of the text within its own context—not so much to explain the text as to provide a provisional set of protocols for contemporary readers of the *Confessions*. To do so we will engage the text on *its* terms, depending on it to disclose the keys for its own interpretation. In so doing we hope to better understand not so much how to resolve the tensions, contradictions, and paradoxes in the text, but how they *do* construct meaning through the integration of the form and content of discourse. I do not claim a naive or objective position in proceeding. Rather, I am conscious that the approach I am taking to the text challenges the scholarly conventions that have governed acceptable interpretations of the *Confessions* for a century, and positions this inquiry and its recommendations for reading the *Confessions* outside of the well-worn debate over Neoplatonism. I believe and am arguing that the commendation of rhetoric in the text confounds the predominant interpretive categories established by that debate.

Initial Coordinates (1.1.1)

Our orientation as readers begins in the title. "Confession" in the Roman world at the turn of the fifth century carries profoundly public connotations: a legal, forensic, and political sense ingrained from the time of the Roman Christian martyrs, or "confessors" (Scott 36–37). Augustine employs the Latin term *confiteri* in its threefold sense: first and foremost he offers a "confession of praise and thanks to God"; second he confesses his sin; and finally he confesses his faith (Bonner 48–50; Brown, *Augustine,* 175).

Before we read a word of his prose, Augustine indicates the public nature of his confessions and guides us to expect praise and blame framed by faith. He not only immediately enacts "confession" in its three movements but also provides a primer to guide our reading as we engage the first chapter of book 1. Therefore, we will examine the passage closely.

> You are great, O Lord, and greatly to be praised: great is your power and to your wisdom there is no limit. (1.1.1)[3]
>
> Magnus es, domine, et laudabilis valde: magna virtus tua, et sapientiae tuae non est numerus. (1.1.1)

Augustine begins with praise addressed to God, a paraphrase combining two verses of Scripture: Psalm 48:1 and Psalm 147:5. The paraphrase is important because in it Augustine shifts from the third-person voice of the psalmists to the intimacy of the second person. Brown notes that by addressing God in the first line Augustine announces the *Confessions* as a philosophical meditation, but that by speaking to God in the second person he transgresses the form: "Such prayers were usually regarded as part of a preliminary stage in the lifting of the philosopher's mind to God. They had never been used, as Augustine would use them throughout the *Confessions,* to strike up a lively conversation with Him" (*Augustine,* 166–67).

The first line employs words *from* God to speak *to* God about God's power and wisdom. These words are not original to Augustine, yet they have been personalized. Having placed God and Scripture first, Augustine confesses about the human race in its relation to God:

> And man, who is part of your creation, wishes to praise you, man who bears about within himself testimony to his sin and testimony that you resist the proud. Yet man, this part of your creation, wishes to praise you. (1.1.1)
>
> et laudare te vult homo, aliqua portio creaturae tuae, et homo circumferens mortalitatem suam, circumferens testimonium peccati sui et testimonium, quia superbis resistis: et tamen laudare te vult homo, aliqua portio creaturae tuae. (1.1.1)

He hints at pride's role as the evidence of sinful opposition against God but reiterates that the proper and innate human desire is to praise God, which can only be restored on God's initiative. Our brief meditation on God as creator and humankind as created with an inclination to speak to God as God also introduces pride, sin, and mortality as disruptive of that innate inclination and knowledge. However, the distant meditation is once again interrupted by a change in voice:

> You arouse him to take joy in praising you, for you have made us for yourself, and our heart is restless until it rests in you. (1.1.1)
>
> tu excitas, ut laudare te delectet, quia fecisti nos ad te et inquietum est cor nostrum, donec requiescat in te. (1.1.1)

The most famous quotation from the *Confessions* shifts our attention from third person singular—the collective "man"—to ourselves with Augustine, who is speaking for/with us. We cannot mistake Augustine's sensitivity to the voice, for in the very next statement he again speaks for himself. This is no editorial "we." By himself he enacts the restlessness that he asserts we share. A series of questions erupts through which Augustine, at a seemingly breathless pace, appeals for a definitive answer on the process through which he and anyone else might come to praise God.

> Lord, grant me to know and understand which is first, to know you or to call upon you? But how does one who does not know you call upon you? For one who does not know you might call upon another instead of you. Or must you rather be called upon so that you may be known? (1.1.)
>
> da mihi, domine, scire et intellegere, utrum sit prius invocare te an laudare te, et scire te prius sit an invocare te. sed quis te invocat nesciens te? aliud enim pro alio potest invocare nesciens. an potius invocaris, ut sciaris? (1.1.1)

Initially, two questions introduce the issues of praising and calling on God (apparently distinct forms of address) and knowing God. These questions result in the hypothetical problem of someone calling on the wrong God out of ignorance. A tentative resolution is offered through a rhetorical question. Then, Augustine introduces the questions of Scripture (Rom. 10:14) on the issue—again rhetorical questions, followed by the scriptural resolution of the relationship between seeking and praising God (see also Deut. 4:29; Prov. 8:17; Luke 11:10; Ps. 40:16; Ps. 70:4; Ps. 105:3–4).

> Yet "how shall they call upon him in whom they have not believed? Or how shall they believe without a preacher?" "And they shall praise the Lord that seek him," for they that seek him find him, and finding him they shall praise him. Lord, let me seek you by calling upon you, and let me call upon you by believing in you, for you have been preached

to us. Lord, my faith calls upon you, that faith which you have given to me, which you have breathed into me by the Incarnation of your Son and through the ministry of your preacher. (1.1.1)

quomodo autem invocabunt, in quem non crediderunt? aut quomodo credent sine preadicante? et laudabunt dominum qui requirunt eum. quarentes enim inveniunt eum et invenientes laudabunt eum. quaeram te, domine, invocans te, et invocem te credens in te: praedicatus enim es nobis. invocat te, domine, fides mea, quam dedisti mihi, quam inspirasti mihi per humanitatem filii tui, per ministerium praedicatoris tui. (1.1.1)

The passage concludes with an orderly presentation of Augustine's answer, which Scripture has expanded from his original questions: (1) faith, which God breathes into Augustine through preaching and the Incarnation, leads to (2) belief, by which Augustine can (3) call on God, which is his means of (4) seeking and finding God, which enables him to praise God, the act of a resting heart.

In this series, which Augustine presents in reverse, the scriptural reference from Romans 10 introduces two elements not to be overlooked in the development of the text. First is the precedence of belief over knowledge. That "belief precedes understanding" is perhaps the most famous of all maxims attributed to Augustine. Here he incorporates the principle without fanfare. But its character in the introduction to the *Confessions* contradicts quite directly the characteristic Neoplatonic elevation of knowledge over belief. He sets a deeply anti-Neoplatonic tone. The second element is the crucial role of the preacher as a catalytic agent for God in the process Augustine describes. He posits rhetoric, eloquence, and oratory as integral to his project. Finally, Augustine indicates that in his present voice he has been through this process and presently stands in faith, though still seeking and calling after God—the very thing he has just enacted.

John K. Ryan says that in this passage the statement "our heart is restless until it rests in you," "sums up Augustine's whole teaching on man's relation to God" (371). For the reader, the statement may begin to trace the outlines of Augustine's teaching on man's relation to God, but the entire first passage sums up nothing, although it moves the reader in important ways. It builds expectations for a dynamic discourse that demands our full attention. The first paragraph is an overture, not a finale: God produces faith in Augustine through the combination of preaching and the Incarnation—an overtly rhetorical formula.

The initial coordinates of the text foreground a concern with order, but not a simple, static, discursive order. The two-way conversation with God quickly becomes a three-way conversation (Brown, *Augustine*, 166), despite some—like McMahon—who claim that Augustine maintains a mode of prayer to God throughout. The changing voices Augustine utilizes with such agility accentuate the textual dynamics, which include inquisition of God as well as praise of God in the reader's presence. Starnes warns of Augustine's sophisticated use of rhetorical questions:

> If this is not appreciated and these questions are taken at face value the work will seem much more open and indefinite than it is. Examples of Augustine's use of this device can be found on almost every page, often mixed in with genuine questions. (*Conversion*, 26)

The warning rightly belies our need to explore in what other ways our reading may suffer from anachronistic blind spots. For instance, we see that Augustine relies heavily on Scripture. In this small segment his statements that present certainties either quote, paraphrase, or echo Scripture. The Latin text gives no indication of when Augustine is quoting Scripture, and translators sometimes err in their notation of Scripture references. Even so, many allusions, partial quotes, and echoes are not referenced at all in the notes of the Latin text or in translation, although they permeate Augustine's discourse.

Situating the Confessions

We come as readers to the *Confessions* as a discrete text, isolated in time and space from the broader cultural discourse in which it emerged. Even if we read it as part of an anthology of Augustine's works, our access to how the text relates to its contemporary circumstances and its historical situation is sorely limited. With familiar texts in our own time and situation this is usually not the case. We have our favorite contemporary authors, speakers, actors, directors, athletes, and musicians. We attend to each performance, composition, or production, and, whether consciously or unconsciously, we note how the one we are currently engaged with relates to others by the same person and how it responds to and interacts with the larger artistic, social, and political situation. For bookies, film critics, book reviewers, and White House correspondents these relations become an obsession, eliminating the isolation of discrete discursive acts.

To engage the *Confessions* we need to cultivate our own sensibilities toward the personal and societal currents to which Augustine responded with this text. We need to know who the *Confessions* was addressed to, the dynamics and situation of Augustine's life at the time, and the conventions of the text's production in form and technique. These factors cannot interpret the *Confessions* for us, they merely help us in our attempt to engage the text on its own terms—in its own habitat. Admittedly, the attempt recreates provisionally and partially. Few people can know a lion well in the wild, and we learn more of the zoo or circus by seeing the lion in a cage there. But at a wildlife park, where the natural situation is re-created, we may learn something of a lion. The better the reconstruction of the lion's everyday life, and the more time we spend there, the better we can understand the animal before us.

Confessing by Request

Augustine pays no homage to the Muses. In writing the *Confessions* he does not respond to a romantic impulse for self-expression or a vision from God. To compose the work is not even his idea. Frederick van der Meer notes that, except for *De trinitate*, all of Augustine's "greater" works "came into being to meet the particular needs of the time" (xvii).

That Augustine writes the *Confessions* in response to numerous requests surfaces within the text as a matter for inquiry (10.3.3–4.6). He asks, "Why do they seek to hear from me what I am?" [quid a me quaerunt audire qui sim] (10.3.3) and reflects that "many men wish to know about this, both men who have known me and others who have not known me. They have heard something from me or about me." [et multi hoc nosse cupiunt, qui me noverunt, et non me noverunt, qui ex me vel de me aliquid audierunt] (10.3.4). He wonders aloud about what they expect to gain from hearing him confess (10.4.5).[4]

These requests could be read as applying only to book 10. However, as late-fourth-century Christians, Augustine's colleagues might beckon for some report on the current state of his soul but would certainly expect the revelations from his past that are contained in the first nine books (Brown, *Augustine*, 158–60). Many of the stories Augustine relates in the *Confessions* were in circulation by word of mouth prior to their writing, and people were eager for them to be published (Gibb and Montgomery, eds., ix; 10.3.4).

The *Confessions* responds to a variety of queries from fellow Christians, and Augustine does not hesitate to direct his discourse specifically to such charitable seekers (Bonner 50–51). The people in question are alternatively referred to as the *spirituales* or *servus Dei*. A loosely affiliated network of highly educated laymen, nuns, monks, priests, and bishops spread throughout the Roman Empire, they seem to be the most likely source of entreaties for the *Confessions* (Brown, *Augustine*, 159–60, 202).[5]

In many senses, Augustine had become the "dean" of the *servus Dei*. The monastery he established in Hippo "became a 'seminary' in the true sense of the word: a 'seed-bed' from which Augustine's proteges were 'planted out' as bishops in the leading towns of Numidia" (Brown, *Augustine*, 143). Hippo itself was quite the cosmopolitan city, the second port of Roman Africa behind Carthage (Marrou 35). Augustine traveled extensively throughout North Africa, often preaching in Carthage and other towns (Bourke 150–51; Meer 12). People from all over the world also came to visit Augustine in Hippo (Brown, *Augustine*, 158).

Meer argues persuasively that to the surprise of most students of Augustine, he was most concerned with the lives of his parishioners and the community in Hippo (xvii). But Augustine's church was not limited to Hippo, or to Africa. It extended throughout the known world (Markus 113; Bourke 150–51). Therefore, when we consider the *Confessions*, Augustine's active contact throughout North Africa and the expanse of the Roman Empire must be taken into account, because the *servus Dei*, his friends at a distance, had requested it (Keenan 61). When he talks to God in the *Confessions* he calls them "your servants, my brothers," and when he addresses them they appear as "brother" in some form (9.2.4, 9.13.37, 10.4.5, 10.4.6, 10.34.51, 10.34.62, 12.26.35). These are not generic terms for Augustine; they refer to the intimate friends who provoked him to compose the *Confessions*.

But the *servus Dei* are not isolated ecclesiastics; they interact on a much wider network as well. Their regular correspondence includes people of various stations of life outside the bounds of the church. Therefore, in addition to the mounting clamor among Augustine's friends, we must expect that "the *Confessions* were intended for circulation outside the Church" (Meer 349). Augustine knows that more people will hear his words than those who originally asked him to compose the work.

The Bishop of Hippo

Although Augustine enjoyed a fine reputation within a circle of friends and correspondents across the Roman Empire, this group would have been relatively small in number compared to the two thousand parishioners that might stand packed into the church at Hippo for a martyr's mass (Meer 23). To the Roman world, Augustine, as bishop of Hippo, would not have been a high-profile individual. In addition to the fact that he was reportedly slight, bald-shaven, and modestly dressed, Meer also indicates that:

> A great deal of his work was that of an ordinary priest; he was the kind of bishop whom the more casual officials cheerfully kept waiting in their anterooms. There was, in fact, beneath the genius, a very humdrum Augustine who lived in what was really a large but very ordinary presbytery and who could be approached by anybody about pretty well any business that his caller fancied. (xvi, 25)[6]

The writing of the *Confessions* began a year or two after Augustine became bishop in Hippo, and immediately upon the completion of his first section of *De doctrina Christiana*, books 1, 2, and part of 3 (Portalie

22; O'Donnell, *Augustine*, 38). He would take at least three years to complete the *Confessions*. One reason for this could be the priority he placed on his duties as bishop. Augustine was a fixture in the community of Hippo, a "public man" of significance to the people who lived there (Brown, *Augustine*, 193, 202). For the Catholic Christians, Augustine preached at least four times a week, and during Lent and other major events on the church calendar he spoke up to seven times a week (Meer 175–76). Catholics and non-Catholics also depended on Augustine as an alternative to the Roman civil courts:

> Perhaps the function that occupied most of his time was the one he discharged in the episcopal court. . . . The civil courts of the provinces were far from being in ideal condition, so that non-Christians as well as Christians flocked to the house of every distinguished bishop. . . . At Hippo there was, naturally, a vast quantity of this work to be done. Augustine generally spent the morning in his court, "fasting," says Possidius, "sometimes until the dinner hour [our eleven o'clock], and sometimes for the whole day." (McCabe 264–65)

As bishop of Hippo, a position he held for thirty-four years, Augustine would be a much more reliable public figure to residents than the Roman governors, who often held their positions for a short time and bore no enduring concern for the town or province (Brown, *Augustine*, 195–97). From the time he ascended to the bishopric, Augustine had relinquished the contemplative life.

Concurrent with his local responsibilities, he also served as a leader in the councils of the African Catholic Church. As W. R. Johnson notes, "His mail brought him news of heresies and factional quarrels: Could he perhaps write a letter on this problem? Would he counter this latest heresy with a letter or a pamphlet?" (227). Although never a primate, Augustine would quickly become the "force of the African Church" (Marrou 35). He and the *servus Dei* of Africa, through their deliberations in the larger councils of African Catholicism, would set the course of church doctrine and policy in Africa, and—to a great extent—for the Western church that was yet to come (Meer 10; Brown, *Augustine*, 24).

In this, we trace an outline of Augustine's ordinary life, but only as a suggestion—one protocol—which anyone who approaches the *Confessions* might wisely pursue independently of this study.[7] For our present purposes, however, we must note at least that as Augustine writes his *Confessions* it appears he is exercising his avocation, not his vocation. By vocation, he is a public figure in an important provincial town, fully engaged in the social and political life of both his parish and the African church, dealing primarily with the everyday concerns of the people of Hippo and maintaining his preaching and catechizing duties. How, in the midst of such burdens, did Augustine write?

Orality and Literacy

How did that holy man, the charitable Augustine, write? O, that he were here with us, even in our presence, to speak to us! For through his voice, its tone and its cadence, we might hear, and hearing might understand, and understanding might read the *Confessions* and freely pursue wisdom, to the delight of that charitable one, and even more so to our own. But if we were to hear that holy and charitable man, would we be reading or listening? Listening indeed. For if a speaker should speak and we should be reading we would not hear, but our reading would be disrupted. Likewise, if we should listen, ever so carefully, while that holy Augustine, charitable though he be, should write to us we would hear nothing but the quill against the parchment. And so if Augustine, the charitable and holy, should write, we should be reading him, and if that same holy and charitable man should speak, we should be hearing him. Thus reading for writing, and hearing for speaking. Yet he speaks to us, and does not write.

The *Confessions*, if we would approximate its own context, must be heard. According to Mikhail Bakhtin, it is no book to curl up with alone:

> It is significant that even today one cannot read St. Augustine's *Confessions* "to oneself"; it must be declaimed aloud—to such an extent is the spirit of the Greek public square still alive in it. (134–35)

To Bakhtin someone might say, "Of course one *can* read the *Confessions* to oneself today." But to do so naively, without at least a conscientious attempt to "hear" the confessions in our mind as we read, would be like claiming to know a song by its lyrics alone—denying the tune any significance. That we must engage the text in its oral context cannot be overemphasized. The *Confessions* themselves expect to be read aloud. One of their most memorable passages announces this expectation. In it Augustine reinforces the cultural norm of reading aloud by introducing Ambrose's unusual practice of silent reading:

> When he read, his eyes moved down the pages and his heart sought out their meaning, while his voice and tongue remained silent. Often when we were present—for no one was forbidden entry, and it was not his custom to have whoever came announced to him—we saw him reading to himself, and never otherwise. After sitting for a long time in silence—who would dare to annoy a man so occupied?—we would go away. We thought that in that short time which he obtained for refreshing his mind, free from the din of other men's problems, he did not want to be summoned to some other matter. We thought too that perhaps he was afraid, if the author he was reading had expressed things in an obscure manner, then it would be necessary to explain it

> for some perplexed but eager listener, or to discuss some more difficult questions, and if his time were used up in such tasks, he would be able to read fewer books than he wished to. However, need to save his voice, which easily grew hoarse, was perhaps the more correct reason why he read to himself, but with whatever intention he did it, that man did it for a good purpose. (6.3.3)

What modern reader would pause to wonder at why another was reading silently? In most circumstances we would wonder about someone who read aloud at length to a group of adults.[8] To us, this scenario may appear comical: a group of people comes by to visit the bishop, watches him read for some time, and then gets up and leaves without speaking a word! (Crosson 152). And as they leave they puzzle over the bishop's rationale, reflecting upon what they would expect to happen if he did read aloud—the unavoidable interruptions for clarification and discussion—and the more likely need for the preacher to preserve his voice.

But Ambrose was exceptional. He violated the expectations of these highly educated professionals and probably the expectations of the writers whom he read. Leo Ferrari captures these expectations succinctly.

> The *Confessions* was written long before *The Gutenberg Galaxy* appeared on the horizon of history. Consequently, both books and readers were extremely rare and the coming together of the two make of reading a highly social occasion.
>
> We must therefore begin by realizing that the *Confessions* was written to be read aloud before an assembled audience, as Augustine himself repeatedly says of it. This means that the text is really a script for dramatic performance. ("Scene," 102)

Production

How the *Confessions* were produced suggests that we might hear them more precisely as a *transcript* of a dramatic performance; a recording utilizing the finest Roman recording technology available: the *notarii*. Documented by reference to Augustine's own testimony in numerous letters and works, Meer provides this synopsis of the most probable means by which the *Confessions* were composed:

> The bishop did not concern himself with the actual labour of writing—no writer of Antiquity ever did that. When he was at home he dictated, and walked up and down as he did so. Even his greater works came into being in this way, for the actual business of writing was too great a physical strain. Moreover, he could command the services of a whole staff of shorthand writers, the *notarii* . . . , who scratched the

> notae and who were probably found from among the clerics of his own household. Every ecclesiastical personage of any importance had one or more *notarii* available, and he also speaks of libraii, who gave him readable copies of what he had dictated, copies which then received from him their final correction. (414)

In the modern sense Augustine did not "write" the *Confessions* at all. He spoke them. He spoke them with the conventional expectation that when they were read, they would be read aloud in the company of many listeners by someone who really knew how to "read," someone skilled in what we would now refer to as oral interpretation.

By contrast, Robert McMahon claims that the sense we get of Augustine's speaking in the *Confessions* is a brilliant literary stroke by Augustine the author to make the text appear as though it were spoken—assuming the author is actually writing (10). McMahon imagines an Augustine so skilled at producing an oral form that he can successfully compose a text that "declares itself to be unrevised" since "speech cannot be revised; it can be retracted only by addition" (10). McMahon, reading through contemporary conventions of literary criticism—and applying a "historico-formalist" approach skillfully—regards the oral character of the *Confessions* as a literary device and considers anyone who interprets the work as genuinely unrevised as "mad," "a perfect literalist" (xiii, 10).

As it turns out, one need be neither mad nor a literalist to receive the text of the *Confessions* as an edited but direct transcript of a series of oral performances by Augustine. His conventional means of textual production alone should acquit us of the notion that our reception of the text as an oral performance is precipitated by a sophisticated literary device. A much more likely scenario, drawing together some of the threads developed thus far concerning Augustine's everyday life as bishop of Hippo, would suggest that the *Confessions* never constitutes the focus of his attention but rather provides a welcome, almost recreational diversion to his mind and soul.

We can picture Augustine, the *servus Dei* and other distant friends in mind, pacing the floor of his church house in Hippo, confessing to them and God with a monk furiously taking shorthand into the late night hours or perhaps all night long. These dictation sessions are a relaxing diversion from the burdens of the bishopric, at least for Augustine (Meer 238, 418). Yet the *Confessions* are no consuming passion. Far from being his only project, they emerge over a period of time in which other works absorb much of his time and attention. During the four years in which Augustine works on the *Confessions* (397–401 A.D.) he also composes portions of at least seventeen other extant works (Portalie 402–3; Brown, *Augustine*, 184–85).[9] Of these, he begins and completes fourteen concurrently with the *Confessions* and begins three that he completes later.[10] Using Meer's estimate of Augustine's preaching schedule, he delivers at least six hundred sermons during the same stretch of time; possibly more than eight hundred.

The everyday demands on the bishop and sheer volume of his works argue that Augustine dictates them *ex tempore*, by far his favored method for public speaking in theory and practice (G. Riley 122; *De doctrina Christiana*, 4.10.25; Meer 413). He customarily works in this fashion, utilizing the monks who serve as his *notarii* to note and transcribe his sermons and correspondence. He will not even engage in a debate without a *notarius* to take minutes and obtain the signatures of witnesses (Meer 416, 418). As Johnson has observed, "What amazes is that out of the relentless torrent of words there came some books of enduring power and beauty, and there came pages that, for their truth and passion, have yet to be surpassed" (227).

Publication

The *Confessions* are recognized as one such book by his contemporaries (Guitton 9). They receive the book as an extended form of correspondence, the distinctions being minimal. In fact, Augustine includes as treatises in his *Retractiones* some works sent as letters (Marrou 55).

> This is partly explained by the way books were published in the ancient world. At this time, (that is long before Gutenberg), to "publish" a work meant simply to put one exemplar-type into circulation, authorizing the readers to make a copy of it. (Marrou 55)

We can only assume that upon completion Augustine sends the *Confessions* to those among the *servus Dei* who initially requested the accounts included in the work. In Augustine's correspondence, though, we find numerous requests for works and various responses. Darius receives a copy of the *Confessions* with Augustine's gratitude for circulating other of the bishop's works (Keenan 81). And while a copy is made in Hippo and sent to a prominent literary figure previously unknown to Augustine, his friend Evodius of Uzalis must send one of his own *librii* to Hippo to copy the work, since Augustine's staff is overwhelmed with other matters (Meer 132).

A certain Count Valerius receives his own copy of the *Confessions*, since he reads every book or letter he can find by Augustine "whenever they happen to come into his hands, even if they are addressed to others" (Keenan 81). Augustine, therefore, confesses with a clear sense of who will certainly read this text. But he also knows that many to whom they have not been specifically addressed will hear his confessions.

Augustine maintained a widespread correspondence with Christian and pagan friends. So while the *servus Dei* asked the questions that sparked the "writing" of the *Confessions,* Augustine does not address them exclusively. He knows that its circulation will extend beyond ecclesiastical boundaries and writes accordingly (Meer 349). Critics will read this work and will attempt to use its contents against him (J. O'Meara, "Fiction," 84; Meer 244). He also adjusts the tone of his discourse to a more cosmopolitan, sophisticated level reserved for more highly educated audiences; a tone he never uses with parishioners in Hippo (Keenan 203).

Reading in the Late Roman Empire

For Augustine while producing the text, and for listeners while hearing it (whether reading it aloud to themselves or listening to a reader), tone was a physical experience in the reception of the text, not an abstract literary concept.

Augustine says he possesses in memory those things he learned and presumably taught of the liberal arts, such as "what literature is, what skill in disputation is, how many kinds of questions there are, and whatever else of such subjects I know" (10.9.16). This seems a vast array in itself but makes up only part of his memory. Kathleen E. Welch, in her book *The Contemporary Reception of Classical Rhetoric: Appropriations of Ancient Discourse,* indicates that the sort of curriculum Augustine would have learned and taught can be characterized as rich in mnemonic formulas designed to cultivate a memory and consciousness "conveyed through speaking" (23).

> The transmission of knowledge was conveyed through devices such as formulas so that they could be remembered and transmitted. The nature of memory made this way of thinking and communicating especially effective. The presence and perhaps the power of the numerical formulas that dominate much of the contemporary reception of classical rhetoric probably originate in the world of primary orality. (23)

Augustine puts just this sort of thought on display early in the *Confessions* in the midst of his discussion of the pear-stealing episode (2.5.11). And this primary oral pattern permeates his discourse, the rhetorical practice of the age. When Augustine reads Aristotle's *Categories,* a work which challenged even his instructors, he finds it easily understandable (4.16.28). One of the reasons may be that he is able to complete Aristotle's thoughts even when they are indicated only by cues in his text. As Welch suggests, one of the crucial skills primary orality develops is the ability to fill in what the speaker or writer has left unsaid in a formula or figure of thought (23). Both Aristotle and Augustine's texts, when they are read by moderns "appear to be unorganized because they are repetitive, sometimes contradictory, and frequently tentative, traits that are expected in speaking, but that become negative in writing" (Welch 24). In *Orality and Literacy,* Walter Ong explains:

> In a primary oral culture, to solve effectively the problem of retaining and retrieving carefully articulate thought, you have to do your thinking in mnemonic patterns, shaped for ready oral recurrence. Your thought must come into being in heavily rhythmic, balanced patterns, in repetitions or antitheses, in alliterations and assonances, in epithetic and other formulary expressions, in standard thematic settings . . . , in proverbs which are constantly heard by everyone so that they come to mind readily and which themselves are patterned for retention and ready recall, or in other mnemonic form. Serious thought is intertwined with memory systems. Mnemonic needs determine even syntax. (34)

In Ong's judgment, the culture in which Augustine lived and moved and dictated the *Confessions* "knew some literacy, but still carried an overwhelming oral residue" (35). In other words, Augustine and many of his friends were highly literate, but discourse was still dominated by primarily oral patterns of *thought*. Eloquence was the standard by which a person's intelligence and education were judged (Keenan 67). In the *Confessions,* Augustine himself gauges people's intelligence and—to a certain extent—their virtue by their eloquence: including Cicero (3.4.7), Hierius (4.14.21), Faustus (5. 6.11, 5.7.13), and Ambrose (5.13.23, 5.13.24).

How do all these factors—Augustine's work in the midst of a primarily oral culture, the method and stimuli for its production, and the means by which the *Confessions* was published—affect us as contemporary listeners? How do they help us hear Augustine's *Confessions*?

Recognizing the conditions under which it was produced helps us adjust our ears to the unique dynamics of the text. We understand that we must listen and hear it as a dramatic performance—a script designed to move human hearts, minds, *and voices.* The individual words guide our reproduction of the sounds, while the figures of speech and thought reproduce the movements of our hearts and minds. Even if we read silently we can accomplish this to some extent, as the *Confessions* itself acknowledges:

> Although my tongue is at rest and my throat silent, yet I sing as much as I wish. (10.8.13)
>
> et quiescente linqua ac silente gutture canto quantum volo. (10.8.13)

The figures of speech and thought become central to our reception of this text. It strongly resists the modern impulse to dichotomize form and content. This is particularly true for Augustine, who insists on the integrity of wisdom and eloquence within the text of the *Confessions* itself as we saw in the last chapter. The integrity of form and content does not mean we should expect a seamless text without gaps or digressions. In fact, quite the opposite is the case. By virtue of its oral characteristics the *Confessions* invites listeners to digress with it and from it, to dispute and engage its questions, even to depart from the text at times for discussion. As we heard from Starnes, this does not suggest that the *Confessions* is a wide-open text that provides readers with no definitive answers, conclusions, or positions.

Yet the gaps and digressions, expected by readers and listeners of the fifth century, who are delighted to fill in such gaps and travel the digressions, can render the text inaudible to the modern heart and mind. Others simply judge them inferior:

> Before him, Paul and the Psalmists alone had thus spoken; to their school Augustine, the pupil of rhetoricians, went to learn: and thus arose the language of the "Confessions." It is not difficult to dissect into its component parts, to discriminate the Biblical element from the rhetorical, and to point out much that is far-fetched, and archaic—frigid conceits and artificial turns. (Harnack 133)

Unless we grasp the cultural expectations embedded in the text, our tendency is either to "dissect" the text and attempt a content reduction to abstract propositions or to consider form in isolation from substance. Such literary criticism, which McMahon applies to the *Confessions,* resists "the dissonance that repetition, contradiction, and an absence of internal unity bring to the formalist-trained sensibility" (Welch 25). Instead of engaging the text on it own terms, McMahon extrapolates an abstract propositional meaning from what he claims is the deep structure of the text. In the introduction to his "essay on the literary form of the *Confessions*" McMahon establishes his coordinates for reading as follows:

> This work does not concern itself primarily with the history of Augustine's life or thought, or with the truth or validity of the positions he avows. . . . This book approaches the *Confessions* "intrinsically": as a literary work that engages its audience in particular ways, possesses a variety of internal patterns, and proceeds in a narrative movement. (xiii)

As he follows through on this commitment, McMahon claims that the entire *Confessions* can be summarized and understood as unified by the single Platonist principle of "return to origins" (xviii). The Platonic reading enables McMahon to categorize the *Confessions* as "central to our tradition of Platonist literary form" (xix). But to arrive at this conclusion requires that the texture of Augustine's work be received as an authorial facade, masking the true, underlying unity of the *Confessions:*

> The return to origins is a fully coherent principle in the temporal unfolding of Augustine the speaker's dialogue with God, yet it has been carefully occulted by Augustine the author. The *Confessions* thus embodies, in its literary form, the dialectic all Christians experience between the obvious disorders in our history and God's providential ordering of all things. (xix)

By ignoring the historical circumstances of Augustine's thought and life McMahon creates space to find a speaker-author distinction "intrinsic" to the text but nowhere suggested or implied. Indeed, more than one "Augustine" inhabits the *Confessions,* but the distinctions between these "Augustines" are symptomatic of Augustine's and the text's temporal existence. They are not a literary device contrived by Augustine, the author, to present the audience with a speaking Augustine, when in fact he is writing. For instance, Augustine cues the audience when he modifies the telling of a familiar story, as in his account of his vision with Monica at Ostia. He says, "Such things I said, although not in this manner and in these words" [Dicebam talia, etsi non isto modo et his verbis] (9.10.26).

We understand from the text that it presents nothing new to God (10.2.2). And given the presence of at least one *notarius,* and likely more than one, Augustine never composed these confessions "alone with God." In this sense it appears that Augustine never had "a room of one's own" in which to write the *Confessions.*

When we encounter what appears as obscurity and find ourselves tempted to generate occulted meanings, perhaps we would do better as readers to recognize that this is a phenomenon of the temporal expanse between cultures, eras, and worlds, rather than to misrecognize reductive meanings that clearly violate the integrity of the text. In the *Confessions,* Augustine is not occulting his heart but opening it. Where he indulges in hidden meanings, we must admit that they are not so hidden to his fifth-century listeners—who would delight in completing his formulas as an exercise in cultural literacy—as they are to today's readers. Augustine's "hidden meanings" engage and delight his contemporaries and resonate, not as a hidden dissonance beneath a melodious tune, but rather with intricate harmonies.

Finally, the *Confessions* emerge under rhetorical circumstances. We mean "rhetorical" here in the sense that they are public discourse directed toward an audience with the intention of influencing their social behavior. Certainly figures and tropes permeate the discourse, and we acknowledge that Augustine does use rhetoric in this distinct but related sense as well. But by insisting that the work is self-consciously rhetorical in our first sense as well, we agree with Scott that "we must understand the *Confessions*, not so much as a literary autobiography or any other kind of literary object, but more as an action intending ultimate significance for the self and others," and that it is "more than a narcissistic act of self-orientation through writing" (40, 41).

When Augustine dictated the *Confessions*, the muses were on break . . . terminally. Augustine's friends, the *servus Dei* called for this work. They did not ask for a literary masterpiece. They wanted to hear Augustine's confessions, a most conventional request from an old established sinner. He responded with a text they could hear and engage in a social context, with public and private implications—a text committed on its own terms to do work in the world. The *Confessions* delivered more than either its speaker or listeners perhaps expected. It was the most widely read of Augustine's works in his own day, and has been so in every generation since.

Explicit Cues for Listeners

The immediate question, as we examine how to read the *Confessions* then, is: How does Augustine do this work through the discourse—especially, what does he expect of his listeners? Throughout the *Confessions* Augustine addresses both God and human beings as listeners. Since the protocols for reading we are trying to develop are not explicitly directed to God, our attention will focus on cases in which Augustine provides overt cues for human listeners. We will consider these cues as they occur in the temporal progression of the text.

Augustine provides sparse directions to listeners early in the *Confessions*. As has been previously noted, the title of the work and its first chapter orient us and use "we" and "us" at certain points where Augustine identifies with listeners in addressing God. Then, at the conclusion of a long paragraph in which he considers the temporality of human life in the context of God's eternal day, he pauses to speak directly to audience members:

> What matters it to me if someone does not understand this? Let him too rejoice and say, "What is this?" Let him rejoice even at this, and let him love to find you while not finding out, rather than, while finding it out, not to find you. (1.6.10)

> quid ad me, si quis non intellegat? gaudeat et ipse dicens: quid est hoc? gaudeat etiam sic, et amet non inveniendo invenire, potius quam inveniendo non invenire te. (1.6.10)

By directing his attention specifically to the audience, he anticipates questions in the minds of listeners—in this case as a result of what will become, even to Augustine, an intricate intellectual challenge. The directions are quite clear: we are to voice any lack of understanding but privilege finding God over finding some particular understanding. But it also presumes that most listeners will be able to follow the discourse.

Early in book 2 comes the recognition that these confessions are directed not only to God but to the people who "come upon these books of mine" [ex particula incidere postest in istas meas litteras] (2.3.5). Augustine raises the "Why write the *Confessions*?" question directly and answers, "That I myself and whoever else reads them may realize from what great depths we cry unto you. And what is closer to you than a contrite heart and a life of faith?" [ut videlicet ego et quisquis haec legit cogitemus, de quam profundo clamandum sit ad te. et quid propius auribus tuis, si cor confitens et vita ex fide est?] (2.3.5). The answer puts us in league with Augustine once again and invokes Psalm 130:1, with echoes from Isaiah and the Psalms.[11] The directions to readers in book 2—this one and a second instance—occur preceding and then in the midst of an account commonly known as the "pear-stealing episode."

The second directive enjoins listeners who view the pear-stealing episode as a sin far beneath them to thank God for his mercy in rescuing Augustine and preserving them from such deeds, since God alone deserves credit for their good works (2.7.15). In all three cases, Augustine provides explicit guides to audience response at key points where he anticipates audience questions.

Between the end of book 2 and book 8 Augustine provides only one cue directed to listeners. It comes in the introduction to book 4:

> Let proud men, who have not yet for their good been cast down and broken by you, my God, laugh me to scorn, but in your praise let me confess my shame to you. Permit me, I beseech you, and enable me to follow around in present recollection the windings of my past errors, and to offer them up to you as a sacrifice of jubilation. For without you, what am I to myself but the leader of my own destruction? What am I, when all is well with me, except one sucking your milk and feeding on you, the incorruptible food? What manner of man is any man, since he is but a man? Let the strong and mighty laugh us to scorn, and let us, the weak and needy, confess ourselves to you. (4.1.1)

inrideant me arrogantes, et nondum slubriter prostrati et elisi a te, deus meus, et ego tamen confitear tibi dedecora mea in laude tua. sine me, obsecro, et da mihi circuire praesenti memoria praeteritos circuitus erroris mei, et immolare tibi hostiam iubilationis. quid enim sum ego mihi sine te nisi dux in praeceps? aut quid sum, cum mihi bene est, nisi sugens lac tuum aut fuens te, cibo qui non corrumpitur? et quis homo est quilibet homo, cum sit homo? sed inrideant nos fortes et potentes, nos autem infirmi et inopes confiteamur tibi. (4.1.1)

The discourse here exemplifies the effect of repetition in a primarily oral text. The beginning of the passage responds to people who, having heard the first three chapters, deride Augustine in his confession, perhaps as McCabe did in the early 1900s:

Now, the *Confessions* may be fine literature, but they contain an utterly false psychology and ethics. About the year 400, when they were written, Augustine had arrived at a most lofty conception of duty and life; he commits the usual and inevitable fallacy of taking the later standard back to illumine the ground of his early career. In the glare of his new ideal, actions which probably implied no moral resistance at the time they were performed cast an appalling shadow. (24–25)

He insists on confessing despite derision and encourages us to stay the course and do the same. The scorners initially laugh at Augustine, but the discourse divides from the scorners and invites us to participate in the *Confessions* collectively. The passage precedes Augustine's narrative about his life as a Manichaean, a dualistic religious sect in which body and spirit were distinguished to such an extent that acts deemed sinful for Christians were attributed to external causes and dismissed as irrelevant for a Manichaean to concern himself with.

The laughter in the face of Augustine's concern with past sin establishes *the* crucial division in audience directions and urges us to take Augustine seriously. From this point on, the overt indicators appeal to a sympathetic audience. In book 8, the conversion narrative, Augustine prompts us to prepare to respond with praise to God as we hear the story (8.1.1).

In book 9 Augustine focuses on postconversion acts and attitudes and support amidst his uncertainty about their sinfulness. He recognizes that some listeners will judge his brief continuation as master of rhetoric in Milan as sinful. He admits that it may have been wrong and asks God (and presumably his brothers) for pardon (9.2.4). Likewise, he anticipates that someone might find his tears at Monica's death sinful. On this account he appeals to our charity (9.12.33). Finally, he asks for prayers for Patricius and Monica for their past sins (9.13.37).

By far the most extended discourse with the audience takes place in book 10. Augustine develops, through the first four chapters of the book, the rationale for confessing in the present. In this sense, the *Con-*

fessions in no way presents itself to the audience as a fully coherent text, and Augustine devotes himself to work through the difficult transition with his readers. He begins simply by foregrounding the presence of the audience in the book and reiterating the disclaimer from book 2, namely, that God has already heard his private confessions and that he is confessing, at this place in the text, exclusively for our benefit (10.1.1, 10.2.2). In this way, the text self-consciously orients itself as speaking to God, but primarily for the sake of the audience.

Augustine grapples out loud with the question of why we might want to hear about his present life. Our interest in the past seems obvious enough, but Augustine takes advantage of the opportunity to introduce his predisposition to speak in the present, not only of himself but also regarding "[a] race eager to know about another man's life, but slothful to correct their own! Why do they seek to hear from me what I am, men who do not want to hear from you what they themselves are?" [curiosum genus ad cognoscendam vitam alienam, desidiosum ad corrigendam suam. quid a me quaerunt audire qui sim, qui nolunt a te audire qui sint?] (10.3.3). He expects us to hear ourselves in his present and to believe in his reports on the basis of a charitable attitude (10.3.3, 10.3.4). He then moves on to specify some of the actions a charitable listener will take. First, a good listener with a "brotherly mind" will respond in prayer for Augustine. This he hopes many readers will do (10.4.5). Second, Augustine calls for appropriate responses to his actions, to love the lovable, lament the lamentable, approve the good, disapprove of the evil, and in everything to maintain love (10.4.5). These themes recur throughout the book (4.6, 33.50, 34.51, 39.62).

The resounding appeal comes to us for charity, prayer, and identification with Augustine as sympathetic followers of God. Beyond maintaining momentum through the dramatic shift from narrative to more speculative discourse, Brown suggests one reason why Augustine might feel a need for support from the audience: "The amazing Book X of the *Confessions* is not the affirmation of a cured man: it is the self-portrait of a convalescent" (*Augustine*, 177).

Augustine returns in book 11 to reminding us that he is not confessing for God's sake, but that our affections might be "roused up" with him to say "The Lord is great, and exceedingly to be praised" [Magnus dominus et laudabilis valde] (11.1.1). We get no more clear directions until book 12.

The listener in book 12 must choose once again to align with Augustine or exit the discourse:

> I desire to converse for a little while in your presence, O my God, with these men who grant that all these things, of which your truth is not silent inwardly in my mind, are true. For those who deny

> these things, let them bark as much as they wish, make only a din for themselves. I will attempt to persuade them, so that they may become quiet and leave open a way into themselves for your Word. (12.16.23)

> Cum his enim volo coram te aliquid conloqui, deus meus, qui haec omnia, quae intus in mente mea non tacet veritas tua, vera esse concedunt. nam qui haec negant, latrent quantum volunt et obstrepant sibi: persuadere conabor, ut quiescant, et viam praebeant ad se verbo tuo. (12.16.23)

We understand from this that if we agree with Augustine about the truth, he wants to continue the conversation. Otherwise, we should bark at the moon, or be persuaded. By the end of the chapter, though, the issue for listeners finally surfaces as presuppositional agreement with Augustine on the authority of Scripture, not necessarily agreement on interpretive particulars.[12]

> But with those who do not assert to be false all these things which are true, but honor your holy Scripture put forth by holy Moses, and like us place it on summit of authority that must be followed, and yet contradict me in some matter, I speak thus: Do you, our God, be judge between my confessions and their contradictions. (12.16.23)

> cum his autem, qui cuncta illa, quae vera sunt, falsa esse non dicunt, honorantes et in culmine sequendae auctoritatis nobiscum constituentes illam per sanctum Moysen editam sanctam scripturam tuam, et tamen nobis aliquid contradicunt, ita loquor. tu esto, deus noster, arbiter inter confessiones meas et contradictiones eorum. (12.16.23)

Both sides of this binary clash are reiterated in proper oral fashion (12.23.32), after which listeners are exhorted to maintain charity when opinions differ between interpreters working from shared assumptions (12.26.35, 12.30.41). The explicit expectations for us are unmistakable, since Augustine is now in the heart of his interpretation of Genesis 1.

As readers we must attend to the cues Augustine makes obvious in the text. For although they are explicit, they make up a minuscule proportion of the text and could easily be missed. These limited overt directions to listeners correlate closely with the situation of the text—appealing primarily to the *servus Dei* and other sympathetic readers, assuming a variety of intellectual levels, anticipating questions and discussion, and expecting enemies and critics. To complete our set of protocols for how to read the *Confessions* we need to turn our attention to a richer, more elusive, yet more substantial set of interpretive keys in the text.

Implicit Cues for Listeners

In 1990 Colin Starnes published a definitive interpretation of the *Confessions* based on the text in its own context: *Augustine's Conversion: A Guide to the Argument of Confessions I–IX*. Starnes, with his command of the language, style, and secondary literature, masterfully provides a resource that alerts the reader of the *Confessions* to minute details and the compounded worldview that Augustine invites us to adopt and enact when we read his text. In an attempt to complement Starnes's approach, I have been explicating *how* Augustine's discourse works to induce us to adopt his worldview, to enhance our ability to read this ancient text.

The conditions, or protocols, necessary for contemporary readers to engage the *Confessions* has dominated our attention, including the text's own initiative; the circumstances under which it was produced, published, and circulated; and the explicit cues it provides for readers. Having observed these coordinates for contemporary readers, we now turn to implicit factors in the text that guide our reading. To a great extent, these are the issues upon which the quality of interpretation turns, because—while being textual cues—they demand specific applications of cultural literacy. Through these implicit textual expectations the *Confessions* resists interpretations guided by keys imported without textual warrant.

Engagement in the Present Voice

A distinguished professor of philosophy, relating his experience of reading the *Confessions*, remarked that the book, especially the Latin text, still moves him to tears when he reads it.[13] The *Confessions*, if an autobiography at all, is an autobiography of the heart (Brown, *Augustine*, 28). It is the heart of the reader, that home of the will, to which Augustine appeals.

Readers regularly report the experience of being moved to participate in this text with a refreshing yet sometimes frightening intimacy, encountering ourselves and our own experience in the *Confessions* as much as Augustine's (McMahon 7). Jean Guitton identifies the *Confessions'* power to engage its readers as a historical constant and says that, "Minds so different as those of Petrarch and St Teresa of Avila were to find in it the story of their own spiritual course. Modern man, too, comes more and more to recognise himself in it" (9).

O'Donnell suggests that Augustine designed the *Confessions* to engender participation and frustrate analysis:

> He makes it possible for every reader to duplicate the process through which he has gone, to go through that process for himself. The very difficulty of the text thwarts analytic detachment and hur-

ries the reader along. Read in this way, the book is no longer Augustine's book, but our own book. (*Augustine*, 122–23)

The self-recognition of readers in the *Confessions* persists, despite Brown's astute observation that "Augustine did not write for us, though he can make us forget this. He wrote for his contemporaries" (*Religion* 11). Augustine makes us forget the historical context of the *Confessions* by omitting details we might expect in an autobiography. Descriptions, careful attention to dates, contemporary historical events, and many names slip into the shadows.[14] Absence of detail may elide the historical situation in which the text was produced, yet this alone hardly accounts for the responses of subsequent readers.

The limitation of defining details creates gaps that invite us as readers to complete them from our own context. In place of Augustine's history, we substitute our own. Starnes observes that in books 1–7 Augustine:

> Shows how he was moved to become a Christian through the objective principles implanted in the created world. These alone are what he describes as operative in his conversion. For his human audience, this means that the first confession is addressed to anyone at all. It does not presuppose that the readers are Christians . . . nor, even more exclusively, that they are Christian philosophers. . . . This first part presumes nothing more than acquaintance with the common realities of human nature, the divine law, and with the objective elements of the Christian gospel and church. (*Conversion*, 1)

The extent of the broad appeal of book 1 continues through the beginning of book 3, when Augustine encounters the *Hortensius*, which marks the beginning of his desire for wisdom. The pear-stealing episode exemplifies how Augustine invites us to participate in this text by narrating a vaguely defined scenario from his own life.

> In a garden nearby to our vineyard there was a pear tree loaded with fruit that was desirable neither in appearance nor in taste. Late one night—to which hour, according to our pestilential custom, we had kept up our street games—a group of very bad youngsters set out to shake down and rob this old tree. We took great loads of fruit from it, not for our own eating, but rather to throw it to the pigs; even if we did eat a little of it, we did this to do what pleased us for the reason that it was forbidden. (2.4.9)
>
> arbor erat pirus in vicinia nostrae vineae, pomis onusta, nec forma nec sapore inlecebrosis. ad hanc excutiendam atque asportandam nequissimi adulescentuli perreximus nocte intempesta, quousque

> ludum de pestilentiae more in areis produxeramus, et abstulimus inde onera ingentia non ad nostras epulas, sed vel proicienda porcis, etiamsi aliquid inde comedimus, dum tamen fieret a nobis quod eo liberet, quo non liceret. (2.4.9)

Perhaps the rise in violent crime committed by children and adolescents today makes us long for such comparatively simple mischief. But the salient point is made in the reading of even this brief narrative. Who has not engaged in or observed just such an act, motivated in just such a way at just such a point in a child's life? The scene changes are easy for us to accomplish as we read ourselves into such narratives supplied by Augustine. The motives are what he defines, ponders, and redefines. But even this narrative pattern does not account for the *Confessions*' enduring power of engagement through the rest of the work and upon current readers. For, in his meditation upon the pear-stealing episode Augustine can take readers along courses they would not ordinarily follow in interpreting such an action.[15]

Augustine is no Pied Piper. A reader may marvel with him as he searches the motives behind such events yet explains them differently. But most continue to listen, because the most direct means by which Augustine engages us as readers is his voice: a voice *we* must animate for him to interpret his own past for us (Flores 2). Although occasionally Augustine speaks to us, as in the directions on how to respond to the work, most often we take the role of sincere parishioners participating in public prayer: we speak *with* Augustine. And this is no artifice. In the public readings of his own day, the reader was a dramatic stand-in for Augustine. We literally become Augustine's voice, even if we "read to ourselves."

> One can read the *Confessions* only by taking the part of the speaker. One cannot read the volume without taking up, in one's own first person, Augustine's *inquisitio veritatis*.
>   One cannot read it without addressing God, whether one believes in God or not. The ongoing present of Augustine's speaking-writing unfolds in the ongoing present of our reading. More precisely, our reading *recreates* Augustine's prayer in our own times and places. Willy-nilly, every reader of the *Confessions* perforce impersonates—takes on the persona of—Augustine. (McMahon 8)

When he composed the *Confessions* Augustine had come to understand reason as an alliance of the affections and intellect (Brown, *Augustine*, 155). His complete integration of thought and emotion in the text is so impressive that Brown can rightly judge the work "a masterpiece of strictly intellectual autobiography," but then attribute its lasting appeal, especially for modern readers, to its "emotional tone" (*Augustine*, 167,

170). That tone is heard and felt when we as readers perform this text in which we hear a man inquire in his present voice into carefully selected recollections that anticipate resonances in us as listeners while we read through our own lives alongside his.

The Persistent Role of the Hortensius

The transition in the text from universal appeals through the experiences of infancy, childhood, and schooling to the unique course of Augustine's life is marked by the introduction of the *Hortensius*, a treatise from which Augustine would secure both a motive and method to seek for the sort of philosophy that could sustain the integration of intellect and emotion necessary for the *Confessions*:

> Among such associates of my callow youth I studied the treatises on eloquence, in which I desired to shine, for a damnable and inflated purpose, directed towards empty human joys. In the ordinary course of my study I came upon a book by a certain Cicero, whose tongue almost all men admire but not his heart. This work contains his exhortation to philosophy and is called *Hortensius*. This book changed my affections. It turned my prayers to you, Lord, and caused me to have different purposes and desires. All my vain hopes forthwith became worthless to me, and with incredible ardor of heart I desired undying wisdom. (3.4.7)

> Inter hos ego inbecilla tunc aetate discebam libros eloquentiae, in qua eminere cupiebam, fine damnabili et ventoso per gaudia vanitatis humanae; et usitato iam discendi ordine perveneram in librum cuiusdam Ciceronis, cuius linguam fere omnes mirantur, pectus non ita. sed liber ille ipsius exhortationem continet ad phiosophiam et vocatur Hortensius. ille vero liber mutavit affectum meum, et ad te ipsum, domine, mutavit preces meas, et vota ac desideria mea fecit alia. viluit mihi repente omnis vana spes, et inmortalitatem sapientiae. (3.4.7)

From this point on, the *Confessions* progresses through Augustine's encounter with Manichaeanism, skepticism, and Platonism. In the secondary literature, this journey is variously identified as "treatment not applied" (Brown, *Augustine,* 176), "turning from one life to another" (Hagendahl 725), "incomplete conversions" (Flores 2–3), or "false relations to God" (Starnes, *Conversion,* 24).

The Failure of the Manichaeans and the Academics

It is generally agreed that the *Hortensius* was a catalyst for Augustine's pursuit of philosophy (Gilson 9; Brown, *Augustine*, 80). In some cases this agreement carries the connotation that Cicero's philosophy was unsophisticated and amateurish by comparison to Greek philosophers and that Augustine abandoned Cicero shortly after his encounter with the *Hortensius*.

Nothing could be further from the truth (O'Donnell, *Augustine*, 3, 90). Augustine never counted the *Hortensius* as part of his failure to achieve rest in God. As we shall see, the *Hortensius* established the method by which he judged every alternative he explored as insufficient and which finally led him to the Garden at Milan. (Starnes, *Conversion*, 61) Only fragments remain of the *Hortensius*, but Vernon J. Bourke's summary helps us get a sense of why it might have so inspired Augustine:

> Among other things, Cicero wrote: "If it is necessary to philosophize, then one must philosophize; if it is not necessary to philosophize, one must still philosophize, for it is only by thinking philosophically that one can show that it is possible to go beyond philosophy" (Muller, ed., frag. 12). Further, the *Hortensius* stressed the importance of a liberal education as a basis for the study of philosophy (frag. 23). Cicero also included a sketch of the history of philosophy: Thales, Socrates, Democritus, Aristotle, Theophrastus, Ariston of Chios, Posidonius, and Nicomachus of Tyre are briefly discussed. The four great ancient virtues (prudence, temperance, fortitude, and justice) are covered (frag. 64). Cicero, writing before the time of Christ, even suggests that the study of philosophy is an ideal preparation for death and a celestial life (frag. 97). (Bourke 3)

Recalling that Augustine was a master of Cicero's works, the *Hortensius* likely supplied a more extensive treatment of wisdom than he would have found in *De oratore* or *Orator* (Brown, *Augustine*, 300). It would have provided the philosophical regimen Cicero advised to complement the treatment of eloquence in those familiar rhetoric texts, where he insisted that the ideal orator be a man of wisdom and eloquence, style and substance, philosophy and rhetoric. Augustine would never abandon these unities. The *Hortensius* was defective, not because of false teaching but because "Christ's name was not in it." This lack could have been ameliorated immediately had Augustine been humble enough to understand Scripture (3.4.8).

> None such as I was at that time could enter into it, nor could I bend my neck for its passageways. When I first turned to Scripture, I did not feel towards it as I am speaking now, but it seemed to me un-

worthy of comparison with the nobility of Cicero's writings. My swelling pride turned away from its humble style, and my sharp gaze did not penetrate into its inner meaning. (3.5.9)

non eram ego talis, ut intrare in eam possem, aut inclinare cervicem ad eius gressus. non enim sicut modo loquor, ita sensi, cum attendi ad illam scripturam, sed visa est mihi indigna, quam Tullianae dignitati compararem. tumor enim meus refugiebat modum eius, et acies mea non penetrabat interiora eius. (3.5.9)

Augustine blames his own pride, not Cicero's writings, for his inability to discern the substance of the Scripture. Interestingly, Augustine states that he wants to "strongly embrace not this or that sect, but wisdom itself, whatsoever it might be" and that without the name of Christ no philosophical approach—as in Cicero—or philosophy in itself could "capture me" (3.6.8) Then, immediately after he bypasses the Scripture he affiliates with a sect!

He departs from the Manichaeans because he finds them of inferior philosophical substance. Faustus, their chief spokesman, Augustine finds most eloquent but inferior intellectually (5.6.11). Augustine never had been able to become a full-fledged Manichaean, and Faustus confirms his intuition.

He spends even less time engaging the work of the Academics, to the extent that Gerald Bonner can say with good warrant that "it is misleading to talk, in any but the widest sense, of a period of Academic scepticism in Augustine's life" (74). The problems with the Academics were that they lacked the name of Christ and that they were Skeptics (5.14.25). Despite the fact that the Academics practiced "a very accommodating kind of scepticism," Augustine targeted them in *Contra academicos*, a dialogue written at Cassiciacum shortly after Augustine's conversion.

Recalling that Augustine first levels the charge of lacking the name of Christ at Cicero—an Academic himself—while relating his discovery of the *Hortensius*, Augustine makes a practical distinction regarding Cicero at this point. He rejects elements of skepticism in Cicero's work, but he forever embraces the integration of philosophy and rhetoric espoused by the master orator of Rome.

Although Augustine moves through and dispenses with skepticism, he does not abandon Cicero's *Hortensius* as a philosophical compass. It resurfaces eleven years after his first reading of it, and Augustine attempts to pursue wisdom once more, guided by the same coordinates:

Anxiously reflecting on these matters, I wondered most of all at how long was that time from my nineteenth year when I had first been fired with a zeal for wisdom. For then I had determined, if wisdom were found, to abandon all the empty hopes and all the lying follies of my vain desires. But see, I was now in my thirtieth year, still caught fast in the same mire by a greed for enjoying present things that both fled me and debased me. All the while I would say to myself: "Tomorrow I will find it! It will appear clearly to me, and I will accept it! Behold, Faustus will come, and he will explain everything! Ah, what great men are the Academic philosophers! Nothing certain can be discovered for the conduct of life! But no, we must seek more diligently; we must not fall into despair!" (6.11.18)

Et ego maxime mirabar satagens et recolens, quam longum tempus esset ab undevicensimo anno aetatis meae, quo fervere coeperam studio sapientiae, disponens, ea inventa, relinquere omnes vanarum cupiditatum spes inanes et insanias mendaces. et ecce iam tricenariam aetatem gerebam, in eodem luto haesitans aviditate fruendi praesentibus, fugientibus et dissipantibus me, dum dico: "cras inveniam; ecce manifestum apparebit, et tenebo; ecce Faustus veniet et exponet omnia. o magni viri Academici! nihil ad agendam vitam certi conprehendi potest? immo quaeramus diligentius et non desperemus." (6.11.18)

We know that the *Hortensius* fired Augustine's zeal for wisdom. It set him "ablaze." Here, he recalls that experience and criticizes the Manichaeans and Academics as falling short of sustaining the quest for wisdom. He attempts to recover the dream. As Augustine proceeds into the introduction of book 7 he also recalls that "from the time that I first began to learn anything of wisdom I did not think of you, O God, as being in the shape of a human body" [non te cogitabam, deus, in figura corporis humani: ex quo audire aliquid de sapientia coepi, semper hoc fugi] (7.1.1). It may be that the reference here foreshadows the one in *De civitate Dei* (22.20) in which Augustine credits Cicero with championing the idea that God is immaterial in the *Tusculan Dialogues* (1.27). Nevertheless, even these brief references reiterate the fact that two sects cannot fulfill Augustine's desire to pursue wisdom, kindled by his interpretation of the *Hortensius* and subject to the name of Christ. The same formula will survive the failure of Platonism as well, to which we must devote more deliberate attention.

The Failure of the Platonists

Considering the way in which the *Confessions* criticize Neoplatonism takes more careful consideration primarily because for more than a century Augustinian scholars have debated whether latent "Neoplatonism" is their motivating force. For a textual critic, this is a relatively straightforward matter, as Starnes so effectively demonstrates (*Conversion*, 182–

99). Numerous respected Augustinian scholars insist that by the time the *Confessions* were written, Augustine had made a full transition from the philosophy of Neoplatonism to Christian orthodoxy.[16] None of these scholars claim that Neoplatonism had no influence on Augustine as a Christian. Quotes and echoes from the *Enneads* are present in the *Confessions,* and Augustine himself credits Neoplatonism for its value and substance despite its many errors. Nevertheless, Augustine speaks clearly and critically about his inability to sustain a pursuit of wisdom through Neoplatonism.

Perhaps the most offensive indictment for a Neoplatonist in these passages is Augustine's use of Scripture to relate the teachings and failings of Neoplatonism (7.9.13–15). To his listeners he makes no reference to exactly which books he has in mind. John J. O'Meara cites this as a problem:

> Take, for instance, the celebrated passage (7.13–15) in which Augustine describes what he read in the Platonist books. He does not say, for example, "I read in some of the *Enneads* of Plotinus, or in the *de regressu animae* (or *Philosophy from Oracles*) of Porphyry, or in these works of both philosophers, translated by Victorinus, of the Father, and Intelligence, and the soul of man and their relations. This enabled me to conceive of a spiritual deity, which released me from a block until then insurmountable to me. It seemed to me as it had seemed to others, that there was a correspondence between these Principles and the Father and the Word of the Christian Trinity." Such a statement would have given us direct information on a crucial episode in Augustine's life where, because of the indirect telling, in spite of the concentrated attention of scholars for a century, obscurity remains. ("Fiction," 84–85)

O'Meara offers this as part of a general complaint that the use of Scripture throughout the *Confessions* fictionalizes it by leaving the reader in obscurity where greater clarity is desired ("Fiction," 84–86). In other words, certain readers want to know certain things, and the use of Scripture obscures the informational certainty. O'Meara almost suggests, like McMahon, that if Augustine had wanted to, he could have made the *Confessions* a scholarly treatise instead (McMahon 7). Since the *Confessions* lacks full documentation of Augustine's sources, O'Meara concludes that Augustine's account must be considered "fictional" rather than factual. Instead of informational clarity, Augustine once again is charged with a literary deceit. O'Meara believes that Augustine is hiding something behind the text that "ought" to be there. In most cases that something is Neoplatonism in one form or another, with Augustine consciously or unconsciously hiding the dominant influence of Neoplatonism under a Christian veneer. The *Confessions* then becomes factually unreliable, but remains a sophisticated literary device.

I am arguing, by contrast, that the *Confessions* could not have been a treatise. To suggest that the form and substance of this text are interchangeable instead of integrational constitutes nothing but arrogance toward the modus operandi of Augustine's entire project. That more specific information about Augustine's life is available to him than what he included in the *Confessions*—details that would help us know more about Augustine—is beyond question. But Augustine's project is not an exercise in self-disclosure (Scott 41; Flores 13). To provide a detailed scholarly history of which books of the Platonists he read and how they influenced him would subvert his purpose in bringing them into the text in the first place. His project is critical. Neoplatonism in the *Confessions* is a *target*, not a subject.

> In order to understand the argument of the *Confessions*, Augustine himself did not think it necessary for the reader to know the authors or the precise content of these [Neoplatonic] works. Not only does he refuse to refer to them by name—which he could easily have done—but he finds it perfectly adequate to describe their content solely in terms of the same teachings which are contained in the Scriptures. Moreover, the effort to locate his sources can be very misleading because it is just this method of working from clues in Augustine to the discovery of his sources and thence back to Augustine that has led to strained interpretations, as Augustine's works are forced to conform with the source that is presumed to explain them. (Starnes, *Conversion*, 182)

Augustine, working through the union of form and substance in the text, accentuates the gulf between Christianity and Neoplatonism (Burnaby 70). His failure when he first encountered the *Hortensius* was pride and the absence of the name of Christ. The temptation of the Platonists is threefold: (1) Pride, "Now I began to desire to appear wise. Filled up with punishment for my sins, I did not weep over them, but rather was I puffed up with knowledge" [iam enim coeperam velle videri sapiens, plenus poena mea et non flebam, insuper autem inflabar scientia]. (2) Distraction, "They might have drawn me away from the solid foundation of religion" [fortasse aut abripuissent me a solidamento pietatis]. (3) Similarity, "I might have thought that if a man studied those books alone, he could conceive the same thoughts from them" [putarem etiam ex illis libris eum posse concipi, si eos solos quisque didicesset] (7.20.26). The overwhelming momentum of the passage teaches the opposites of these as well, not pride but humility; not presumption but contrition; not books of the Platonists but the "Sacred Scriptures." Thus in 7.20 he explicates—regarding the incomparable value of Scripture versus the books of the Neoplatonists—what he has so vividly enacted in 7.9.

Even Augustine's invocation of the "Gold from the Egyptians" metaphor, whereby he acknowledges that he recovered truths of great value from the Neoplatonists, accentuates his departure from them (7.9.13–15). Hagendahl contends that Augustine's practice in such cases cannot be characterized as a synthesis of pagan and Christian, but as the "strong subordination of what is borrowed property" (729). The Israelites were not sharing the gold with the Egyptians, they were "redeeming" it from their slave masters. And they left.

Augustine's departure from Neoplatonism to Christianity in the *Confessions* is not precipitated by a philosophical quarrel over minor details. The division is fundamental.

> Augustine's insistence on the error of the same Platonism that had led him to the true knowledge of God may seem confusing but is absolutely essential to understanding the radical difference he sees between Platonism and Christianity—a difference which is central to the logic of the remainder of the *Confessions*. (Starnes, *Conversion*, 194)

The heart of that difference is clearly the Incarnation (Marrevee 71–72). At the time the *Confessions* were composed, the Incarnation constituted *the* social and philosophical divide between Neoplatonists and Christians, to the extent that Neoplatonists would publicly display the gospel of John 1:1 but never John 1:14 (Brown, *Augustine*, 102). Not that the Neoplatonists denied that Jesus lived and was "a man of surpassing wisdom, whom no other man could equal" [de excellentis sapientiae viro, cui nullus posset aequari] (7.19.25)—this Augustine found acceptable within the constraints of the Neoplatonic system. Rather, the doctrine that God had taken on flesh—that Jesus was deity, not part of the divinity that we all share—became the issue upon which Augustine departed from Neoplatonism. The division occurred in two directions: (1) that Logos (Christ) became a discrete human soul in one person—Jesus; (2) that Christ was not a man made divine, but God himself become a man. Both reinforce the radical difference between God and human beings as Creator and creature versus souls as emanating from Logos. Without the Incarnation, the Neoplatonists had only Logos and could not entertain the name of Christ incarnate within their system.

Before the Garden at Milan: The Quest Begins

When Neoplatonism fails to sustain his search for wisdom, Augustine turns to the church. The priest, Simplicianus, reinforces Augustine's departure from Neoplatonism and urges him toward conversion (8.2). Starnes summarizes Simplicianus's tactic:

> He recognized that Augustine's difficulty did not lie in his knowledge of God but in his inability to submit his will to that of Christ. Seeing the similarity between the cases of Victorinus and Augustine, he told him the story of Marius' conversion. He did so not to show the rapport between Christianity and the philosophical knowledge of God but to show the absolute difference between the two relations to his knowledge, embodied in the philosopher's presumption and the Christian's humility. . . . The whole story is placed in the contest of the will, of humility, and of exhortation—as opposed to knowledge, pride, and instruction. (*Conversion*, 218)

On the heels of Simplicianus's narrative of Victorinus's conversion comes the story of Saint Anthony as related by Augustine's friend and fellow African, Ponticianus (8.6). Through these narratives—confessions within the *Confessions*—Augustine anticipates his own conversion narrative and teaches us how to respond to it (O'Donnell, *Augustine*, 98).

Relating his thoughts during these narratives, Augustine recognizes that his desire to search for wisdom has not yet been realized:

> Many, perhaps twelve, of my years had flown by since that nineteenth year when by reading Cicero's *Hortensius* I was aroused to a zeal for wisdom. Yet still I delayed to despise earthly happiness, and thus devote myself to that search. For the bare search for wisdom, even when it is not actually found, was preferable to finding treasures and earthly kingdoms and to bodily pleasures swirling around me at my beck. (8.7.17)

> quonium multi mei anni mecum effluxerant—forte duodecim anni—ex quo, ab undevicensimo anno aetatis meae, lecto Ciceronis Hortensio, excitatus eram studio sapientiae, et differebam contempta flicitate terrena ad eam invetigandam vacare, cuius non inventio, sed vel sola inquisitio, iam praeponenda erat etiam inventis thesauris regnisque gentium, et ad nutum circumfluentibus corporis voluptatibus. (8.7.17)

Augustine moves through twelve years and the failings of three "sects" or philosophies. Each proves to be a digression from wisdom. That is, the Manichaeans, Academics, and Platonists do not represent incremental progress toward wisdom, an evolution of his thought. Although he learns something from each—and he acknowledges intellectual growth through each sect—they represent detours from the path toward wisdom. Having read the Platonists, he was "pushed backwards in my search" and kept on "the road to perdition" [et repulsus sensi, quid per tenebras animae meae contemplari non sinerer] (7.20.26). He seeks only for a place from which he can begin a genuine search for wisdom, with coordinates taken from the *Hortensius*.

Therefore, we can see in the text that Augustine never moves beyond the *Hortensius*. It is not another failed philosophical system or sect. Augustine recognizes the pitfalls of such systems in his first reading of Cicero's treatise, despite his subsequent excursions into them. The *Hortensius* is different. Augustine consistently utilizes it as providing a method—subject to the name of Christ—for pursuing wisdom.

We find confirmation of the persistence of this work within the *Confessions* and subsequently in Augustine's life. In addition to the preceding discussion of Augustine's repeated references to the *Hortensius*, we must note, given O'Meara's concern about the books of the Neoplatonists, that Augustine chooses to identify this text and its author specifically, and to discuss its contents in his own words rather than in the words of Scripture. Cicero is mentioned by name or by commonplace elsewhere in the *Confessions* (3.4.8, 5.6.11), and Augustine quotes directly from the *Tusculan Dialogues* in at least one place (1.16.25).[17] Augustine continued to study the *Hortensius* at Cassiciacum and Thagaste after his conversion and baptism, respectively (Hagendahl 493, 555). Furthermore, later in his life he recommends the *Hortensius* "to his own students so that it might work in them the same effect it had in him," a practice consistent with Augustine's frequent and sometimes lengthy quotation of it in works that span his Christian life (Starnes, *Conversion*, 79).[18] In sum, Augustine never abandoned the definitive statement on wisdom he discovered in the *Hortensius*. As James J. O'Donnell states, the *Hortensius* "was the spur to all his searches for truth" (*Augustine*, 90).

Fulfillment of the Ciceronean Ideal: The Incarnation

Wisdom and philosophy are not equivalent terms in Cicero. Eloquence and philosophy may exist independently, as may associated dialectical pairs—form and content, style and substance, emotion and reason, manner and matter. But in Cicero, "wisdom is knowledge embodied in speech" (DiLorenzo 258).

> Cicero held that "the nature of rhetoric is determined by its relation to philosophy, and that relationship is essentially one of content and expression, of things (*rea*) and words (*verba*)." The two, philosophy and rhetoric, cannot be separated, they are interdependent, and if one is pursued without substantially grasping the other they are rendered useless. From Cicero's time onward (as even before) there was an ever widening rift between philosophy and rhetoric and this separation culminated in the sophistic method of oratory. In sophistry it was not considered essential that an orator also be a philosopher.

> Eloquence was the key to a successful rhetoric and philosophy became a completely separate art. Philosophers were to think and orators to speak. (G. Riley 116)

To wit, Henri Marrou's indication that studying the liberal arts and philosophy together, as suggested in the *Hortensius,* was a radical proposition for the Sophists of the Late Roman Empire:

> Literary education was not usually opposed, as it is with us, to a scientific education, but rather to Philosophy, to that stern calling of the philosopher who values the truth of thought and the obligations it entails above the conceits of fine speaking. It is possible to describe the development of ancient education as a counter-point in two voices, in which Rhetoric and Philosophy in turn prevail over each other, are opposed, or reunite for a time in an attempt at synthesis. (17–18)

On this basis, the initial *Hortensius* passage in the *Confessions* merits closer inspection; for in the context of the dominant understanding of the relationship between liberal arts (that is, rhetoric) and philosophy, the terms employed by Augustine may carry more freight than a naive reading might suggest. The statement about Cicero in 3.4.7, "cuius linguam fere omnes mirantur, pectus non ita" is translated by Ryan close to the literal Latin as "whose tongue almost all men admire but not his heart." Outler renders the same phrase, "whose language almost all admire, though not his heart" (64). Warner translates it, "a man whose style, though not his heart, is almost universally admired" (56). Starnes, in his commentary on books 1–9, says that the *Hortensius* "was included in the curriculum because of Cicero's exemplary eloquence," and then translates the phrase "whose tongue almost all men admire—though they don't pay so much attention to what he teaches" (60).

Starnes's explanation of this translation is fascinating in connection with our discussion. He says in a footnote:

> The opposition here between lingua and pectus is doubtless that suggested by Testard (Vol. 1, p. 18) who, following Cicero, sees in it the distinction between rhetoric and philosophy. That Augustine had in mind a distinction between form and content is confirmed in the last sentence of the same section. . . . See also Courcelle (Recherches, pp. 59–60) who argues that the distinction was not so much an either/or as a both/and. (*Conversion,* 79)

Starnes, translating by the spirit rather than the letter of the passage, captures the sense Hagendahl perceives when he interprets Augustine's statement on Cicero as "tacit opposition to the prevailing opinion" (588). Augustine is not merely summarizing popular opinion toward Cicero but waving a red flag to challenge status quo philosophy and rhetoric—that is to say, the entire Roman educational system. Augustine aligns himself with neither philosophy nor rhetoric as mutually exclusive, but with Cicero, the first seriously to attempt an integration of both, which he called wisdom (G. Riley 111).

From this perspective we might ask why Augustine persists in using the *Hortensius* as a philosophical compass but rejects wisdom as being fulfilled in the quest itself. What does he need beyond Cicero? Here we recall that the *Hortensius* exemplifies the strong religious impulse inherent in the philosophy of Augustine's day.[19] As an exhortation to philosophy, the *Hortensius*, unlike the *De oratore* or *Orator*, not only treats wisdom as the union of philosophy and rhetoric, knowledge and eloquence, but demands control of fleshly desires as well—expanding Cicero's own definition of wisdom to be the union of three rather than two elements (Hagendahl 496).

Therefore, Cicero provides a construct which Augustine can fully affirm, plus a plausible integration of two of the three elements: philosophy and rhetoric. However, even when Augustine had only a vague association with the name of Christ, he recognized that nothing inherent in the *Hortensius* could satisfy its own demand for control of his desires—that is, his will. Once Augustine discovers himself as a synthesis of being, understanding and will, Cicero can help him with the first two, but his will constantly disrupts whatever progress he can otherwise initiate (13.11.12).

As we learn, Augustine does not become a Ciceronean, for Cicero simply supplies the prerequisites for the pursuit of wisdom. Augustine becomes a Christian. The Ciceronean integration, the wisdom for which the *Hortensius* had made him burn, could be fulfilled exclusively in Christ incarnate: the human embodiment of Wisdom. Through his incarnation, Christ perfectly integrates philosophy and rhetoric, form and content, and exercises his passions perfectly in the body.

> But our life came down to us, and he took away our death, and he slew it out of the abundance of his own life. He thundered forth and cried out to us to return hence to him, into that secret place from which he came forth to us. For he came first into the Virgin's womb, wherein our human nature, our mortal flesh, was espoused to him, lest it remain forever mortal. And from there he came forth "as a bridegroom out of his bridal chamber," and he "rejoiced as a giant to run the way." For he did not delay, but he ran forth and cried out by words and deeds, by death and life, by descent and ascension, crying out for us to return to him. (4.12.19)

> Et descendit huc ipsa vita nostra et tulit mortem nostram, et occidit eam de abundantia vitae suae, et tonuit clamans, ut redeamus hinc ad eum in illud secretum, unde processit ad nos in ipsum primum virginalem uterum, ubi ei nupsit humana creatura, caro mortalis, ne semper mortalis; et inde velut sponsus procedens de thalamo suo exultavit ut gigans ad currendam viam. non enim tardavit, sed cucurrit clamans dictis, factis, morte, vita, descensu, ascensu, clamans, ut redeamus ad eum. (4.12.19)

Therefore, Augustine could arrive at the point of producing these confessions only via the Garden at Milan. In that experience he had no mystical or Platonic vision. He heard a voice, picked up the Scripture, read it, believed it, and acted upon it—a predominantly discursive event. The fragment of Scripture he read—"Not in rioting and drunkenness, not in chambering and impurities, not in strife and envying; but put you on the Lord Jesus Christ, and make not provision for the flesh in its concupiscences" [non in comissationibus et ebrietatibus, non in cubilibus et inpudicitiis, non in contentione et aemulatione, sed induite dominum Iesum Christum, et carnis providentiam ne feceritis in concupisentiis] (8.12.29)—finally satisfied the prerequisites laid out in the *Hortensius*. Nothing else could sustain the pursuit of wisdom to which Cicero had exhorted him. At the midpoint of the *Confessions* Augustine is finally ready to begin his own quest for true wisdom.

> A decade before writing the *Confessions,* Augustine "moved imperceptibly into a new world." He no longer strives to become a perfect, God-like individual, modeled after pagan philosophers, but realizes that such a project is futile. . . . This shift in outlook is indicated by a change of metaphors. Previously, Augustine viewed human life as a task of ascent, now his metaphor for living is to be on the way. (Kristo 126–27)

The Incarnation immediately reorients Augustine from the vertical and ahistorical to the horizontal and temporal plane. But his conversion at the Garden of Milan cannot be reduced to a purely existential religious experience. It is no momentary encounter. In the garden, Augustine finally embraces the incarnate Word in His full integrity. This integrity, which the Word accomplished and now initiates in Augustine, had otherwise eluded Augustine.

Cicero repeatedly had prodded Augustine, especially through the *Hortensius,* to pursue truth, goodness, and happiness with wisdom (O'Donnell, *Augustine,* 3, 90). But Augustine could find no practitioners of Cicero's paradigm for wisdom—the marriage of philosophy's knowledge and self-control to rhetoric. Finally, the incarnate Word integrates the eternal Word of the Neoplatonists—that Logos within their philosophical system—with a second sense of Logos, the rhetorical sense—the act of speaking. Augustine embraces these two senses of Word as inseparable in the Incarnation, situating rhetoric positively at the center of his entire enterprise.

My reading departs radically from the predominant assumptions guiding interpretation of the *Confessions* on exactly this point. O'Connell goes so far as to claim that the Incarnation is unimportant in the *Confessions* because the Incarnation is unimportant in the church until after the fourth century. Similarly, Teselle devalues the Incarnation in the *Confessions* based on his assumption that Augustine was preoccupied with God the Father to the exclusion of the Son in the Trinity.

But the Incarnation functions monumentally in the text of the *Confessions*, guiding the style and substance of Augustine's discourse. The Incarnation provides initiative for the *Confessions* with rhetoric as its servant (1.1.1); the Incarnation defines Cicero's shortcomings (3.4.8); the Incarnation diagnoses the errors of the Manichaeans (5.3.5); the Incarnation constrains Augustine from the intellectual appeal of the Skeptics (5.14.25); the Incarnation illuminates the crucial flaw of the Platonists (12.9.13–15). Augustine expresses the discursive impetus that drives his conversion to completion as the imperative to "put on the Lord Jesus Christ," an embrace of the Incarnation (13.12.29).

In Augustine's terms, what he embraces is the speaking, embodied, Logos, who brings eternal wisdom into the contingency of temporal life. This "Lord Jesus Christ" becomes a model for temporal life because through the Incarnation the Logos volitionally enters time to enact and embody eternal principles of goodness and wisdom, producing a coherent and fully integrated life in a world defined by its contingent, temporal frame.

In the *Confessions* Augustine enacts the quest for wisdom that has been realized for him at the Garden of Milan—one in which human beings participate temporally. He emphasizes the rhetorical sense of the incarnate Word immediately, tying it to the role of the preacher as the main avenue through which people can receive faith and seek God (1.1.1)

Ambrose the Preacher: Model of True Eloquence

In Augustine's case, the preacher is Ambrose, who frustrates Augustine's attempt to maintain a critical distance and perform a formalist analysis of the bishop's eloquence divorced from the substance of his discourse. Some have labeled Ambrose as a prime contact between Neoplatonism and Augustine (Marrou 28). However, Ambrose seems to have a keen consciousness regarding the conflict between Neoplatonism and Christianity. He praises Simplicianus, his spiritual "father," for his ability to distinguish the rift between the truths of Christianity and

Neoplatonist philosophy (Starnes, *Conversion*, 217). Ambrose read Greek fluently and was quite learned in Greek philosophy, never hesitating to exploit such knowledge when it advanced the claims of Christianity (Brown, *Augustine*, 84). That is, as Campenhausen explains, Ambrose was somewhat opportunistic in his appropriation of the "Gold of the Egyptians":

> Ambrose was willing to learn from the Neo-Platonists. He adopted, for instance, their conception of substance; yet what he was looking for was not a new metaphysic. Problems of this kind he did not pursue. All that mattered to him was to define the revealed Christian truth in an intellectually neat and consistent form and thus make it unassailable. His knowledge of God as such is not a conclusion of his systematic thinking, but is based on the Holy Scripture. (99)

Augustine may notice that Ambrose occasionally borrows the technical vocabulary of Neoplatonism (O'Donnell, *Augustine*, 6). But it is Ambrose's eloquence that revolutionizes Augustine's rhetoric by pointing him to wisdom (Colish 28). In Ambrose's sermons, Augustine finds form and content finally indivisible (5.13.23–14.24). So Ambrose, the model bishop, foreshadows what Augustine later explicates about the proper approach to preaching—subordinating ascents of mysticism to the integration of form and substance, words and deeds, in the here and now:

> Therefore, let your ministers now work upon the earth, not as upon the waters of infidelity by preaching and speaking through miracles and mysteries and mystic words, where ignorance, mother of wonder, is made attentive out of fear of these secret signs. . . . But let them work as upon the dry land, separated from the whirlpools of the great deep. Let them be a pattern to the faithful by living before them and by arousing them to imitation. For thus do men truly hear, not merely to hear, but also to do. (13.21.30)

> Operentur ergo iam in terra ministri tui, non sicut in aquis infidelitatis, annuntiando et loquendo per miracula et sacramenta et voces mysticas, ubi intenta fit ignorantia mater admirationis in timore occultorum signorum . . . sed operentur etiam sicut in arida discreta a gurgitibus abyssi, et sint forma fidelibus vivendo coram eis et excitando ad imitationem. sic enim non tantum ad audiendum sed etiam ad faciendum audiunt. (13.21.30)

Ambrose's preaching is not perfect. He merely points to perfect integration through the Incarnation. And the same Incarnation not only justifies the *Confessions*—by it they are authorized: "Yet this your Word would be but little to me, if he had given his precepts in speech alone and had not gone on before me by deeds. I do this by deeds as well as by words" [et hoc mihi verbum tuum parum erat si loquendo praeciperet, nisi et faciendo praeiret. et ego id ago factis et dictis] (10.4.6). The Incarnation stands not as a means to accomplish human ascent but as a contrast to the obsession with ascent (10.42–43).

Augustine introduces the portion of *De doctrina Christiana* completed prior to the *Confessions* with a parallel passage that subordinates the individual, mystical, and visionary to the corporate, social, and rhetorical:

> We should not tempt Him in whom we have believed, lest, deceived by the wiles and perversity of the Enemy, we should be unwilling to go to church to hear and learn the Gospels, or to read a book, or to hear a man reading or teaching, but expect to be "caught up to the third heaven," as the Apostle says, "whether in the body or out of the body," and there hear "secret words that man may not repeat," or there see Our Lord Jesus Christ and hear the gospel from Him rather than from men.
>
> We should beware of most proud and most dangerous temptations of this kind and think rather that the Apostle Paul himself, although prostrated and taught by the divine and heavenly voice, was nevertheless sent to a man that he might receive the sacraments and be joined to the church. And the centurion, Cornelius, although an angel announced to him that his prayers had been heard and his alms recognized, was sent to Peter for instruction. He not only received the sacraments from him, but was also taught what should be believed, what should be hoped, and what should be loved. And all of these things in both instances might have been done by an angel, but the condition of man would be lowered if God had not wished to have men supply His word to men. (5–6)
>
> neque temptemus eum cui credidimus, ne talibus inimici versutiis et perversitate decepti ad ipsum quoque audiendum evangelium atque discendum nolimus ire in ecclesias aut codicem legere aut legentem praedicantmque hominem audire et excpectemus rapi usque "in tertium caelum sive in corpore sive extra corpus," sicut dicit apostolus, et ibi audire "ineffabilia verba quae non licet homini loqui," aut ibi videre dominum Iesum Christum et ab illo potius quam ab hominibus audire evangelium.
>
> Caveamus tales temptationes superbissimas et perculosissimas magisque cogitemus et ipsum apostolum Paulum, licet divina et caelesti voce prostratum et instructum, ad hominem tamen missum esse ut sacramenta perciperet atque copularetur ecclesiae; et centurionem Cornelium, quamvis exauditas orationes eius elemosinasque respectas ei angelus nuntiaverit, Petro tamen traditum imbuendum,

> per quem non solum sacramenta perciperet sed etiam quid credendum quid sperandum quid diligendum esset audiret. Et poterant utique omnia per angelum fieri, sed abiecta esset humana condicio si per homines hominibus deus verbum suum ministrare nolle videretur. (5–6)

Augustine's appropriation of Cicero in the *De doctrina Christiana* has been so well documented that it hardly bears repeating here.[20] The irony, however, occurs when we realize that book 4—where Cicero's work is appropriated most clearly—was not published until approximately thirty years after the first three books began to circulate in 396. However, Meer claims from his study of Augustine's sermons that book 6 "had been lived and experienced long before it was written down" (413).

By the time he writes the *Confessions*, Augustine is a fifth-century bishop. His primary task is to teach and preach the Word of God. He leads us through the *Confessions* to teach, delight, and perhaps move us—the threefold process of rhetorical performance shared by Cicero and Augustine.[21] The *Confessions*, like the sermons, exercises a priori the rhetoric of book 4 of *De doctrina Christiana,* but it also teaches the same rhetoric. In other words, the *Confessions* engages us as a self-consciously rhetorical discourse.

Augustine suggests a positive view of rhetoric which corrects the empty eloquence of the Second Sophistic, demanding that eloquence be accompanied by substance. One of the ways he makes the necessity of this union explicit in the *Confessions* is through self-criticism of his speech before the emperor:

> I sought only to please men, not to instruct them, but only to please them. For this reason, you broke my very bones under the rod of your discipline. (6.6.9)

> sed placare inde quaerebam hominibus, non ut eos docerem, sed tantum et placarem. propterea et baculo disciplinae tuae confringebas ossa mea. (6.6.9)

Clearly the right goal would be to instruct—that is, to tell the truth—rather than merely to please the listeners with lies (6.9.9). Augustine, having pointed to the primacy of instruction, follows immediately with a narrative in which he seeks to please his students *in order to instruct* them, with the positive outcome of having moved at least one, Alypius.

> By chance, there was a passage to be read lying in my hands. As I was explaining it, I thought that a comparison with the circus would be apropos, by which what I wished to say would become both

clearer and more pleasant to those whom such madness held captive by means of some biting sarcasm at their expense. (6.7.11)

et forte lectio in manibus erat, quam dum exponerem et oportune mihi adhibenda videretur similitudo cirecensium, quo illud quod insinuabam et iucudius et planius fieret, et cum inrisione mordaci eorum, quos illa captivasset insania. (6.7.11)

Augustine similarly relates a story about how Monica encourages, and sometimes persuades, other women in Thagaste to use certain tactics to avoid being beaten by their husbands:

> She would give them serious advice in the guise of a joke. From the time, she said, they heard what are termed marriage contracts read to them, they should regard those documents as legal instruments making them slaves. Hence, being mindful of their condition, they should not rise up in pride against their lords. Women who knew what a sharp-tempered husband she had to put up with marveled that it was never reported or revealed by any sign that Patricius had beaten his wife or that they had differed with one another in a family quarrel, even for a single day. (9.9.19)[22]

> haec earum linguam, veluti per iocum graviter admonens, ex quo illas tabulas, quae matrimoniales vocantur, recitari audissent, tamquam instrumenta, quibus ancillae factae essent, deputare debuisse; proinde memores conditionis superbire adversus dominos non oportere. cumque mirarentur illae, scientes quam ferocem coniugem sustineret, numquam fuisse auditum aut aliquo indicio claruisse, quod Patricius ceciderit uxorem, aut quod a se invicem vel unum diem domestica lite dissenserit. (9.9.19)

The second story incorporates not only the combination of instruction and pleasure, but accentuates the unity of the speaker and her words, which is evident to her listeners. We might consider these isolated narratives as "process stories" that alert us to the kind of discursive strategy that permeates the entire text. Because in most cases Augustine subtly but effectively integrates teaching and narrative, the teaching comes primarily while Augustine is using the first person, present voice. His strategy confirms the suggestion that Augustine frequently conflates narrative and argument (Milovanovic-Barham 6).

We cannot take more than a few brief examples to demonstrate this strategy. First, in 4.4.7, Augustine introduces a narrative segment on the death of an unnamed friend in this way:

During those years, when I first began to teach—it was in the town in which I was born—I gained a friend, my equal in age, flowering like me with youth, and very dear to me because of community of interests. As a boy, he had grown up with me, we had gone to school together, and had played games together. But in childhood he was not such a friend as he became later on, and even later on *ours was not a true friendship, for friendship cannot be true unless you solder it together among those who cleave to one another by the charity "poured forth in our hearts by the Holy Spirit, who is given to us."* Yet it was sweet to us. [Emphasis added.]

In illis annis, quo primum tempore in municipio, quo natus sum, docere coeperam, conparaveram amicum societate studiorum nimis carum, coaevum mihi et conflorentem flore adulescentiae. mecum puer creverat et pariter in scholam ieramus pariterque luseramus. sed nondum erat sic amicus, quamquam ne tum quidem sic, uti est vera amicitia, quia non est vera, nisi cum eam tu agglutinas inter haerentes sibi caritate diffusa in cordibus nostris per spiritum sanctum, qui datus est nobis. sed tamen dulcis erat nobis.

The emphasized segment of this passage shows Augustine's agility at moving from narrative to criticism and back to narrative. For readers, the momentum of the discourse takes us right through our brief lesson on true friendship and back to the story. As we read along in the first person, Augustine has us shifting tense in midsentence, marshaling scriptural support from Romans 5:5 for his view on friendship and then returning to the narrative.

In another instance, where Augustine is relating his school experience, he says, "I would have learned nothing unless forced to do it. *No one does good against his will, even if what he does is good.* Nor did those who drove me on do well" [non enim discerem, nisi cogerer. nemo enim invitus bene facit, etiamsi bonum est quod facit. nec qui me ugebant, bene faciebant] (1.12.19, emphasis added).

In this case, like the earlier one, the kinds of strategies Augustine employs, using voice, person, and tense to inject commentary into narrative are obvious. They do vary, and not all of the text is a sustained narrative, even in the first nine books. But these examples suffice to alert the reader to how nimble Augustine can be in his instructional strategies.

Augustine reveals and advocates the efficacy of the integration of form and content, enacting it in his own present voice—a temporal, discursive process (McMahon 150). Augustine's voice draws us into a dialogue, expecting social engagement and response (Henry 18–19). Interpretation of deeds and words are central to our participation, and as we progress through the text, Augustine explicitly and implicitly provides the instruction we need to participate (Scott 39; Gilson 227).

Through the *Confessions,* Augustine attempts an enactment of a genuine pursuit of wisdom, built on the expectations of fifth-century orality and the conventions of cultural literacy that attend his particular place, time, and audience. He treats at least two factors as universals— the Incarnation and the pursuit of Wisdom. But he particularizes them in his experience and situation, and thus invites us into his audience. By the delightfulness of his discourse he gains our ears, to teach us how to read the Incarnation—the Word in Deed—as the integral point which ultimately grounds our own pursuit of Wisdom—that is, genuine happiness. In saying this, we do not summarize what the *Confessions* means; we merely acknowledge and argue for a crucial set of directions Augustine divulges to readers who would engage his *Confessions* on its own terms.

Chapter 3

The Significance of Incarnational Wisdom in Time

The *Confessions* is most comfortably read today as an antique Latin autobiography, a nostalgic exemplar for a genre to be named more than a thousand years after its publication. As Gerald Bonner has noted, "It is customary for readers of the *Confessions* to devote their attention to the first nine books, to pay some regard to the tenth, and to neglect the last three" (48). The autobiographical approach releases us from the more demanding reading of books 10–13, which comprise approximately one-half of the volume.

The inclination to abandon the text somewhere between book 9 and 10 is understandable (Meer xv). Book 10 does not follow from book 9 with chronological precision (Bonner 47). But the *Confessions* invites us to proceed across the temporal gap between the past of book 9 and the present of book 10. The move reflects that, in his own context, Augustine could expect readers to be well acquainted with his intervening experience as monk, priest, and bishop. In other words, information we might consider essential to an autobiography Augustine dispenses with as extraneous, since he is not composing one (O'Donnell, *Augustine,* 83).

Continuing through the entire *Confessions,* instead of stopping after book 9, we experience the shift to book 10 as a radical departure from our generic expectations for autobiography. It similarly transgresses the early Christian confessional form. Augustine's contemporary readers were asking for books 1–9. Early in book 10 it appears that they asked for the final four books as well, but Augustine does not deliver quite what they might have expected in these later books (Brown, *Augustine,* 177–78). He says in a letter that one purpose of the *Confessions*—presumably including his catalogue of present sins in book 10—is to "present himself as he is" to keep friends and admirers from giving him undeserved praise (Keenan 81).

Though Augustine violates ancient and modern conventions, on its own terms the *Confessions* presents itself as unified. Augustine makes a simple move from a narrative of his past life—permeated with instruction and reflection—to his present encounter with himself, God, Creation, and the Scripture. Augustine's present ruminations and excursions are more clearly exegetical and didactic but do not dispense with narrative altogether (Jay 1047). They address questions and issues anticipated in books 1–9.[1] In the process, Augustine creates a dynamic, almost metaphorical, interaction between the first and second half of the *Confessions*. Neither should be read in isolation.

Vernon J. Bourke claims that great benefit awaits us if we work through the last four books of the *Confessions* with Augustine, books of "cardinal importance" in understanding Augustine's development (8). But the benefit we can gain from engaging the last four books can only come by continuing Augustine's quest for wisdom with him. He tells us as much when he introduces book 10.

Robert Meagher helps us see what is at stake if we participate *with* Augustine in discourse rather than looking *at* his text (4–5). He says, "While we pride ourselves as the most widely traveled and learned of ages, our studies amount all too often to sheer tourism, free of spiritual risk and growth" (4). Meagher charges us with a consensual "recourse to the periphery of human spiritual life," which he terms a "dogmatic obsession . . . always avoiding the center, the substance, of serious human thought" (4).

There can be no doubt that Augustine is engaged in serious human thought and that human spiritual life abides at the center of that thought. Therefore, we may risk much by reading books 10–13 and joining him, even provisionally, in the pursuit of wisdom via the incarnate Word. We can join him because Augustine the writer and what he writes become contemporary to us for the first time in books 10–13. They are written both from his present and The Present of the incarnate Word. But joining Augustine means serious consideration of the Incarnation on Augustine's terms, a union of form, substance, and morality.

Therefore, the risk is spiritual, but not *only* spiritual. Augustine will push the limits of philosophy, semiotics, theology, rhetoric, psychology, sociology, and other modern intellectual disciplines *at the same time*. As W. R. Johnson has suggested, the closer one gets to Augustine's work, the more difficult it is to separate these intellectual strands into discrete threads (228–29). Johnson observes that in Augustine perhaps the distinctions are not important (228). Indeed, Augustine's transversal of our disciplinary boundaries is positively crucial despite the contemporary enigma that may result. For if we acknowledge that Augustine embraces the incarnate Word axiomatically, applying that Word to all thought and action, and we approach the *Confessions* as integrational in a disciplinary sense, then to export its spiritual substance is to violate its integrity.

To negotiate the second half of the *Confessions* demands not necessarily a Christian reader, but one who will practice a willing suspension of disbelief and temporarily disavow notions that divide the religious and/or spiritual from intellectual life. As B. B. Warfield has said of Augustine:

> It is thus in the last analysis, supernaturalism versus naturalism that he turns to; and this is far from the same thing as rationality versus irrationality—except, indeed, on the silent assumption that the supernatural is an absurdity, an assumption which was decidedly not Augustine's. (164–65)

The spiritual risk—the one we may feel most keenly—is that journeying with Augustine in his quest for wisdom may produce in us a spiritual experience that challenges our assumptions by its integrity. And we should not underestimate Augustine on this point. Augustine's faith is no anti-intellectual fundamentalism. He is not a Late Roman televangelist. As Colin Starnes has noted:

> To put this in its bluntest form, Augustine has shown that ancient philosophy failed in the face of Christianity not because it was drawn from human reason, but because it was not sufficiently faithful to the demands of reason insofar as the philosophers turned, at the crucial moment, from Wisdom to folly. By ignoring this aspect of Augustine's teaching the critics erred not so much by their insistence on the will, but by their failure to do so as thoroughly as did Augustine who certainly had to enter the church voluntarily—not because this route opposed human reason but because it was the only rational choice in which his will could find its integrity. (*Conversion*, 284–85)

As we discussed in the previous chapter, Augustine's account of finding his integrity centers on the incarnate Word. The *Confessions*, as we consider books 10–13, takes us along with Augustine on his journey toward wisdom, which is entirely contingent upon that Word. To travel this road is not to become a "follower" of Augustine, but to take the path of wisdom with him. Along the way we will find him expressing a more complete Christianity—a type not ordinarily found in our experience—and perhaps the only sort worthy of pursuit and practice (Starnes, *Conversion*, 285). The manifest value of adopting Augustine's spiritual assumptions for this journey—the benefit commensurate to the risk—resides in exploring first how the incarnate Word leads to wisdom and then how Augustine's theorizing on this basis might enrich our own discursive theory and practice today.

Our quest with Augustine takes us immediately to the issue of how—empowered by the incarnate Word—he pursues wisdom. His conversion stokes his philosophical desire and curiosity (Crosson 158). For Augustine, the problems that animate the first nine books of the *Confessions* are not abandoned but intensified. "It is only in the final four books of the *Confessions* that Augustine really begins to fathom the full implications of his own guiding questions" (Scott 41). Therefore, his encounter with the incarnate Word energizes and permeates the entire inquiry. What may surprise us is the decisive role discourse plays in these later books. The incarnate Word is not an empty symbol. Its dynamic function drives Augustine's consideration of memory, time, and interpretation.

Memory

In book 10 Augustine begins to consider the questions raised in the first nine books. He first raises memory as a prominent issue in book 1 while reflecting on how he learned to speak. In this defining moment he introduces memory as crucial to epistemology, inherently semiotic, and psychosocial in movement.

> But I myself, with that mind which you, my God, gave me, wished by means of various cries and sounds and movements of my limbs to express my heart's feelings, so that my will would be obeyed. However, I was unable to express all that I wished or to all to whom I wished. (1.8.13)

> sed ego ipse mente, quam dedisti mihi, deus meus, cum gemitibus et vocibus variis et variis membrorum motibus edere vellum sensa cordis mei, ut volutati pareretur, nec valerem quae volebam omnia nec quibus volebum omnibus. (1.8.13)

A rhetorician from the start, Augustine reports that his memory both retained and then produced the words he needed to progress as an active member of human society.

> I pondered over this in memory: when they named a certain thing and, at that name, made a gesture towards the object, I observed that object and inferred that it was called by the name they uttered when they wished to show it to me. That they meant this was apparent by their bodily gestures, as it were by words natural to all men, which are made by change of countenance, nods, movements of the eyes and other bodily members, and sounds of the voice, which indicate the affections of the mind in seeking, possessing, rejecting, or avoiding things. . . . When my mouth had become accustomed to these signs, I ex-

pressed by means of them my own wishes. Thus to those among whom I was I communicated the signs of what I wished to express. I entered more deeply into the stormy society of human life, although still dependent on my parents' authority and the will of my elders. (1.8.13)

pensebam memoria: cum ipsi apellabant rem aliquam et cum secundum eam vocem corpus ad aliquid movebant, videbam et tenebam hoc ab eis vocari rem illam, quod sonabant, cum eam vellent ostendere. hoc autem eos velle, ex motu corporis aperiebatur, tamquam verbis naturalibus omnium gentium, quae fiunt vultu et nutu oculorum ceterorumque membrorum actu et sonitu vocis indicante affectionem animi in petendis, habendis reiciendis fugiendisve rebus. . . . per haec enuntiabam. sic cum his, inter quos eram, voluntatum enuntiandarum signa conmunicavi; et vitae humanae procellosam societatem altius ingressus sum, pendens ex parentum auctoritate nutuque maiorum hominum. (1.8.13)

Gestures, he claims, are natural and naturally understood. But he could only learn words by listening to others; the words themselves revealed no necessary connection to the objects they signified. Among numerous references to memory prior to book 10, this eighth chapter of the first book anticipates Augustine's first foray into wisdom, the necessary founding move in which he questions himself about how memory and knowledge work.[2]

While inviting us into book 10, Augustine teaches us that as listeners we can have no proof of his truthfulness (10.3.3). The reason is, we do not have access to his heart (10.3.4). He claims he does not lie, but we can have no assurance of it. Yet the burden of truth rests with us as listeners. If we listen with charity, we will believe that he tells us the truth (10.3.3–4). He forces the issue of truth in human speech, distinguishing our sensory perceptions from truth. In fact, his skepticism about the persuasive efficacy of our reception of language alone leads him to say that Christ would have been "but little to me" if his speech had not been confirmed by deeds (1.4.6). Augustine announces that he will be attempting to imitate this union of words and deeds, then confesses further that the incarnate Word *does* have access to his heart. It is through this Word that Augustine can proceed, though uncertain about himself, since "not with doubtful but with sure knowledge do I love you, O Lord. By your Word you have transfixed my heart, and I have loved you" [Non dubia, sed certa conscientia, domine, amo te. percussisti cor meum verbo tuo, et amavi te] (10.6.8).

Augustine does not doubt the reality of the things we perceive, but finds them to be unverifiable (G. Riley 176). He does doubt our judgments based on sense perception. We share the power to perceive with animals. What sets us apart is reason, the ability to question, a matter of will:

The Significance of Incarnational Wisdom in Time   87

In them [animals], reason has not been placed in judgment over the senses and their reports. But men can ask questions, so that they may clearly see the invisible things of God, "being understood by the things that are made."

However, through love for such things they become subject to them, and in subjection they cannot pass judgment on them. Nor do things answer those who ask unless they are men of judgment. They do not change their voice, that is, their beauty, when one man merely looks at them and another both looks at them and questions, so as to appear one thing to this man, another to that. It appears the same to both: it is silent to one, but speaks to the other. Nay, rather, it speaks to all, but only those understand who compare its voice taken in from outside with the truth within them. (10.6.10)

non enim praeposita est in eis nuntiantibus sensibus iudex ratio. homines autem possunt interrogare, ut invisibilia dei per ea, quae facta sunt, intellecta conspiciant, sed amore subduntur eis et subditi iudicare non possunt. nec respondent ista interrogantibus nisi iudicantibus, nec vocem suam mutant, id est speciem suam, si alius tantum videat, alius autem videns interroget, ut aliter illi appareat, aliter huic, sed eodem modo utrique apparens ill. muta est, huic loquitur: immo vero omnibus loquitur, sed ill. intellegunt, qui eius vocem acceptam foris intus cum veritate conferunt. (10.6.10)

Again, Augustine charges the listener with responsibility to discern truth. Perceptions prohibit demonstrative proofs but do not negate reason. Augustine assumes that people and at least some animals share sense perceptions in common. What differs is the critical faculty—reason, a faculty dominated by "hearing." Clearly, the sense he reflects on is sight, yet we reason based on hearing whatever these objects of our perception say. Our hearing is determined by what we love. The words Augustine hears from them are "Your god is not heaven and earth, nor any bodily thing" [non est deus tuus caelum et terra neque omne corpus] (10.6.10). We find the truth through discourse, which is based on perceptions. This discursive work takes place in the "fields and spacious palaces" of memory, "where are treasures of countless images of things of every manner, brought there from objects perceived by sense" [campos et lata praetoria memoriae, ubi sunt thesauri innumerabilium imaginum de cuiuscemodi rebus sensis invectarum] (10.8.11).

Notice how Augustine himself reveals his own inner dialogue while considering this question. Images are taken from external senses, whether by direct experience or by testimony, and from these images in memory we speak internally and externally (10.7.14). But the memory contains more than these "sensible" images; it contains "intelligible" things as well. Intelligibles themselves reside in memory, and so differ from images of external things perceived by sense (10.10.17). A geometrical axiom exists in memory, the sun does not. But the axiom, like all intelligible things, is something other than language (10.12.19).

Augustine must note that intelligible things are other than language because, like the sensible images in memory, they are considered through speech. Therefore, to exercise critical judgment, both sensible images and intelligible things must be presented from memory via sensible discourse. "I combine one another of the likenesses of things . . . with things past, and from them I meditate upon future actions, events, and hopes" [ex eadem copia etiam similitudines rerum vel expertarum vel ex eis, quas expertus sum, creditarum alias atque alias et ipse contexo praeteritis; atque ex his etiam futuras actiones et eventa et spes, et haec omnia rursus quasi praesentia meditor] (10.8.14). The relationship between the contents of memory and discourse suggests two crucial points in the progress of Augustine's inquiry.

The first point is that memory drives Augustine's epistemology. All knowledge, internal and external, depends on it to some extent.

> Augustine recognizes that memory is central to all knowledge claims. . . . Since every knowledge claim involves memory (in that any knowledge claim involves preconceptions) and, strictly speaking, a knowledge claim is never only about the putative object of the knowledge claim. In fact, a knowledge claim is a complex. I have been taking Augustine to be saying that memory is always part of this complex and that memory, then, is central to any epistemology. (Bubacz, "Factual Memory," 192)

Bubacz's indication that Augustine's view of memory applies universally bears further consideration. Augustine recognizes the existence of a priori principles in mind, intelligible objects existing universally but accessible *only* through the learning process (Colish 36; Bubacz, "Illumination," 42). He says, "Whence and how did these things enter into my memory? How, I do not know, for when I learned them I did not give credence to another's heart, but I recognized them as true and I entrusted them to my heart" [unde et qua haec intraverunt in memoriam meam? nescio quomodo; nam cum ea didici, non credidi alieno cordi, sed in meo recognovi] (10.10.17). Augustine concludes that intelligible objects are hidden in memory but are not useful until they are conceived through learning.

Some may equate his epistemological account of intelligibles with Plato's theory of recollection as narrated in the *Phaedrus*. However, there is a subtle but crucial distinction in the *Confessions*. Simply stated, Plato explains recollection as knowledge of Truth recognized in earthly beauty that corresponds with earlier out-of-body experiences of soul with the heavenly Ideal. By contrast, Augustine's theory of illumination explains cognition (versus recognition) and collection (versus recollection) of intelligibles—already existing in mind but in a disordered and hidden state (10.11.18).

The second point is that discourse animates Augustine's learning process and memory in the *Confessions*. Learning cannot take place apart from the ability to name the images and objects within memory. Although the name is not the object, the name must be present for memory to access the object.

> We have heard this name, and we all confess that we all desire the reality: we do not take delight in the mere sound of the word. When a Greek hears it in Latin, he finds no delight in it, since he does not know what has been said. We are delighted, just as he is also if he hears it in Greek. For neither Greek, nor Latin is that reality which Greeks and Latins and men of other tongues long to possess. . . . This could not be unless that very thing for which this is the name were retained in their memory. (10.20.29)
>
> audivimus nomen hoc et omnes rem, omnes nos adpetere fatemur; non enim solo sono delectamur. nam hoc cum latine audit Graecus, non delectamur, quia ignorat, quid dictum sit; nos autem delectamur, sicut etiam ille, si graece hoc audierit; quoniam res ipsa nec graeca nec latina est, cui adipiscendae. . . . qod non fieret, nisi res ipsa, cuius hoc nomen est, eorum memoria teneretur. (10.20.29)

As Marcia Colish states, "Since he holds that learning takes place through the transient, sensory medium of language, the memory is essential to the existence of sustained cognition of any kind" (36). So speech and thought are counterparts in memory, consistent with Augustine's early report of his entrance into society by the acquisition of language. But the fact that active memory depends upon signification—the ability to connect the sound that signifies to the image or the thing itself (10.15.23)—forces us to acknowledge that because the particular languages in which we think enter memory through sense perceptions, even principal thought cannot be proven. Therefore, as Bubacz has noted, "memory claims (and other knowledge claims) are important in the degree to which they have utility, in the degree to which they help us order our lives and to anticipate the future. This makes Augustine seem a pragmatist" ("Factual Memory," 192).

He seems so not only to us but to himself, for he recognizes that will interprets the contents of our memory to order our lives. It is a practical process. He introduces the blessed life as an example of a universal, intelligible object upon which our desires work. "If they [all men] could be asked in one language whether they wish to be happy, they would answer without hesitation that they wish this" [nota est igitur omnibus, qui una voce si interrogari possent, utrum beati esse vellent, sine ulla dubitatione velle responderent] (10.20.29). When asked what they desired, they would say the words "happy life," presenting a common intelligible object from memory (10.23.31).

Augustine defines the joy that is pursued as joy in truth, which is none other than joy in God (10.23.33). He admits, however, that he himself has experienced counterfeit joys, ones which he pursued in place of God (10.21.30). And when we pursue counterfeit joy, though we know the intelligible truth, we misjudge that truth and "hate the truth for the sake of that very thing which they have loved instead of the truth" [itaque propter eam rem oderunt veritatem, quam pro veritate amant] (10.23.34). The necessity of calling forth objects of memory via language means that in thought and speech, even fixed, intelligible truth is never immediate. Language is the mediator; the relation between sensible and intelligible, outer and inner thought is always constituted in words (Brown, *Religion and Society*, 10). But the problem is not with language; the problem remains with the will:

> Everywhere, O Truth, you give hearing to all who consult you, and at one and the same time you make answer to them all, even as they ask about varied things. You answer clearly, but all men do not hear you clearly. All men ask counsel about what they wish, but they do not all hear what they wish. Your best servant is he who looks not so much to hear from you what he wants to hear, but rather to want what he hears from you. (10.26.37)

> veritas, ubique praesides omnibus consulentibus te simulque respondes omnibus diversa consulentibus. liquide tu respondes, sed non liquide omnes audiunt. omnes unde volunt consulunt, sed non semper quod volunt audiunt. optimus minister tuus est, qui non magis intuetur hoc a te audire quod ipse voluerit, sed potius hoc velle quod a te audierit. (10.26.37)

Comparing Augustine's analysis of our reasoning about an intelligible object—the happy life—with the earlier passage quoted about the reception of sense perceptions confirms the fact that in both cases we reason discursively through memory, and will controls our responses.

The whole quest through memory for Augustine has not been a simple exposition of the psychological phenomenon we call memory, with its attendant social implications. The *Confessions* here takes us on Augustine's discursive adventure at the center of which is the enigma of where God is in relationship to memory. It appears to Augustine first that God must be in his memory:

> But where within my memory do you abide, Lord, where do you abide? What kind of abode have you fashioned for yourself? What manner of sanctuary have you built for yourself? (10.25.36)

> sed ubi manes in memoria mea, domine, ubi illic manes? quale cubile fabricasti tibi? quale santuarium aedificasti tibi? (10.25.36)

Augustine reviews his memory, ruling out the places where sensory images and affections are stored. Upon further consideration, he rules out the possibility that God is his mind: "Nor are you the mind itself, because you are the Lord God of the mind." But being neither in a place nor the mind itself, Augustine still asserts that God dwells in his memory (10.25.36). He has determined that God is not a mental phenomenon or construct but the Creator of mind, which forces him to reframe his question from *where* God is in his memory to *how* God came to dwell in memory.

> Where then did I find you, so that I might learn to know you? You were not in my memory before I learned to know you. Where then have I found you, if not in yourself and above me? There is no place, both backward do we go and forward, and there is no place. (10.26.37)

> Vbi ergo te inveni, ut discerem te? neque enim iam eras in memoria mea, priusquam te discerem. ubi ergo te inveni, ut discerem te, nisi in te supra me? et nusquam locus, et recedimus et accedimus, et nusquam locus. (10.26.37)

God cannot be located in human memory or be equated with the human mind, which can be remembered. Such mental location would be merely a species of comprehension, and no one can comprehend God. To know that God inhabits one's memory and mind does not mean that one can necessarily "find" God there. There is no question that God still "dwells" in memory, but he must shift his perspective from the human mind and memory comprehending God to the acknowledgment that God—radically Other than Augustine—reveals Himself in Augustine's memory and mind. Augustine recognizes God as outside and above his memory, yet able to dwell independently within him even when his attentions are focused elsewhere (10.26). So he must continue in the enigmatic knowledge that God is entirely other than Augustine—both above him in an irreducible transcendence, and yet within him with a pervasive immanence. God thereby overwhelms Augustine literally and figuratively through each of the five senses (10.27).

Having worked through a provisional construct of memory, Augustine applies it to his present life. He rehearses his struggles with temptations of will, acknowledging the limited accuracy of his own mental reports:

> So do I seem to myself, but perhaps I am deceived. Within me are those lamentable dark areas wherein my own capacities lie hidden from me. Hence, when my mind questions itself about its own powers, it is not easy for it to decide what should be believed. (10.32.48)

> ita mihi videor; forsitan fallar. sunt enim et istae plangendae tenebrae, in quibus me latet facultas mea, quae in me est, ut animus meus de viribus suis ipse se interrogans non facile sibi credendum existimet. (10.32.48)

These difficulties are repeated as he reviews his progress and failure in the face of the threefold character of sin: lust of the eyes, lust of the flesh, and pride of life. Augustine presents his postconversion persona as a riddle to himself (10.33.50), entangled and caught by his eyes (10.34.53), distracted by vain curiosities and worthless thoughts (10.35.57), and ignorant in his self-deceit and pride (10.37.62). R. A. Markus notes that in book 10, "Augustine had come to terms with the impossibility of penetrating into the darkness of his own self" (124). In each specific case, as he doubts himself he repeatedly appeals to the incarnate Word for mercy as the source of his hope for the presently elusive integrity and wisdom he seeks.

Remembering that the wisdom Augustine pursues—that blessed life—consists of the integration of knowledge, eloquence, and moral self-control, he has promoted a practical epistemology grounded in memory and interdependent with discourse, in which will determines the quality and clarity of knowledge. He is conscious that he cannot reason unless he can remember, and he cannot remember without recourse to words (which are also in memory). But the failure of his postconversion will prompts Augustine to judge the epistemology that he elaborates as insufficient in itself to sustain his quest for wisdom. His fundamental discovery through the process is the resolution of his question about God's relations to memory and knowledge.

> And I myself, who found all this, who went over all these things, and strove to mark off and value each thing in accordance with its excellence, taking some things as sense reported them, questioning about others that I felt were intermingled with myself, numbering off and distinguishing the very messengers of sense, and then in the wide treasure of memory scanning certain things, laying away certain others, and drawing forth others still—I myself was not you. Not

even when I did these deeds, that is, not even that power of mine by which I did them, not even that was you. For you are that abiding light which I consulted concerning all these things as to whether they were, as to what they were, and as to what value they possessed. (10.40.65)

> nec ego ipse inventor, qui peragravi omnia et distinguere et pro suis quaeque dignitatibus aestimare conatus sum, excipiens alia nutantibus sensibus et interrogans, alia mecum conmixta sentiens, ipsosque nuntios dinoscens atque dinumerans, iamque in memoriae latis o pibus alia pertractans, alia recondens, alia eruens: nec ego ipse, cum haec agerem, id est vis mea, qua id agebam, nec ipsa eras tu, quia lux es tu permanens, quam de omnibus consulebam, an essent, quid essent, quanti pendenda essent. (10.40.65)

God, Augustine concludes, is radically other than himself. If God is, He must be radically other, given the inherent uncertainty of Augustine's epistemology tainted as it is by unverifiable perceptions (sensibles and language, which implicates intelligibles) and incontinent will. That Augustine appeals to Christ the mediator as the means to continue his quest for wisdom may seem unremarkable. But having reached his conclusion about God's distinct being—completely outside of human sensibility and intelligibility—Augustine makes progress toward explicating how the incarnate Word could "fix" his heart. Given Christ's otherness as God, his mediation and intersession breaks into sensible and intelligible experience in a different way. By his incursion into memory, the incarnate Word retains "something like men and something like God" (10.42.67) to mediate between God and humankind and address the problem of the will.

Here we make a mistake if we interpret Augustine's statements as a simple twentieth-century "spiritualized" answer or an appeal to religion to explain the inexplicable. In the terms Augustine has laid out for us, he is working through the implications of radical otherness visiting itself in humility and love upon the human condition. Augustine confesses his own lack of wisdom and dependence on the incarnate Word, not in the form of an anti-intellectual, reductive religiosity, but to pause and check his coordinates before embarking on the next inquiry, one which will build upon and extend the discussion of memory in time (Grant 24–25).

Time and Eternity

In his first volume of *Time and Narrative,* Paul Ricoeur admits that he does a certain amount of violence to Augustine's *Confessions* in serving the purposes of his own project (1:5). Ricoeur's statement that Augustine "inquires into the nature of time without any apparent concern for grounding his inquiry on the narrative structure of the spiritual autobiography developed in the first nine books of the *Confessions*" must be counted as part of Ricoeur's violation (1:4). The questions of time taken up in book 11 and their resolution surface throughout the narrative of the first nine books. These prefigurations accentuate Augustine's conflation of narrative and argument and point to the fuller treatment of the issue to which we will now attend. Discourse, speech in particular, dominates Augustine's consideration of time and eternity.

Augustine introduces the gulf between the temporality of human speech and eternity as the guiding issue for book 11. In the process he reminds us that he speaks in this format not to meet any need in God, but for us (11.1.1). As we engage this second inquiry into the *Confessions*, we should note that Augustine acknowledges his official role as preacher and bishop. He offers his precious time to us as what remains "free from need of replenishing my body and my mental powers and the demands of such service as we owe to other men, and such as we do not owe yet we render" [liberas a necessitatibus reficiendi corporis et intentionis animi, et servitutis, quam debemus hominibus, et quam non debemuset tamen reddimus] (11.2.2).[3] In this recreation from routine duties, Augustine alerts us to the iconicity of his discourse: he speaks to us in time about speech in time. After offering the service of his "thought and tongue" he gestures toward the prophet Moses's feigned lack of eloquence—asking God to "circumcise" both his inner and outer lips (11.2.3). Though the first few verses of Genesis will preoccupy his scriptural exegesis for the remainder of the *Confessions*, he thereby opens himself to the entire canon of Scripture:

> Let me confess to you whatsoever I shall find in your books, and let me "hear the voice of praise," and drink you in, and consider "the wonderful things of your law," from that beginning, wherein you made heaven and earth, even to an everlasting kingdom together with you in your holy city." (11.2.3)

> confitear tibi quidquid invenero in libris tuis, et audiam vocem laudis, et te bibam, et condiderem mirabilia de lege tua ab usque principio, in quo fecisti caelum et terram, usque ad regnum tecum perpetuum sanctae civitatis tuae. (11.2.3)

Here stands biblical time, a distinct teleology, not circular, not a return to the garden, but a journey from one distinct beginning to another—from the garden to the city. We should not expect the interpretation of Genesis 1 as the first installment of a commentary on the whole Bible, for in the economy of the church Fathers, Genesis 1 stands proxy for the whole of Scripture—its interpretation will complete the *Confessions*:

> We have here a preview of the content of the last three books: they will explicate the Genesis account of creation in which the whole history of creation is summed up. (The seventh day of creation is the day of eternal rest towards which the holy city proceeds; the first six days represent, *inter alia*, the six ages of man.) The last three books are thus an emblem of all scriptural study since they treat in detail a passage of scripture that stands for the whole. (O'Donnell, *Augustine*, 115)

Augustine more than genuflects toward what we might call the ultimate metanarrative of Western culture. The inquiry itself begins with an invocation to God for help in interpreting the Scripture:

> I beseech you by your Son, our Lord Jesus Christ, "the man of your right hand, whom you have confirmed for yourself," as your mediator and ours, through whom you have sought us when we did not seek you, and sought us so that we might seek you, your Word, through whom you have called to adoption a people of believers, among them me also. (11.2.4)

> obsecro per dominum nostru Iesum Christum filium tuum, virum dexterae tuae, filium hominis, quem nos quaesisti non quaerentes te, quaesisti autem, ut quaereremus te, verbum tuum, per quod fecisti omnia, in quibus et me, unicum tuum, per quem vocasti in adoptionem populum credentium, in quo et me. (11.2.4)

Augustine asks specifically for mediation from Christ. He overtly employs the formula for the pursuit of wisdom from book 10: (1) recognizing his moral insufficiency; (2) wanting what he will hear, instead of hearing what he wants; and (3) calling upon the incarnate Word—"in whom are hid all the treasures of wisdom and knowledge"—who alone can serve as a temporal, human mediator and maintain his eternity with God the Father.

Word as Arbiter of Truth

Without the incarnate Word, Augustine cannot hope to understand the Scripture, in this case Genesis 1:1. He has no way to establish the written words of Moses as true (11.3.5). Even if Moses could explain what he meant, Augustine would only have access to the prophet's written words and voice—sensible signs unverifiable on their own. The *Confessions* had long since affirmed the truth and authority of the entire Bible (6.5.7). Now Augustine develops the basis for receiving the Scripture and all Creation as authentic and authoritative revelation. That basis is eternal speech.

> Truth, neither Hebrew nor Greek nor Latin nor barbaric in speech, without mouth or tongue as organ, and without noise of syllables, would say to me, "He speaks the truth.". . . Therefore, since I cannot question him who was filled by you, and thus spoke true words, I entreat you O Truth, I entreat you, O my God, "spare my sins." Do you who granted to him, your servant, to speak these true words, grant to me that I may understand them. (11.3.5).

> nec hebaea nec graeca nec latina nec barbara veritas sine oris et linguae organis, sine strepitu sylla barum diceret: "verbum dicit,". . . quum ergo illum interrogared non possim, te, quo plenus vera dixit, veritas, rogo, te, deus meus, rogo, parce peccatis meis, et qui illi servo tuo dedisti haec dicere, da et mihi haec intelligere. (11.3.5)

God himself breaks into the cycle of sensible uncertainty to confirm the truth of Scripture by testifying to its veracity. Augustine believes that Moses spoke truthfully because of God's presence within him when he wrote the words of Genesis. But this is not enough. In human language true speech is insufficient on its own to produce understanding in a listener. The external words must be somehow verified internally. As listeners, Augustine piques our interest with this paradoxical speech of God, understandable, though without human form in language, production, or structure. But he digresses before elaborating on the voice of God.

Returning to his text, Augustine says that through the voice of self-evidence, heaven and earth assert that they were created (11.4.6).[4] Augustine asks, "How did you make heaven and earth?" The answer is, in a way completely other than human making: "What exists, for any reason except that you exist? You spoke, therefore, and these things were made, and in your Word you made them" [quid enim est, nisi quia tu es? ergo dixisti et facta sunt, atque in verbo tuo fecisti ea] (11.5.7). By considering the Creation, Augustine's inquiry expands to the entire scope of human experience and knowledge. Even more important for our own inquiry, Augustine leads us to affirm that speech precedes all material existence, including the existence of humanity.

This Word becomes Augustine's sole arbiter of truth and is named Truth itself. All words uttered by created beings, even when commissioned by God, must be confirmed internally. Augustine refers to the inner and outer ear, which correspond to his reference to inner and outer lips at the beginning of the book. The outer ear, as in the discussion of memory, perceives words of ordinary discourse:

> These words of yours, formed for a certain time, the outer ear reported to the understanding mind, whose interior ear was placed close to your eternal Word. Then the mind compared these words

> sounding in time with your eternal Word in its silence, and said, "It is far different; it is far different. These words are far beneath me. They do not exist, because they flee and pass away. The Word of my God abides above me forever. (11.6.8)

> et haec ad tempus facta verba tua nuntiavit auris exterior menti prudenti, cuius aurus interior posita est ad aeternum verbum tuum. at illa comparavit haec verba temporaliter sonantia cum aeterno in silentio verbo tuo et dixit: "aliud est longe, longe aliud est. haec longe infra me sunt nec sunt, quia fugiunt et praetereunt: verbum autem dei mei supra me manet in aeternum." (11.6.8)

Augustine leaves no doubt about the process of discerning truth. The rightly ordered mind makes a comparative judgment of the created, temporal, resonant words in the outer ear against the creative, eternal, silent Word in the interior ear. James J. Murphy notes the role of interior truth in Augustine as explicated in *De magistro*, which Murphy reads as a "natural talent" to "discriminate the true from the false" ("Metarhetorics," 206). In this case, however, there should be no confusion between the intelligible objects which abide in memory as considered in book 10 and the eternal Word of book 11. This Word is no skill or item of memory or in any other way a human faculty or possession. Neither is the Word static. If we follow Augustine carefully here, together we may find ourselves quite out of our depth.

> So you call us to understand the Word, God with you, O God, which is spoken eternally, and in which all things are spoken eternally. Nor is it the case that what was spoken is ended and that another thing is said, so that all things may at length be said: all things are spoken once and forever. Elsewise, these would already be time and change, and neither true eternity nor true immortality. (11.7.9)

> Vocas itaque nos ad intellegendum verbum, deum apud te deum, quod sempiterne dicitur et eo sempiterne dicuntur omnia. neque enim finitur, quod diecebatur, et dicitur aliud, ut possint dici omnia, sed simul ac sempiterne omnia: alioquin iam tempus et mutatio, et non vera aeternitas nec vera immortalitatis. (11.7.9)

Augustine continues to instruct us rhetorically, and we should recognize that he has accentuated the chasm between temporality and eternity, between which the only analog is speech (Jordan 196; Ricoeur 1:5, 24). The implication of this relationship is that temporality, not expression, separates words from Word (D. W. Johnson 43). The emphasis on the temporal/eternal distinction prepares Augustine to define the Word in more specific terms, not only as eternal expression but also as the temporal mediator. The Word of God speaks temporally in the flesh through the Gospel to produce belief and speaks eternally as "the sole good Master" to confirm the truth of that belief (11.8.10). From this we see that the "interior Truth" of which Augustine speaks is Christ himself, and that in his attempt to imitate Christ, instructional discourse would have to be primary. The Word was not only made flesh but maintains full status as Creator (11.9.11).

An Account of Eternity

The basic coordinates of Augustine's argument in book 11 have been laid out with his explication of the discourse of the incarnate Word in time and eternity. However, the argument remains undeveloped and does not account for anticipated objections, which he addresses. In the process, Augustine presents a sophisticated philosophy of time that rests on his observation of oral discourse rather than being tied in some way to the movements of the universe (Vance 21; Ricoeur 1:14).

The question Augustine anticipates is: "What was God doing before he made heaven and earth?" [Quid faciebat deus, antequam faceret caelum et terram?] (11.10.12). This query provokes numerous related questions, all of which treat eternity with skepticism. These inquisitors Augustine terms as "carnal" because they have not compared temporality with eternity, but rather ask temporal questions as though eternity were a super-temporality of some sort instead of an altogether different dimension. Therefore, as Augustine has related from his own experience, they can claim no stability of heart. In fact, Augustine casts doubt on his own stability and denies that his human words can provide stability to others (11.11.13).

The direct inquiry into the nature of time begins with a defining statement on eternity: "You have made all times, and you are before all times, and not at any time was there no time" [omnia tempora tu fecisti et ante omnia tempora tu es, nec aliquo tempore non erat tempus] (11.13.16). In terms of Augustine's argument, he preempts any notion that eternity is a derivative of time (Ricoeur 1:22). From this point he raises the question to which the remainder of the book will be devoted:

> What is time? Who can easily and briefly explain this? Who can comprehend this even in thought, so as to express it in a word? Yet what do we discuss more familiarly and knowingly in conversation than time? Surely we understand it when we talk about it, and also understand it when we hear others talk about it.
>
> What, then, is time? If no one asks me, I know; if I want to explain it to someone who does ask me, I do not know. (11.14.17)[5]

> quid est enim tempus? quis hoc facile breviterque explicaverit? quis hoc ad verbum de illo proferendum vel cogitatione comprehenderit? quid autem familiarius et notius in loquendo comemoramus quam tempus? et intellegimus utique, cum id loquimur, intelligimus etiam, cum alio loquente id audimus. quid est ergo tempus? si nemo ex me quareat, scio; si quarenti explicare velim, nescio. (11.14.17)

The question demands an answer that Augustine can not easily produce. Engaging his subsequent deliberation on the issue should remind us of the dangers of reducing his argument to a simple series of summary propositions. We might easily do so, for Augustine's philosophy of time, extracted from its moorings in the *Confessions,* maintains much of its provocative character. However, the extraction dispenses with the philosophy of discourse that pervades every mention of temporality we have thus far seen. To fall prey to the "lure of the informational" here compromises our interpretation of the *Confessions,* which cannot be complete without Augustine's enactment of the almost futile task of learning anything within the constraints of human discourse (Welch 23).[6] Augustine makes this prominent by juxtaposing language and time.

In the first place, Augustine attempts to discern the nature of past, present, and future. The process he works through is a toilsome effort to discover what he can *say* to us truly about these three aspects of time. He comes to a conclusion of sorts in which he attempts to elucidate the status of our inquiry:

> It is now plain and clear that neither past nor future are existent, and that is not properly stated that there are three times, past, present, and future. But perhaps it might properly be said that there are three times, the present of things past, the present of things present, and the present of things future. These three are in the soul, but elsewhere I do not see them: the present of things past is in memory; the present of things present is in intuition; the present of things future is in expectation. If we are permitted to say this, then I see three times, and I affirm that there are three times. It may also be said that there are three times past, present, and future, as common usage incorrectly puts it. This may be stated. Note that I am not concerned over this, do not object to it, and do not criticize it, as long as we understand what we say, namely that what is future is not now existent, nor is that which is past. There are few things that we state properly, and many that we speak improperly, but what we mean is understood. (11.20.26)

> quod autem nunc liquet et claret, nec futura sunt nec praeterita, nec proprie dicitur: tempora sunt tria, paeteritum, praesens et futurum,

> sed fortasse proprie diceretur: tempora sunt tria, praesens de praeteritis, praesens de preasentibus, praesens de futuris. sunt enim haec in anima tria quaedam, et alibi ea non video: praesens de praeteritis memoria, preasens de praesentibus contuitus, praesens de futuris expetatio. si haec permittimur dicere, tria tempora video fateorque, tria sunt. dicatur etiam: tempora sunt tria, preateritum, praesens, et futurum, sicut abutitur consuetudo, dicatur. ecce non curo nec resisto nec reprehendo, dum tamen intellegatur quod dicitur, neque id, quod futurum est, esse iam, neque id, quod praeteritum est. pauca sunt enim, quae proprie loquimur, plura non proprie, sed agnoscitur quid velimus. (11.20.26)

This passage represents the way Augustine conducts the entire inquiry into the nature of time. Ricoeur points out that Augustine follows this rhetorical path, wending his way through the possibilities, moving from problem to resolution, to the inherent impasse of that resolution, to another resolution throughout the discussion (1:6). In this segment at least two things occur simultaneously. On the one hand, Augustine has progressed in his project by moving the commonsense past, present, and future into the mental present, satisfying his concern that these three aspects of temporality exist in the face of the realization that the past and future do not exist as times separate from the present. This will prove to be a significant step in our inquiry with him. On the other hand, the transition in the passage from "plain and clear" to "that we speak improperly, but what we mean is understood," manifests Augustine's sensitivity to the difficulty human language poses for both comprehension in speech and hearing. He shows us how time and human discourse implicate one another.

From the question of "What is time?" Augustine next confronts the related question of measuring time. Introducing the question, he focuses once more on what ordinary language we use to talk about lengths of time, but speaks only on the basis of his belief that God will hear and assist him in the process.

He continues, through the discussion of measures, to make explicit the dilemma that language presents. As the introduction to the problem of measures comes to a close he says, "We say these things, and we hear them, and we are understood, and we understand. They are most clear and most familiar, but again they are very obscure, and their solution is a new task" [dicimus haec et audiviums haec et intellegimur et intelligimus. manifestissima et usitatissima sunt, et eadem rursus nimis latent, et nova est inventio eorum] (11.22.28).

Understanding time is obscured internally and externally, which pushes Augustine to seek aid from God. "I see that time is a kind of distension. Yet do I see this, or do I only seem to myself to see it? You, O Light, will show this to me" [video igitur quandam esse distentionem. sed video? an videre mihi videor? tu demonstrabis, lux, veritas.] (11.23.30). The difficulty of deliberation pushes Augustine to the limit, so that he calls himself one "who does not even know what I do not know!" [ei mihi, qui nescio saltem quid nesciam!] (11.25.32). And when he concludes the discussion, he must argue against the objections of his own mind that time is a psychological phenomenon (11.27.36). The example he uses of the progression of reciting a psalm provides a fuller disclosure of Augustine's use of discourse in relation to the mind to show how time consists in our looking forward with expectation to the future, which passes through the present into our memory of things past. In the psalm, the expectation must depart through our performance, which causes our memory of the psalm to grow. So we measure expectations and memories, which both exist only as we bring them into the present through discourse (11.18.23). Then Augustine applies the example:

> What takes place in the whole psalm takes place also in each of its parts and in each of its syllables. The same thing holds for a longer action, of which perhaps the psalm is a small part. The same thing holds for a man's entire life, the parts of which are all the man's actions. The same thing holds throughout the whole age of the sons of men, the parts of which are the lives of all men. (11.28.38)

> et quod in toto cantico, hoc in singulis particulis eius, fit atque in singulis syllabis eius, hoc in actione longiore, cuius forte particula est illud canticum, hoc in tota vita hominis, cuius partes sunt omnes actiones hominis, hoc in toto saeculo filiorum hominum, cuius partes sunt omnes vitae hominum. (11.27.38)

So subtly does Augustine intermingle discourse and temporal life, even to the expanse of world history, that we might miss it unless we attended in advance to his unremitting connection between thought, speech, and action in this inquiry that is purportedly "about" time. When Augustine approaches the issue of measurement, he says, "I measure time, I know. Yet I do not measure the future, because it does not yet exist; I do not measure the present, because it is not extended in space; I do not measure the past, because it no longer exists" [tempus metior, scio; sed non metior futurum, quia nondum est, non metior praesens, quia nullo spatio tenditur, non metior praeteritum, quia iam non est] (11.26.33). As his deliberations close, time no longer measures objects; it measures people—individuals, communities, and the entire human race—extended in memory and expectation but living in a moment with no measurable extent.

The Incursion of the Incarnation in Time

For Augustine, the result of the deliberation is a humbling one. He says, "But since 'your mercy is better than lives,' behold, my life is a distention, or distraction" [Sed quoniam melior est misericordia tua super vitas, ecce distentio est vita mea] (11.29.39). He returns to the incarnate Word from this discussion of time in isolation. "But 'your right hand has upheld me' in my Lord, the Son of man, mediator between you, the One, and us, the many, who are dissipated in many ways upon many things" [et me suscepit dextera tua in domino meo, mediatore filio hominis inter te unum et nos multos, in multis per multa] (11.29.39). The incarnate Word empowers Augustine's expectation of eternity and makes it purposeful in the midst of a temporal life in which "I am distracted amid times, whose order I do not know, and my thoughts, the inmost bowels of my soul, are torn asunder by tumult and change" [at ego in tempora dissilui, quorum ordinem nescio, et tumultuosis varietatibus dilaniantur cogitationes meae, intima viscera animae meae] (11.29.39).

Through his appeal to the Truth, Augustine finally finds a place to stand and summarizes his argument against the objections that motivated this extended temporal deliberation by reinforcing the radical distinction between eternity and our temporal experience (11.30–31). We feel that distinction with Augustine most profoundly as the distinction between an unstable, disintegrating temporality versus a stable eternity in which we find integrity (Kristo 138). He amplifies in book 11 what he injects briefly amidst the narrative of his past life: that by our own lights we cannot escape the endless deferral of being called temporality (4.10.15).

We cannot elude time to participate in the stability of the eternal by any power of mind or body, but eternity can and does stabilize time (Ricoeur 1:29). Our stability comes via the Incarnation, through which the Word takes on flesh and thereby participates fully in temporality (Burnaby 76). Although the Incarnation is the ultimate act of humility, the mediator accomplishes it without abandoning his eternity (10.43.68). Therefore, he brings eternity into our temporal experience (Guitton 44–45; McMahon 128). As Colin Starnes puts it:

> By his Incarnation God reveals something about himself that cannot be deduced from any consideration of the divine law. He shows us that the temporal belongs to him as much as does the eternal. By making himself a temporal means to an eternal end God has shown that he regards our temporal situation just as much as our eternal status. (*Conversion*, 220–21)

God's valuation of temporal experience is made manifest by the fact that union with Christ always takes place as situated in time (Adam 48–49).

Both the process and experience of conversion and the subsequent life of faith occur in our temporal experience (Grant 29, 31–32).

The incarnation also makes temporal wisdom a genuine possibility. Through his mediation of eternal and temporal, the Word incarnate unifies our temporal sensibilities and eternal, intelligible truths (Starnes, *Conversion,* 100; Starnes, "Exegesis," 347).

> This is your Word, which is also the beginning because it also speaks to us. Thus in the Gospel he speaks through the flesh, and this word sounded outwardly in the ears of men, so that it might be believed, and sought inwardly and found in the eternal truth. (11.8.10)
>
> ipsum est verbum tuum, quod et principium est, quia et loquitur nobis. sic in evangelio per carnem ait, et hoc insonuit foris quribus hominum, ut crederetur et intus quareretur, et inveniretur in aeterna veritate. (11.8.10)

Augustine considers the Incarnation itself as essential, because through it we gain the temporal access we need to learn wisdom. The Word incarnate demonstrates perfect integration of substance, words and deeds.

Through the temporal discourse of book 11, Augustine tests the limits of human knowledge concerning time and eternity. His consideration of the issue persists today as one of his most profound contributions to human thought. In it, he reveals imprecision and error in human reason left to its own temporal devices. He attends in particular to the uncertainty and instability of discourse. In our attempts to formulate discourse, we see wisdom frustrated by our temporal inability to think or speak clearly, a problem in which the mutual insufficiency of thought and speech implicate each other. Augustine's repeated query, "What can I say?," is answered by what God gives (11.2.3). The answer in its simplicity is the Incarnation, through which the integration we have come to associate with Augustinian wisdom can alone be found.

In the progression of the *Confessions* this deliberation on time serves as a precursor to interpretation, an act dependent upon the connection between temporal and eternal (Colish 25). But for the moment, we may say with Augustine that the incarnate Word secures temporal knowledge. Because we experience the union of time and eternity in discourse, we recognize that Augustine's epistemology depends not on *ratio* but on *oratio* (Guitton 61). He is not engaged in a quest pursued through sanctimonious prayer. The incarnate Word, by stabilizing his present, enables him to continue his "lively conversation with God" in our midst (Brown, *Augustine,* 167).

In sum, Augustine's faith is directed toward eternity, but his life is fully engaged in his sociohistorical context. Despite the fact that Augustine's influence will permeate the middle ages, Augustine's own world is not medieval. The people of late Roman antiquity viewed their age as one of enlightenment and high culture, especially advanced in literary taste. Augustine had participated fully in this high culture and had enjoyed its material abundance (Brown, *Religion and Society,* 13). The incarnation does not constitute an escape—intellectual or spiritual—from an undesirable material life. The Word incarnate empowers Augustine to pursue wisdom, that full integrity of being. In memory, the Incarnation secures the will, restoring Augustine's faculty of right reasoning. In time, the Incarnation secures knowledge, the product of reason. The third element of wisdom—discourse/eloquence—remains unsecured.

We have heard in his *Confessions* that Augustine can speak only from temporality stabilized by the Incarnation—which integrates time and eternity. Enacted in time, the incarnate Word is relevant to humanity, whether in expectation or memory:

> He was shown forth to saints of old, so that they might be saved through faith in his coming passion, even as we are saved by faith in his passion now past. For as man, he is mediator, but as the Word, he is in no middle place, since he is equal to God, and God with God, and together one God. (10.43.69)

> hic demonstatus est antiquis sanctis, ut ita ipsi per fidem futurae passionis eius, sicut nos per fidem praeteritae, salvi fierent. in quantum enim homo, in tantum mediator, in quantum autem verbum, non medius, quia aequalis deo et deus apud deum et simul unus deus. (10.43.69)

Yet the same incarnate Word is eternally relevant, and always in the present:

> He departed from our eyes, so that we might return into our own hearts and find him there. He departed, but lo, he is here. He would not stay long with us, and yet he does not leave us. He departed from here, whence he has never departed. (4.12.19)

> et discessit ab oculis, ut redeamus ad cor et inveniamus eum. abscessit enim et ecce hic est. noluit nobiscum diu esse et non reliquit nos. illuc enim abscessit, unde numquam recessit. (4.12.19)

Augustine himself integrates his quest for wisdom with discourse, considering memory and epistemology in book 10; eternity and time in book 11. He discerns that the incarnate Word participates in both, investing our temporal and epistemological lives with eternal significance. The question we are therefore led to is: Given the effect of the incarnate Word on the will and knowledge, how might the Incarnation be manifested in that other aspect of wisdom: expression?

The *Confessions* expects to provoke such questions and warrants them, as we heard in the narrative of Ambrose's exceptional practice of silent reading. Augustine works at the end of an era that Kathleen E. Welch categorizes as a "period of intense language theorizing" (22). The remainder of this chapter, as well as chapters 4 and 5, considers how Augustine theorizes about language in the *Confessions*. In the process, we continue to engage the *Confessions* on its own terms, but more evidently pursue how Augustine leads us through his confessional quest to enrich our own wisdom.

Semiotics

Throughout the *Confessions* the way we hear and speak in temporality is a semiotic process. In one sense, we cannot speak of Augustine's theorizing as semiotics at all. Semiotics was neither named nor conceived as a discrete theoretical area in his day, but is a modern study. On the other hand, Augustine's theory and practice of signification departs from classical language and sign theories (Todorov, *Theories*, 1–19; Eco, *Semiotics*, 33). The departure is so pronounced that Augustine has been credited with articulating the first definitive semiotic viewpoint.[7] The equivalent status he proposes between linguistic and nonlinguistic signs qualifies Augustine's sign theory as distinctively semiotic.[8] As Umberto Eco notes, "Fifteen centuries before Saussure, he will be the one to recognize the *genus* of signs, of which linguistic signs are a *species*" (33).

The discovery of Augustine's semiotic sensibilities challenges us to resist categorizing Augustine's theory exclusively in terms of his Stoic and Platonic predecessors (Manetti 157; D. W. Johnson 31; McMahon 148). Semiotics provides us with a new perspective from which to examine his sign theory and to explore Augustine's preoccupation with discourse in the *Confessions*.

Augustine's book 1 account of how he acquires language outlines his semiotic consciousness. He conjectures that to converse he had to learn the word necessary for him to refer to a specific thing. But to learn that word he first had to know what people meant. He could grasp what they meant (that is, what they had in mind) by observing their verbal and nonverbal action in conjunction (1.8.13). The signs he observed were not self-evident from the things to which they referred. Neither were the words and gestures self-evident indicators of what the adults had in mind. Therefore, Augustine had to gather instances of signs in connection both to their referents and to the thought of the speaker within a particular social context. The immediate result of this first entrance into conversation for the young Augustine was tempestuous social engagement: "I entered more deeply into the stormy society of human life" [et vitae humanae procellosam societatem altius ingressus sum] (1.8.13).[9]

His discussion of language acquisition early in the *Confessions* parallels key factors that the few contemporary scholars exploring Augustine's semiotic sensibilities have identified, primarily from *De magistro* and *De doctrina Christiana*. The three factors are that Augustine (1) understands the relation between the signifier and signified within the sign itself to be arbitrary; (2) recognizes that signs communicate by inference; and (3) grounds significance in social consent allied with cultural and syntactical context.

Augustine recognizes the conventional relation between a sign and its referent, a development clearly attributable to his attention to Stoic and Platonic sign theory (Manetti 157). The radical departure, surpassing these preceding sign theories, occurs in the arbitrary relation he posits between signifier and signified within the verbal sign (Kelly 52–54, 63). On every level, meaning is inferred relationally within the sign, without reference to any external object (Eco, *Semiotics*, 34, 39–42). Eugene Vance points to Augustine's distinctiveness on this issue:

> Clearly, Augustine's insistence upon the arbitrary nature of the bond between the signifier and signified went against the grain of that tradition that is commonly called "Cratylism," after the opinion of one of Socrates' interlocutors, who held that words are in some obscure way replicas of the substances that they name. Such doctrines had persisted in movements distinct from Platonism—for example, in Stoic theories of language. (25)

The inclusion of words in sign theory distinguishes Augustine as semiotic in the modern sense. The arbitrary relation within the sign function—the relation by which Louis G. Kelly attributes Augustine with a fuller sense of the verbal sign in time than Saussure—will distinguish him as semiotic in the postmodern sense (54). Kelly suggests that Augustine subordinates his theory of signs to other concerns. He says, "any discussion beyond the basic nature of the sign function in language was not relevant to Augustine's aim of validating his view of both teaching and learning" (63). The suggestion represents a common view of Augustine's treatment of sign theory: that he develops it as an addendum to justify existing commitments.

Despite its assumed subordinance, Augustine's semiotic theory dominates his view of language, with implications much broader than pedagogy. Eco implies that Augustine, by recognizing language as a sign function, problematizes any equivalence theory of linguistic meaning and opts for an inferential model of meaning. Giovanni Manetti clarifies Eco's point:

> Once Augustine has proposed his conception of words as signs, this change of perspective results in a series of inevitable modifications.

> In earlier theories of language, the relationship between linguistic expressions and their contents was conceived of as *a relation of equivalence*. . . . The motivation for this was epistemological and concerned the possibility of working directly on language, rather than on objects of reality, since language was understood to be a system for the representation of reality (even though inevitably mediated through the mind). In contrast, the relationship between a sign and the thing it referred to was understood to be *a relation of implication*, thanks to which the first term, by the mere fact of existing, enabled the passage to knowledge of the second term. (159)

In other words, signs depend on other signs to establish their meaning. Augustine argues in *De magistro* that the meaning of signs can be understood by the use of other signs, whether words, the pointing of a finger, gestures, or by demonstrating (book 3). We will recall that he enacts this theory for us in the *Confessions* through the "acquisition of language" narrative, in which by learning to read such signs he enters into human discourse and society (1.8.13). In Augustine's view, good listening demands not only knowledge of the specific sign, but its relation to other signs, or its context (Sirridge 187). Augustine had to attend to both the gestures that accompanied the words he was trying to learn, and to hear them "set in their proper places in different sentences" [in variis sententiis locis suis posita] before he could use them to communicate (1.8.13).

Augustine's semiotics certainly applies to teaching and learning. But the application extends into pedagogy from the more basic foundation of signification. All signs teach. They serve as external prompters for internal actions (Murphy, "Metarhetorics," 206; Manetti 162; Colish 16–17). The transition from the equivalence model of meaning to the implicational model of meaning makes language itself an instructional institution (Eco, *Semiotics,* 34ff.; Manetti 167).

That institution, the one in which Augustine participates with outer lips and ears, is decidedly social. Through memory and language, speech and thought, we can share meaning between people (Kelly 50, 64). But the meanings we share reflect the arbitrary nature and function of the signs we use. Our signs "mean" only by common consent (Vance 24–25). Augustine explains this aspect of his sign theory in *De doctrina Christiana,* book 2:

> The single sign *beta* means a letter among the Greeks but a vegetable among the Latins. When I say *lege,* a Greek understands one thing by these two syllables, a Latin understands another. Therefore, just as all of these significations move men's minds in accordance with the consent of their societies, and because this consent varies, they move them differently, nor do men agree upon them because of an innate value, but they have a value because they are agreed upon. (2.24.37)

> "beta" uno eodemque sono apud "Graeco litterae, apud Latinos holeris nomen est, et cum dico "lege," in his duabus syllabis aliud Graecus, aliud Latinus intellegit—sicut ergo hae omnes significationes pro sua cuiusque societatis consensione animos movent, et quia diversa consensio est, diverse movent nec ideo consenserunt in eas homines quia iam valebant ad significationem, sed ideo valent quia consenserunt in eas. (2.24.37)

Distinctions between Greek and Latin occur in books 10 and 11 as illustrations of the success or failure of signs in the *Confessions,* as do distinctions between Hebrew and Latin (10.12.19; 10.20.29; 11.3.5). The relationship between time and society is not missed either. Both *De doctrina Christiana* and the *Confessions* advance the importance of cultural knowledge for language comprehension and respect differences in times and cultures. In both cases, the issue surrounds interpretation of practices recorded in Scripture that conflict with Augustine's contemporary social customs (*De doctrina Christiana* 3.12.18–14.22; *Confessions* 3.7.12–15). Placing the sign function within the temporal flux of human society and language exacerbates the theoretical instability of discourse found in the arbitrary relations between signs and their referents and within the sign between signifiers and signifieds.

To this point, we have briefly considered key elements of Augustine's semiotic viewpoint on human signification. While we have considered them in isolation, the nature of the sign, the shift from equivalence to inference in meaning, and the temporal situation of meaning in discourse and society are clearly interdependent. Given the semiotic theory at work, we can begin to see why discourse recurs as an irrepressible root issue that asserts itself plainly throughout the *Confessions.*

Reflecting on book 10 and memory, signs animate our memory and are prerequisite to epistemology. Access and use, even of intelligible things which reside in memory a priori, demand sensible discourse. We find ourselves unable to produce demonstrable proofs about anything because we depend on signs to mediate all knowledge. Disordered will compounds the problem of knowledge, leaving Augustine with the uncertainty and error of self-knowledge—an unstable self. By introducing temporality in book 11, Augustine presents human knowledge in discourse as unstable, obscure, and ambiguous.

In both cases we have seen how Augustine appeals to the incarnate Word to mediate these dilemmas. Considered in terms of Augustine's quest for wisdom, the incarnate Word stabilizes memory by inhabiting the mind and speaking right moral order to the will from the inside, restoring the ability to reason. In similar fashion, through the Incarnation the eternal Word participates in temporality, investing the elusive present and temporal knowledge with provisional stability. By establishing Augustine's semiotic coordinates we have seen the intensification of the discursive paradox he faces. In the quest for wisdom, Augustine seems to frustrate his own purposes by positing a view of discourse that cannot possibly deliver the substance of the wisdom he seeks—understanding, certainty, and truth. Furthermore, how the Incarnation can satisfactorily stabilize discourse itself remains unclear. But this is the impasse that must be overcome by Augustine if he is to maintain his quest and ever hope to attain wisdom. He accomplishes this, perhaps surprisingly, through rhetoric.

Truth

The studies which examine Augustine's prescience of contemporary semiotic theory criticize him on two counts. First, his comprehensive semiotic theory never materializes due to the distractions of practical issues. Second, he is accused of working through the entire semiotic system only to apply it within a narrowly religious context.

John Deely and Tzvetan Todorov are the prime spokesmen for the view that Augustine's semiotic theory serves ulterior religious motives. Todorov suggests that in terms of semiotics, Augustine was ignorant and did not realize what he was doing, although we may appreciate him in spite of himself (41–42). He was driven by his need "to enlarge the category of transposed meaning in order to permit him to include Christian allegory" (35). Deely, likewise, seems compelled both to acknowledge Augustine's apparent semiotic sophistication, "with distinctions that establish the semiotic point of view and sweep over the horizon of prelinguistic, linguistic, and postlinguistic semiotic phenomena," and then to dismiss it as developed, "only for the sake of narrowly identifying the specific case of conventional signs instituted by God, namely the words of Scripture and the Sacraments of the Church." (17)

The *Confessions* alone, in its broad consideration of the human condition and relentless discursive self-consciousness, exposes the inadequacy of this view. Eco suggests that Augustine's semiotic sensitivity produced the opposite effect, broadening what might otherwise have become a much narrower religious focus and applying a semiotic approach in general:

> In *De Doctrina Christiana* Augustine decides that, in order to understand the Scriptures, the exegete must know physics, geography, botany, mineralogy. Thus the new Christian civilization accepts and introduces . . . into the interpretive circle. . . all the knowledge of classic civilization. (*Semiotics,* 151)

Augustine maintained and expanded his cultural and scientific literacy after his conversion and ordination. In fact, when Galileo defended himself against ecclesiastical narrow mindedness, he appealed to the bishop of Hippo as the model exegete who took the entire scope of revelation and experience as his interpretive province (Crombie 74–75). The charge that Augustine was engaged in bibliolatry seems difficult to sustain against documentary evidence in Augustine's work.

That Augustine was too engaged with practical social concerns to develop a complete semiotic theory to rival those of the nineteenth and twentieth century is an entirely different matter (Gilson 3). The charge cannot be denied. Augustine could not be bothered with theory for its own sake: he was preoccupied with lived social discourse, not an abstract sociology of language (Kelly 60). He was a critic, professor, and bishop. Any theoretical position he held was only as good as its application within the crucible of commonplace social intercourse. We might recall that throughout his preconversion narrative, Augustine subjected every alternative philosophy and sect he encountered to close scrutiny, not only for its theoretical sufficiency but for its "streetworthiness"—that is, its practical resonance with lived experience, especially the wisdom lived by its representatives.

Therefore, in the case of semiotics, Augustine's movement is not from basic semiotic principles to a finely tuned theoretical treatise. He moves from semiotics to rhetoric, the social application of signs, to persuade others to right action ("Metarhetorics," 205). To make the social move, Augustine must somehow address the impasse between wisdom as he understands it and a sign theory that, by its very nature, seems to undermine any commonsense expression or reception of eternal truth or knowledge.

The question of negotiating this impasse may be more pertinent to us than to Augustine. How can rhetoric, working on a semiotic theory riddled with contingency and temporality, speak about eternal truth with a straight face? As we shall see, Augustine comes to his position facing the fact that human discourse left to itself results in radical discontinuity that negates the possibility for nonillusory communication (Brown, *Religion and Society*, 29).

A few scholars have recently identified and tried to deal with problems similar to the one we encounter with Augustine. We will look at two: Julia Kristeva in her essay "The True-Real" and F. G. Bailey in his book *The Prevalence of Deceit*. Kristeva and Bailey address similar tensions between truth and reality. In his introduction, Bailey discusses two basic answers to the question "What is truth?"

> One (somewhat sophisticated) is that truth is a matter of convention, what people agree to be true (truth as coherence, or "intersubjectivity is objectivity," as the jargon goes). . . . Truth is then somewhat optional, unconstrained by nature, a matter of collective choice, manmade.

The other truth (common sense and my simple positivism) is an imperative, theoretically leaving no room for argument: God's truth, anchored in nature, an objective reality to which all must conform and correspondence with which decides whether a statement is true or false. . . . Reasonable civilized people put one point of view against another, testing each in turn, until they jointly uncover the truth, which . . . is waiting out there in the world to be uncovered. (xviii)

For the purposes of our discussion, it is important to note how Bailey mediates these two contemporary views of truth. He argues that although they appear to be in direct conflict, we do best "when sitting on the fence" between them, although he admits that "the linkage between experience [the correspondence theory of truth] and ideas [the coherence theory of truth] is extremely loose" (xxii). Finally, however, Bailey finds no fence upon which he may sit, and aligns himself more strongly with coherence because what he calls "basic lies" that present themselves as objective truth determine our social interaction (xviii, xx). These illusory truths, whether ideological or religious, are socially constructed and instantiated, but not so deeply that they cannot be challenged or merely endured depending on the pragmatic consequences of such actions (129).

Kristeva, through the process of an extended psychoanalytic/semiotic discussion, outlines two views of truth similar to Bailey's. But she sees no satisfactory bridge between the views, though she seeks one. Her study draws out the semiotic implications of the views, which I will attempt to summarize briefly. The first view presented is the correspondence view. In semiotic terms, the person holding to the correspondence theory of truth accepts the truth of the signifier at the expense of disavowing reality (226). Classical philosophy and positivistic science characterize this view of truth, which Kristeva sees as connected to Plato's *Cratylus*—which asserts the necessary correspondence between the sentence and truth—and the *Metaphysics,* in which Aristotle finds statements true inasmuch as they state whatever is (220). Truth can therefore be demonstrated by language. Kristeva labels this view of truth "psychotic," consistent with its abandonment of reality for the sake of truth (226–27).

She presents her coherence view as the disavowal of the truth of the signifier in favor of accepting reality (226). Modern philosophy and rhetoric characterize this view of truth, which identifies truth as the condition of coherence within the context of a particular system of signs (221). Truth, therefore, resides in sentences themselves, submitting to no necessary connection outside of discourse. In this case, truth is determined by its "semblance," an intensification of plausibility (226). Kristeva labels this view "neurotic," in touch with reality but relativistic regarding truth (226–27).

Kristeva's views of truth advance our discussion by their explicit semiotic implications. Furthermore, by contrast to Bailey, she presents these two theories of truth as mutually exclusive. One must either preserve artificial truth (correspondence) or accept subjective truth (coherence) (222). But as helpful as the taxonomies she provides may be, they pale in comparison with the questions she asks of them—questions that remarkably situate Augustine in the midst of a contemporary discussion of why these exclusive views of truth are insufficient.

> I feel more and more that a separate place must be set aside for so-called artistic discourse. If there is any disavowal, it is introduced in the minutiae of such a practice (in each word, sound, color, rhythm . . .) such that these are never "pure signifiers" but always "word" and "flesh" and consequently situate themselves at the very heart of the distinction between these extremes and/or their identity to the extent that they are a microscopic exploration of murder *as* resurrection. (227)

The coincidence between Augustine and Kristeva in the logic of the preceding statement is somewhat surprising. Kristeva is trying to locate a distinctively semiotic place, including linguistic and nonlinguistic signs, where signifiers themselves become incarnate only to face death and resurrection. She understands the religious implications, and they compare favorably with her desired position for artistic discourse. Religious discourse "maintains the existence of the signifier as real but retains the dogmatic and rhetorical conditions which produce plausibility and truthful demonstration" (227). Artistic discourse dispenses altogether with the issue of truth "but succeeds in bestowing plausibility on the signifier and the real," whereas in coherence, plausibility only applies to the real (227).

The alleged superiority of artistic discourse over religious discourse for Kristeva lies in her assertion that religious discourse can so completely bridge the gap between correspondence and coherence theories of truth only by "postulating the impossible as faith" (227). In her conclusion, she claims that the "balm" of religion is,

> [a] discourse that creates plausibility through fictional devices . . . and economizes on the signifier as truth and/or as death: castration, and rejection or refuse. And apart from these solutions? There still remains that language-practice in which the true is the beautiful. But can one learn to write? And anyway, who can write alone? The mystery remains, but today its backdrop is a void. (236)

In the *Confessions*, Augustine long considers faith impossible too—a conglomeration of fictions (3.7–10, 4.4.7–8, 5.10.20–11.21, 5.14.24). He tries to find stability in aesthetics, much as Kristeva suggests, but the void to which she refers makes the aesthetic road finally unpassable:

> I did not know all this at the time, but I loved lower, beautiful creatures, and I was going down into the depths. I said to my friends: "So we love anything except what is beautiful? What then is a beautiful thing? What is beauty? What is it that attracts us and wins us to the things we love? Unless there were a grace and beauty in them, they could in no wise move us." . . . This consideration welled up in my mind out of the depths of my heart, and I wrote the books called "On the Beautiful and the Fitting." (4.13.20)
>
> Haec tunc non noverum, et amabam pulchra inferiora, et ibam in profundum et dicebam amicis meis: "num amamus aliquid nisi pulchrum? quid est ergo pulchrum? et quid est pulchritudo? quid est quod nos allicit et conciliat rebus, quas amamus? nisi enim esset in eis decus et species, nullo modo nos ad se moverent.". . . et ista consideratior scaturriit in animo meo ex intimo corde meo, et scripsi libros "de pulchro et apto." (4.13.20)

By now perhaps we can see that Augustine takes seriously what Kristeva identifies as the integration of coherence and correspondence theories of truth through religious discourse. However, Augustine's discourse is not religious if by that we mean to limit its scope to ecclesiastical, liturgical, devotional, or religious studies contexts. His view of the discourse that can accomplish this integration is comprehensive (Kuhns 25; Guitton 47, 49). His position can be best explained in semiotic terms which point to a rhetorical integration of these seemingly exclusive versions of truth. As we should expect, the integration comes through the incarnate Word.

The Incursion of the Incarnation in Language

Augustine argues in the *Confessions* that God Himself speaks within this semiotic system through His incarnate Word, and that His Word is Truth. In other words, the Incarnation functions as a sign, the semiotic expression of Truth and reality (D. W. Johnson 47). Like Kristeva, we have seen that Augustine demands more than mere language, more than Holy Writ disconnected from experience. He is looking for a sign in the fully semiotic sense: the union of words and deeds (4.13.19; 10.4.6). Not only is the incarnate Word expressed in word and deed, but in its ultimate expression the signifier died. What Kristeva speculates about murder *as* resurrection, Christ actuates by his murder *and* resurrection.

> How have you loved us, from whom he who "did not think it robbery to be equal to you" became "obedient even unto death, even to the death of the cross," he alone being "free among the dead," having power of laying down his life, and having power of taking it up again.

> For us, he is before you both victor and victim, and therefore victor for the reason that he is victim. (10.43.69)
>
> In quantum nos amasti, pater bone, qui filio tuo unico non pepercisti, sed pro nobis inpiis tradidisti eum! quomodo nos amasti, pro quibus ille non rapinam arbitratus esse aequalis tibi factus est subditus usque ad mortem crucis: unus ille in motuis liber, potestatem habens iterum sumendi eam, pro nobis tibi victor et victima, et ideo victor, quia victima. (10.43.69)

Using Kristeva's semiotic paradigm, the incarnate Word provides temporal mediation by his perfect union of words and flesh, but his victimage alone would have no enduring semiotic efficacy. It would merely be one more fleeting moment. The resurrection of the same incarnate Word secures the bridge Kristeva identifies between the reality and truth of the signifier and the reality and truth of the referent, investing it with eternity. But it does more. All wisdom and knowledge reside in the Incarnation because the incarnate Word fully integrates speech and thought with Truth (Gadamer in D. W. Johnson 86). In other words, the incarnate Word secures the entire sign function, unifying the signifier (speech) and signified (thought)—which together constitute the sign—with its referent (object) by necessary rather than arbitrary relations. The relations are necessary because they are eternal relations, despite the fact that they are expressed temporally.

For Augustine then, truth by correspondence exists, but neither in a Platonic nor positivistic sense. Truth is found in its correspondence to the eternal, incarnate Word, the substance and expression of wisdom. On the eternal plane, to which Augustine's expectations are directed, and from which the Word speaks to our inner ear, knowledge is direct, unmediated. But while the Incarnation produces expectations for and glimpses of eternity, we continue in temporality and the semiotic web of arbitrary relations within the sign function. As Kristeva correctly speculates about religious discourse, the Incarnation integrates coherence and correspondence which creates a space for rhetorical action that neither relativizes truth via sheer intersubjectivity nor negates reality by pretense of direct knowledge of all truth, whether material, ideational, or both.

The incarnate Word does not present truth by altering temporality, but by enacting eternal wisdom within our temporal experience and memory. As it stabilizes the elusive present, it likewise secures the reality of the sign function, so that we can be certain that truth exists and know some things truly, even if not completely or perfectly (Colish 54; Jordan 196). That is, the Incarnation creates the space we need in time to function rhetorically and participates in that rhetorical context:

> Thus in the Gospel he speaks through the flesh, and this word sounded outwardly in the ears of men, so that it might be believed, and sought inwardly, and found in the eternal Truth where the sole good Master teaches all his disciples. (11.8.10)
>
> sic in evangelio per carnem ait, et hoc insonuit foris auribus hominum, ut crederetur et intus quareretur, et inveniretur in aeterna veritate, ubi omnes discipulos bonus et solus magister docet. (11.7.10)

The Incarnation works *significantly*, and in that sense it is semiotic and stabilizes language simultaneously. This passage, however, like others in the *Confessions*, highlights the Augustinian commonplace that "belief precedes understanding" (1.1.1, 6.4.6, 6.5.7, 6.5.8, 10.3.3–4). Here we begin to see the application of Augustine's semiotic sensibilities and his attendant commitment to truth worked out in rhetorical practice and theory.

From Semiotics to Rhetoric

Augustine may have first fulfilled the conditions for semiotics in a way suggested in his own mind by the Incarnation. But his sign theory was not motivated, as far as we can tell, by any zeal for reform. The participation of the incarnate Word in temporality and human discourse indicates that neither is inherently flawed, even if both may be surpassed in eternity (Sutherland 143). All things were created by the Word in speech (11.9.11). Time itself was created as well (11.14.17). Furthermore, in his own practice Augustine maintains his confidence in ordinary language (Ricoeur 1:18).

The problem of ambiguity and obscurity, discordance and disintegration, and the division between eloquence and knowledge is a psychosocial disorder Augustine calls "original sin" (1.7.11–12; Vance 27). For Augustine, we saw earlier that this disorder is a matter of the heart or will, with implications for interpretation and epistemology (Gilson 227). It is manifested in the performance of discourse—that is, in rhetoric. In himself, Augustine sees sin as a failure easily diagnosed in his own rhetoric and in the Second Sophistic, both of which appear in the *Confessions* through stories of his preconversion rhetorical practice and departure from the rhetoric school in Milan. But as we have seen, where sin erupted the incarnate Word responded in kind, redeeming Augustine's rhetoric and moving him from the false rhetoric of the Second Sophistic to a rhetoric of truth (Colish 25; Sutherland 142, 152).

The means by which the Incarnation moves Augustine toward true rhetoric—rhetoric in the service of wisdom—is love *(caritas)*. By this love, the incarnate Word does the rhetorical work of integration that makes wisdom possible.

> Love—this is what Augustine means—is the confounder of all antitheses. It breaks the line between the here and the here-after, between change and the changeless, time and eternity. It is peace in conflict, contemplation in the midst of action, sight piercing through faith. For in love, the divine meets the human: heaven comes to earth when Christ is born, and man rejoices in the Truth. (Burnaby 82)

In terms of rhetoric, Augustine posits that love is a prerequisite to belief, the motivation for speaking, and a necessary element for valid interpretation (4.12.19, 10.3.3–4; Sutherland 148). Murphy suggests that Augustine shifts the emphasis of rhetoric from the speaker to the listener, a shift accomplished only upon recognition that love demands communication and supplies the only temporal hope for overcoming ambiguity in rhetorical transactions ("Metarhetorics," 207–8).

We have seen Augustine grapple with the instability of epistemology, temporality, signification, and truth. In every case, radical discontinuities have been mediated intellectually by the Incarnation, the starting point of Augustine's quest for wisdom. Furthermore, we have observed how some of the questions Augustine is pursuing, and the sign theory from which he is working, parallel contemporary issues. Finally, we have suggested that through *caritas,* the incarnate Word transforms Augustine's rhetoric.

To complete our quest for practical wisdom with Augustine, we will turn from the questions of memory, time, and semiotics to consider books 12 and 13, in which he concentrates on interpretation and expression, working out the implications of an incarnational rhetoric. Augustine gives precedence to the critical act—listening—in these concluding books. But we will not limit ourselves exclusively to the final books, because if it is read with charity, the entire *Confessions* is an interpretation—a critical reading of Augustine's life and ours.

Chapter 4

Rhetorical Interpretation

Current critical theorists have made it their project to "deconstruct" and "demythologize" central "metanarratives" of Western culture, the Bible being a prototype. Applied to Scripture, such critical terms function as a euphemistic veneer for attacks against Christian orthodoxy in its many variations. Therefore, as perhaps the most effective postapostolic advocate and shaper of Christian orthodoxy for both Catholics and Protestants, Augustine's approach to textual interpretation has escaped sympathetic scrutiny by the pundits of postmodern criticism. Nevertheless, interpretive practice emerges as the primary activity in Augustine's quest—his pursuit of wisdom empowered by the incarnate Word—a practice in the *Confessions* that shares many core assumptions with postmodern criticism.

What James J. Murphy notes about *De doctrina Christiana* applies equally to the *Confessions,* namely that it "contains certain principles of discourse which are important in their own right" (*Rhetoric,* 61). The immediate contemporary value in reading the *Confessions* as a discourse on interpretation rests in our ability to discern where Augustine's discursive sensibilities correspond with dominant interpretive assumptions of today and where he interrogates those assumptions.

Engaging interpretation in the *Confessions* challenges us, not because Augustine obscures his interpretive coordinates but because Scripture is the focus of interpretation. Enacting his commitment to the unity of form and content, Augustine's *Confessions* are as much about interpretation as they are about Christianity and its Scriptures. Scholars scorn presumption about historical and cultural context in approaching ancient texts. In this case we need to amend our own unfamiliarity and ineptness with the texts Augustine interprets, rather than discounting

Augustine's reflections on interpretation as irrelevant based on the naive assertion that he considers *only* Scripture.[1]

For Augustine and the readers of the *Confessions* in its own era, consideration of religious questions is integral to philosophical, political, and social issues. Faith and religion are not exiles from mainstream public and intellectual life (Markus 167; Shiel 23; Meer 134). scriptural interpretation serves as a common means of negotiating such questions. Even Augustine's uneducated parishioners exercise agility with biblical texts (Meer 133, 428). More recently, however, critics have demonstrated a penchant for anachronistic reduction of Augustine's work to narrow religiosity. Semiotic historians Tzvetan Todorov and John Deely suggest that Augustine's early advances in their field occur despite his ignorance of what he is actually doing. They assume that he seeks only to justify the allegorical interpretation of Scripture (Deely 67; Todorov 35, 41–42).

Attending specifically to interpretation, in "Interpreting the *Variorum*" Stanley Fish asserts that "it has always been possible to put into action interpretive strategies designed to make all texts one, or to put it more accurately, to be forever making the same text" (170).[2] He claims that Augustine's interpretive precepts in *De doctrina Christiana*—ones restated and applied in the *Confessions*—constitute such a strategy. Fish says, "It is dazzlingly simple: everything in the Scriptures, and indeed in the world when it is properly read, points to (bears the meaning of) God's love for us and our answering responsibility to love our fellow creatures for his sake" (170).

Fish may seem accurate, as far as he goes; but he does not go far. His gloss on Augustine to decry monistic interpretive schemes depends upon ignorance of Augustine's work and belies in Fish a simplistic understanding of God's love, human love of God, and love of neighbor. Indeed, in *De doctrina Christiana* (1.36.40–41) and the *Confessions* (12.25.35) Augustine does indicate that the right *end* of interpretation is charity, and that even interpreters who arrive at interpretations which produce charity via mistaken methods have done some good.[3] But when Fish represents Augustine's interpretive strategy as "forever making the same text" he (or his interpretive community) misappropriates Augustine's work, confusing what Augustine says interpretation *should produce* with interpretation itself.

Therefore, my inquiry into the *Confessions* attempts to reconsider, reconstitute, and rehabilitate Augustine's approach to interpretation, examining the interpretive approach of the *Confessions* in books 12 and 13.

Augustine, having established the epistemological and temporal prerequisites to interpretation in books 10 and 11, can now proceed with this preeminent activity in his quest for wisdom. Whereas Cicero's rhetorical activity was dominated by the forensic context, Augustine shifts to textual interpretation. As noted in chapter 1, Augustine equates rhetorical invention and interpretation.

At this point, the character of the interpretive act becomes crucial because it reveals the pervasiveness of rhetoric in the economy of Augustine's sense of wisdom. Definitionally, Scripture is rhetoric for Augustine in that its truths cannot be proven demonstrably. They must be believed. The Scripture speaks publicly, for the ultimate purpose of moving people's wills. Therefore, interpretation is rhetorical invention, in that speakers are given the task of appropriating and adapting the truths of Scripture—many and various—to the temporal circumstances of their local communities through public discourse.

The interpreter serves a vital, Janus-faced role to complete a rhetorical transaction between text and community. For Augustine, "word" carries the polymorphus sense of both written and spoken discourse. But in either case, interpretation addresses a rhetorical text and interprets it as a rhetorical performance, not merely as an intellectual, literary exercise.

With Todorov and Deely, some might suggest that Augustine's interpretive invention applies exclusively to scriptural exegesis and preaching. This may be. However, the *Confessions* argues otherwise. For the moment, in books 12 and 13 it is true that Augustine uses Scripture as the paradigmatic text from which to develop his interpretive approach.

Book 12: Augustine on Rhetorical Interpretation

Perhaps by way of apology to the reader, Augustine begins book 12 by explaining that any inquiry—any quest upon which we embark—necessarily generates a barrage of words (12.1.1). He has purportedly started his consideration of Genesis in book 11, but only makes it through the first verse. In book 12 he will progress one verse further. Inquiry by the ignorant—with whom Augustine aligns himself—requires more words than answers from the wise, but Augustine maintains hope that he will approach such answers with God's help. The account of wordiness propels him into consideration of Genesis 1:2 and a book-length digression about interpretive practice.

The initial words of Genesis 1:2 puzzle Augustine and present the problem which he must resolve in this book, namely, how to live with the unavoidable ambiguity of temporal textuality. Book 11 established that God created the heavens and the earth out of nothing by speaking it into existence (11.5.7, 11.7.9, 11.9.11). However, we now encounter a created formlessness that cannot logically be absolutely nothing, since it is something made, yet is without form (12.3.3). The puzzlement is accentuated by the complete inability to name the formlessness, by which Augustine indicates the intimate relationship between naming and knowledge (12.4.4). The digression continues as we reflect on how heavily the negative figures into the process of definition:

Hence, when thought seeks what mind may attain to in it, and says to itself, "It is not an intelligible form, like life, or like justice, because it is the matter of bodies. Nor is it a sensible form, because what may be seen and what may be sensed is not found in what is invisible and unordered," when human thought says such things to itself, does it not strive either to know it by not knowing it, or to be ignorant by knowing it? (12.5.5)

Ut, cum in ea quaerit cogitatio, quid sensus attingat, et dicit sibi: "non est intelligibilis forma sicut vita, sicut iustitia, quia materies est corporum, neque sensibilis, quoniam quid videatur et quid sentiatur in invisibili et incomposita non est," dum sibi haec dicit humana cogitatio, conetur eam vel nosse ignorando vel ignorare noscendo? (12.5.5)

Augustine briefly discloses his conception of how the negative permeates thought, which he represents as internal discourse. This principle of negativity finally enables the expression of the formlessness of Genesis 1:2 as a process analogous to a "transition from form to form I suspected to be made through something formless and not by means of absolute nothing" [eundemque transitum de forma in formam per informe quiddam fieri suspicatus sum, non per omnino nihil] (12.6.6). Still, knowledge of this formlessness is elusive enough that comprehending it stretches the limits of language. Augustine names it variously "an unformed near-nothing" [informe prope nihil], "a nothing-something" [nihil aliquid], and "an is-is-not" [est non est] (12.6.6). Even these manufactured metaphors seem insufficient.

Through this process, the bishop takes the notion of formlessness and introduces the ordinary workings of human thought as so inseparable from semiotic sensibilities, from discourse and imagination, that content—a genuine something—is inconceivable apart from a namable form. We are shown to be dependent on form, and speech about form, as integral to our understanding substance, something, anything. But process destabilizes knowledge and form because it is a mode of time that introduces change. "Out of this formlessness, out of this almost-nothing, you made all things, of which this mutable world stands firm, and yet does not stand firm" [de qua informitate, de quo paene nihilo faceres haec omnia, quibus iste mutabilis mundus constat et non constat] (12.8.8).

The mutability can be checked through "partaking of the eternal" [particeps tamen aeternitatis tuae] (12.9.9). Augustine himself can partake only through God's speech to him, the Truth which he seeks and receives through his "interior ear" [aurem interiorem] (12.10.10–11.12). The temporal position of humanity is reinforced by a discussion of God in eternity and creatures that partake of eternity immutably, yet which are not co-eternal with God (12.11.13–14, 12.12.15). Augustine—trying to interpret in the stable instability of temporality—contrasts interpretive knowledge with knowledge in eternity:

> I interpret the heaven of heaven as the intellectual heaven, where it belongs to intellect to know all at once, not in part, not in a dark manner, not through a glass, but as a whole, in plain sight, face to face, not this thing now and that thing then, but, as has been said, it knows all at once, without any passage of time. (12.13.16)

> sic intemirm sentio propter illud caelum caeli,—caelum intellectuale, ubi est intellectus nosse simul, non ex parte, non in aenigmate, non per speculum, sed ex toto, in manifestatione, facie ad faciem; non modo hoc, modo illud, sed, quod dictum est, nosse simul sine ulla vicissitudine tomporum (12.13.16)

Augustine's temporal situation means that he, the interpreter, cannot know all at once, but must operate with partial and comparatively dim knowledge. Even the Truth he receives through his interior ear is not complete. But he knows enough to distinguish between those with whom he will continue to discuss interpretation, and those who are in no position to address the text as interpreters. Augustine refuses to entertain the comments of those "enemies" of the Scripture who object to the book of Genesis outright (12.14.17). The objectors to Scripture he prays would be slain by God with a "two-edged sword," a reference to Hebrews 4:12, invoking the same Scripture to which they object, that they might live. He is willing to continue with others:

> Not objectors to the book of Genesis but praisers of it, and they say: "The Spirit of God, who by his servant Moses wrote down these things, did not will that all this be understood from these words. He would not have what you say taken from them, but something different which we say."
>
> To these men I thus make answer as follows, with you, O God of us all, as our judge. (12.14.17)

> ecce autem alii non reprehensores, sed laudatores libri Geneseos: "non" inquiunt "hoc voluit in his verbis intelegi spiritus dei, qui per Moysen famulum eius ista conscrptsit, non hoc voluit intelligi, quod tu dicis, sed aliud, quod nos dicimus." quibus ego te arbitro, deus omnium nostrum, ita respondeo. (12.14.17)

The answer provided addresses not the alternative readings these contradictors of Augustine will suggest, but rather seeks agreement on theconditions established in the first sixteen chapters of book 12 (12.15.18–22). What we have received in these early chapters of book 12 is a primer on the conditions within which interpretation takes place. Interpretation, as inquiry, progresses discursively through multiplication of words. The problem to be addressed by interpretation is the ambiguity of language in time—temporal meaning being established through dependence on the negative in discourse. From the scriptural text, Augustine insists on the union of form and content and a certain semiotic stability produced by the initiative of eternal speech in the temporal context. The eternal provides access to Truth in time but never complete Truth all at once. Augustine approaches interpretation with a firm recognition of the limits of temporal knowledge but with enough confidence in the existence of eternal Truth and partial access to it to validate interpretation as a worthy and positive venture.

In other words, Augustine is not immediately concerned about the truth of the details he presents in his reading of Genesis 1:2, but in the truth of his approach to interpretation. He is developing an interpretive community and a shared goal from which to discuss the exegesis of the text rather than defending the validity of his own interpretation. And this community is exactly what he secures in the *Confessions:* a community of interpreters who agree on the authority of Scripture and love the text (12.16.23).

Finally, Augustine is ready to consider the actual alternatives presented in reading Genesis 1. He introduces numerous interpretations, some which argue over what Moses intended; others which contest the meaning of words (12.17.24–26). But regardless of objections to his own reading and the alternatives suggested, Augustine refuses to "contend in words" [verbis contendere] (12.18.27). This is the point at which Fish's analysis of Augustine proves so inadequate.

In validating interpretation, Augustine bounds it by rules that address the function of interpretation, not restrictive interpretive methodology. He appears to be more concerned about what interpretation does than any specific truth determined by it. Augustine's test is simple: Does the interpretation promote charity and build up others? Or, does the interpretation promote contention and subvert others? The goal of interpretation "is charity, from a pure heart, and a good conscience, and an unfeigned faith" [caritas de corde puro et conscientia bona et fide non ficta] (12.18.27). But this does not produce the single text that Fish seems to expect. Instead, the interpretations multiply:

> What harm comes to me, O my God, "light of my eyes" in secret, if I zealously confess these things to you, what harm comes to me, if various meanings may be found in these words, all of which are true? What harm comes to me, I say, if I think differently than another

thinks as to what he who wrote these words thought? All of us who read strive to trace out and understand what he whom we read actually meant, and since we believe him to speak the truth, we dare not assert that he spoke anything we know or think to be false. Therefore, while every man tries to understand in Holy Scripture what the author understood therein, what wrong is there if anyone understand what you, O light of all truthful minds, reveal to him as true, even if the author he reads did not understand this, since he also understood a truth, though not this truth? (12.18.27)

quae mihi ardenter confitenti, deus meus, lumne oculorum meorum in occulto, quid mihi obest, cum diversa in his verbis intellegi possint, quae tamen vera sint? Quid, inquam, mihi obest, si aliud ego sensero, quam sensit alius eum sensisse, qui scripsit? omnes quidem, qui legimus, nitimur hoc indigare atque conprehendere, quod voluit ille quem legimus, et cum eum veridicum credimus, nihil, quod falsum esse vel novimus vel putamus, audemus eum existimare dixisse. dum ergo quisque conatur id sentire in scripturis sanctis, quod in eis sensit ille qui scripsit, quid mali est, si hoc sentiat, quod tu, lux omnium veridicarum mentium, ostendis verum esse, etiamsi non hoc sensit ille, quem legit, cum et ille verum nec tamen hoc senserit? (12.18.27)

Taking Fish's notion that Augustine, the interpreter, must find a way to reproduce one exclusive meaning from every text, the most astonishing directive we find in the previous passage may be that Augustine expects interpreters of Scripture to arrive at multiple true and distinct meanings, none of which are necessarily exclusive. He also expects that: (1) Various interpreters may judge the intention of a writer differently. (2) All interpreters attempt to discern what the writer actually meant. (3) An interpreter may understand a truth unintended by the writer but revealed by Truth himself.

Augustine immediately reinforces the multiplicity of true readings by reciting a litany of truths from Genesis 1:1 (12.19.28). Then, from Genesis 1:1 and Genesis 1:2, he suggests that different speakers might choose to apply any of these true interpretations to deliver in a speaking context, reminding us that many of the *Confessions'* early listeners were bishops or clerics of one sort or another (12.20.29, 12.21.30).

At this point in book 12 Augustine concludes the discussion of Genesis 1 to focus directly on interpretive issues. First, he dispenses with the naive literalist who questions whether one can infer beyond the specific recorded words of Scripture (12.22.31). Augustine himself has already done this by importing Psalm 115:16 into his discussion of Genesis 1:1. The second interpretive issue—the one which will occupy Augustine through the rest of the book—regards predictable points of disagreement between interpreters:

> I see that two types of disagreement may arise when anything is uttered by means of signs by truthful reporters. One concerns the truth of things, the other is argument about the intention of the speaker. In one way we inquire what may be true with regard to the process of creation; in the other way as to what Moses, that excellent servant of your faith, wished the reader and hearer to understand by his words. (12.23.32)

> duo video dissensionum genera oboriri posse, cum aliquid a nuntiis veracibus per signa enuntiatur, unum, si de veritate rerum, alterum, si de ipsius qui enuntiat voluntate dissensio est. Aliter enim quareimus de creaturae conditione, quid verum sit, aliter autem quid in his verbis Moyses, egregius domesticus fidei tuae, intellegere lectorem auditoremque voluerit. (12.23.32)

As Augustine introduces the problems of intentionality and truth we should remember that he considers these issues in relation to Scripture, a text he views as inspired by God and without error (6.5.7, 7.2.3). He believes that it expresses eternal Truth and that the writers wrote truthfully. The Truth and truths of Scripture are confirmed for Augustine in his "interior ear" by the voice of the Word incarnate. But Augustine's temporality limits him to partial knowledge, which when generalized to other interpreters allows that multiple true meanings will be produced even from Scripture. Finally, the partial nature of truth in interpretation finds its corollary in the partial knowledge of truth in Scripture possessed by the writers, which produces the problem to which Augustine will turn his attention. Therefore, interpreters need to consider both the intended meaning of the writer—in the case of Genesis, Moses—and the intended meaning of the Author, who is Truth. In other words, there are more truths in the text than the writer could know, Moses being a temporal creature like Augustine, yet the text is not without its authority.

By his reinvocation of charity, Augustine reminds us that interpretation takes place within a community for the sake of that community (12.23.32). He finds that he more readily maintains confidence in truth about things through interpretive inquiry than certainty about the writer's intention. When we interpret, we believe that we understand the writer's intention. However, determining that intention precisely is impossible, because we have only indirect, mediated access to the mind of another:

> I see that the truth could have been spoken, whichever of these was said. But which of them he meant by these words, this I do not see

in the same manner. However, whether it was either of these, or some further meaning which I have not mentioned, that this so great a man gazed at in his mind, when he uttered these words, I have no doubt that he saw the true meaning and stated it correctly. (12.24.33).

video quippe vere potuisse dici, quidquid horum diceretur, sed quid horum in his verbis ille cogitaverit, non ita video, quamvis sive aliquid horum sive quid aliud, quod a me commemoratum non est, tantus vir ille mente conspexerit, cum haec verba promeret, verum eum vidisse apteque id enuntiavisse non dubitem. (12.24.33)

As a result, Augustine himself rebukes the interpreter who would exclude another's interpretation in favor of his own, not because the interpretation itself is necessarily false but because such interpretive insistence offends against truth and charity. In both cases, the offending interpreter assumes an anticommunitarian posture driven by pride, not the love of truth, which is always held in common (12.15.34). Again we see that charity in no way demands that interpretation produce a single, authoritative meaning. Instead, it seems to generate multiple, harmonious meanings that, inasmuch as they are true, belong to the community as a whole. "See how stupid it is, amid such an abundance of true meanings as can be taken out of these words, rashly to affirm which of them Moses chiefly meant, and with pernicious quarrels to offend against charity, for the sake of which he spake everything, whose words we try to expound" [iam vide, quam stultum sit in tanta copia verissimarum sententiarum, quae de illis verbis erui possunt, temere adfirmare, quam earum Moyses opotissimum senserit, et perniciosis contentionibus ipsam offendere caritatem, propter quam dixit omnia, cuius dicta conamur exponere] (12.25.35).

That true interpretations belong to the community implies that interpretation itself is a rhetorical performance for communal benefit. Augustine reveals his own performative ambitions, desiring eloquence like Moses to reach listeners from the simplest to those with the greatest understanding (12.26.36). He argues that interpretation cannot exhaust the resources of Scripture. The words of Scripture are a fountain which supplies a manifest variety of true interpretations for listeners at different levels of understanding, different times, and different places—rewarding those who devote themselves to labor and discussion over truths in the text (12.27.37; 12.32.43).

Within this variety of true, proper, but incomplete interpretations there are limits: "He who understands 'In the beginning he made heaven and earth' as if it meant, 'At first he made,' has no valid interpretation of 'heaven and earth' except as meaning the matter of heaven and earth" [At ille, qui non aliter accipit: in principio fecit, quam si diceretur: primo fecit, non habet quomodo veraciter intellegat caelum et terram, nisi materiam caeli et terrae intellegat] (12.19.40). We should note that Augustine is describing his own interpretation, using the limits of interpretation as a means to validate his own reading within those limits—in essence to provide an interpretation of his own meaning. Even while indicating the limitations to interpretation, he nowhere articulates rules for valid interpretation. We might infer some general assumptions about right reason guiding interpretive validity. But Augustine assigns his criticism of interpretation to the relation of interpreters to the community, text, and proper ends of interpretation rather than to any particular interpretive theory or method.

By moving through steps that legitimate the interpretation offered of heaven and earth as the "matter of heaven and earth," he returns to the discussion of form and matter introduced in 12.3. The oral analogy—the priority of sound to melody—from which Augustine works in this case is worth our careful consideration, particularly because it occurs within a text we have identified as being produced in an oral culture for oral performance:

> Who can mentally perceive so subtle a thing as to be able to distinguish without great labor how sound may be prior to a melody? The reason is that a melody is formed sound, and, whereas an unformed thing can exist, what does not exist cannot be formed. In this way, matter is prior to what is made out of it: it is not prior because it makes the thing, for contrariwise it is itself made, and it is not prior by any interval of time. We do not at an earlier time utter formless sounds without the melody, and at a later time adapt or fashion them into the form of a song. . . . When it is sung, its sound is heard, for there is not first a formless sound that is afterwards formed into a melody. (12.29.40)

> quis deinde sic acutum cernat animo, ut sine labore magno dinoscere valeat, quomodo sit prior sonus quam cantus, ideo quia cantus est formatus sonsu, et esse utique aliquid non formatum potest, formari autem quod non est non potest? sic est prior matreies quam id, quod ex ea fit, non ideo prior, quia ips efficit, cum potius fiat, nec prior intervallo temporis; neque enim priore tempore sonos deimus informes sine cantu et eos posteriore tempore in formam cantici coaptus aut fingimus. . . . cum enim cantatur, auditur sonus eius, non prius informiter sonat et deinde formatur in cantum. (12.29.40)

Augustine determines that sound is not prior to melody in power, time, or choice, "but it is prior in origin, for a melody is not formed so that there may be sound, but sound is formed so that there may be a melody" [sed prior est origine, quia non cantus formatur, ut sonus sit, sed sonus formatur, ut cantus sit.] (12.29.40). Through this analogy, used by Augustine to interpret the words of Genesis 1:2, he promotes the integration of substance and style in an utterance that corresponds closely to speech as well as reinforcing the generic form/matter relationship. Substance must exist for form to have something to fashion, but substance cannot exist without being fashioned. If we grasp this subtlety, we will have grasped not only Augustine's reading of the scriptural truth at the moment of creation—that formlessness was prior in origin but not in discernible time—but we will also have understood the dynamic integration of his approach to interpretation.

Right interpretation comes from God, not in a mystical, visionary way, but in a community constituted by God on the basis of love, not pride (12.18.27, 12.25.34–35, 12.30.41). It can be simple or complex. It can be multiple, diverse, adapted to time, place, and situation. This is always the case, according to Augustine: "Through him [Moses] the one God has adapted the sacred writings to many men's interpretations, wherein will be seen things true and also diverse" [per quem deus unus sacras litteras vera et diversa visuris multorum sensibus temperavit] (12.31.42). The meanings come from God, not from the writer, although the writer's intention is assumed to be consistent with the best interpretations, the most thorough understanding. Yet the possibility remains that the writer, like any given interpreter, could hardly foresee the applications in later times that God had prepared in advance:

> But to us, Lord, you point out either that meaning or such other true meaning as pleases you. Hence, whether you uncover the same meaning to us as to that servant of yours, or some other meaning on the occasion of those words, you will still nourish us and error will not delude us. (12.32.43)

> nobis autem, domine, aut ipsam deomstras aud quam placet alteram veram, ut, sive nobis hoc quod etiam ille homini tuo sive aliud ex eorundem verborum occasione patefacias, tu tamen pascas, non error inludat. (12.32.43)

Finally, Augustine recognizes how many words he himself has committed to the first two verses of Genesis, and confesses, promising to limit his own interpretation to a single meaning. He does not resolve the Truth/intention tension, acknowledging that accurately determining the intention of Moses would be best, "and if I do not attain to it, I would still say that which your Truth willed by his words to say to me, which also spoke to him [Moses] what it willed" [quod si assecutus non fuero, id tamen dicam, quod mihi per eius verba tua vertas dicere voluerit, quae illi quoque dixit quod voluit] (12.32.43).

We should expect to see in this single meaning not the execution of some exclusive simple strategy, but a performance fashioned consistently with the interpretive conditions so carefully established through the inquiry of book 12.

Book 13: *An Interpretive Case Study*

The interpretation of Genesis presented in the *Confessions* is not exclusive, even for Augustine. By the time the book 13 commentary occurs, he has already produced two interpretations of the Genesis creation account: *De Genesi contra Manichaeos,* a refutation of Manichaean objections to Genesis that he completed in 389, and *De Genesi ad litteram liber imperfectus,* an attempt at a literal exegesis of the first three books of Genesis that was never completed due to Augustine's self-professed inadequacy for the task in 393 (Brown, *Augustine,* 74; Portalie 402). He would return to Genesis a year after completing the *Confessions* to begin *De Genesi ad litteram,* a literal exegesis of the creation account with a marked resemblance to the more limited consideration in books 11–13. Eugene Portalie notes the similarity between the *Confessions* and *De Genesi ad litteram,* and concludes that even in this last study, which stretched from 401 to 414, Augustine does not advocate his interpretation as the definitive or exclusive reading:

> Augustine presented his theory with great reserve and without condemning other interpretations, "denying no one the liberty of understanding the passage better." "In ignorance we hazard a guess." On the other hand, he energetically demanded freedom to defend his own system. Never perhaps was he so severe to Catholics as he was here towards those involved in contradictions because they had raised their solution to the status of a dogma—and this in the most pious and humble of his books, the *Confessions.* (142)

Augustine's repeated interpretations of the same scriptural text follows obviously from one of his main justifications for multiple interpretations from book 12: the necessity for new interpretations of eternal truth in time. Temporality presents a complex of dynamics wherein, despite the immutability of eternal truth, the interpreter, audience, and language necessarily change. Therefore, we can begin to understand why prior to his ordination Augustine might confidently rebut Manichaean objections to the Genesis creation account, only to doubt his competence to interpret the same passages shortly after his ordination. In the first case, Augustine is a new convert, zealous to refute the errors he perceives in the cult from which the gospel liberated him. In the second, Augustine finds himself humbled by his ignorance of the Scriptures and the burden of his appointment to teach them. He had taken the limitations of his own biblical knowledge seriously enough to petition Valerius, the bishop who preceded him in Hippo, to grant him leave for intensive study prior to his ordination as priest—a request Valerius honored.[4]

We ought to pay as much attention to the changing situations of audiences as to changes for the interpreter when considering the effects of temporality on interpretation. In *De Genesi contra Manichaeos*, Augustine had a clearly defined audience to which the interpretation was addressed. The audience of book 13 is as clearly defined, and quite a different group of listeners. I submit that book 13 may be the most problematic segment of the *Confessions* for the contemporary reader, because rather than turning into an abstract exercise in speculative theology it applies the interpretive coordinates from book 12 to a specific audience. Book 13 presents not a refutation of Manichaeans but an exhortation to the audience of the *Confessions* in its historical context.

Therefore, to approach this final book of the *Confessions* we need to recollect our sense of Augustine's expected listeners, namely the *servus Dei* and sympathetic correspondents—Christian or otherwise—along with those who might encounter the *Confessions* through community readings or later publication. The most charitable readers of book 13 would likely be a predominantly ecclesiastical, highly educated audience. However, if we as contemporary readers want to grasp the significance—even the merely temporal significance—of book 13, we must do so by first cultivating and then keeping our historical wits about us. The context of this text still holds through book 13, and the focus sharpens. With that context in mind, we may hear Augustine preaching quite literally to the choir.

Recitation of Orthodoxy

Augustine takes his listeners seriously, whether addressing common parishioners in Hippo, select audiences in Carthage, or critical scholars of the day (Marrou 57). He effectively gauges his rhetoric to their competence, attitude, culture, and faith (Murphy, "Metarhetorics," 208). His pulpit rhetoric is supple. As Hans von Campenhausen reports:

> Depending of the occasion, time, and audience, the sermons were entirely different. The speaker, Augustine thinks, must not bring a ready-made idea along, but must continually have an eye to his hearers. . . . The essential thing is that his sermon reach the congregation, i.e. be heard with understanding, joy, and obedience. . . . Above all, it must be clear and really lead to the word of the Bible. This last is the crucial point: even more important than popularity is the demand for substance and relevance. (220–21)

He practices this from the broadest scope of his rhetorical approach to the most minute details of his sermons and other works. He will deviate from classical Latin usage or deploy colloquialisms where they are necessary to reach his audience (Kelly 60; Meer 421). This becomes, for Augustine, a matter of prescriptive principle as well as practice (*De doctrina Christiana* 4.10.24–25). Therefore, we should expect book 13 to be well tuned to its hearers.

Indeed, the first thirteen chapters of the book distinctively belie the *servus Dei*. They introduce this final confession as articulating Augustine's statement of faith; the doctrinal essentials from which he proceeds. He defines his faith positively, inviting a sympathetic audience to affirm their orthodoxy. His contributions to Christian orthodoxy began long before the *Confessions*—almost immediately upon his ordination as a priest in Hippo—engaging religious and/or philosophical cults and heresies within the church (Brown, *Augustine*, 141–42).

In this case, true to the form identified by Campenhausen, Augustine concludes the whole matter of the *Confessions* with interpretation of a biblical text. From this text he renders the fundamental tenets of orthodoxy, which he expounds to benefit his listeners.

Augustine begins by summarizing his own origin and conversion as initiated and completed by God's employment of words (13.1.1). This introductory chapter recalls Augustine's temporality in contrast to God's eternity and his need for God in contrast to God's complete independence from him. But the meditation is not egocentric, for its concluding direction frames the purpose for this inquiry as both personal *and* corporate: "I am such a one as may serve you and cultivate you, so that because of you it may be well with me, for from you comes the fact that I am one with whom it may be well" (13.1.1). Augustine sees himself as part of a community and part of the Creation at large always distinct from, but in relation to, God.

For contemporary readers, or worshipers accustomed to sermons or homilies long on popular moral appeals and short on scriptural exegesis, Augustine may appear to be freelancing or digressing. However, to *his* contemporaries—especially the *servus Dei*—and to us if we have ears to hear it, Augustine is explicating his doctrine of God through a measured exegesis of the second half of Genesis 1:2 through 1:3. In it he expounds God's nature, the Trinity, and the doctrine of Man as the image of God.

He first presents the doctrine of God as radically other than all spiritual and material Creation with a brief reconsideration of the original state of Creation's formlessness. The Creation, made without any necessity, "subsists out of the fullness of your goodness, to the end that a good that would profit you nothing, and that was not of your substance and thus equal to you, would nevertheless not be non-existent, since it could be made by you" (13.2.2). The Word, that is the Word incarnate, is revealed as the one who fashions form out of formlessness (13.2.2). Augustine articulates the completeness of the divide between God and his Creation in legal terms: neither spiritual nor material creatures have any claim on God (13.2.2–3).

Before reiterating the total self-existence and self-sufficiency of God in chapter 4, Augustine contrasts his continuing "labor in obscurity" with God's blessedness in Himself (13.2.3–3.4). The crucial distinctions made here place the present Augustine squarely in the midst of the Christian orthodoxy of his own day and leave little room for confusion with his past associations with Manichaeanism, skepticism, and Platonism. God is distinct from the Creation, which He created as a volitional expression of His own goodness. Augustine recognizes himself as a creature, radically other than God, with no internal means of achieving union with God in any Platonic or Neoplatonic sense. All of this he gleans from Genesis 1:1–3. But he is not finished. In book 11 Augustine argued that "the beginning" mentioned in Genesis 1:1 refers to the incarnate Word (11.8–9). So before he gets to book 13 he has two out of three members of the Trinity intact in the passage. Now he moves to the end of Genesis 1:2 to establish the presence of the Trinity in the Creation narrative (13.5.6). The scriptural text mentions the Spirit explicitly, yet Augustine questions why this occurs so late, after the Creation is initiated. The answer moves him into a full discussion of the doctrine of Man.

According to Augustine, late inclusion in the narrative emphasizes the Spirit's work in raising people up despite their fall into lust (13.7.8). He appeals to a variety of quotations from Pauline epistles to confirm the Spirit's charitable work, which enlightens both the goodness of God and the subordinate greatness of humanity in its appropriate, intermediate place:

> every obedient intelligence in your heavenly city had cleaved to you and found rest in your Spirit which is borne unchangeably over every changeable thing. Otherwise even the heaven of heaven would be a darksome deep within itself, but now it is light in the Lord. For in that very restless misery of spirits flowing away and displaying their own darkness, when stripped of the garments of your light, you sufficiently reveal how great you made the rational creature. For in no wise is any being less than you sufficient to give it rest and happiness, and for this it is not sufficient to itself. (13.8.9)

> et inhaereret tibi omnis oboediens intelligentia caelestis civitatis tuae et requiesceret in spiritu tuo, qui superfertur incommutabiliter super omne mutabile. alioquin et ipsum caelum caeli tenebrosa abyssus esset in se; nunc auterm lux est in domino. nam et in ipsa misera inquietudine defluentium spirituum, et indicantium tenebras suas, nudatas veste luminis tui satis ostendis, quam magnam ratio-

> nalem creaturam feceris, cui nullo modo sufficit ad beatam requiem, quidquid te minus est, ac per hoc nec ipsa sibi. (13.8.9)

Neither is the rational creature by itself, or in any sense isolated from others in its experience. Distinction does not equal isolation. The ascent Augustine champions in this interpretation of Scripture is not only initiated by God's Spirit, it is a communal ascent:

> We ascend steps within the heart, and we sing a gradual psalm. By your fire, by your good fire, we glow with inward fire, and we go on, for we go upwards to "the peace of Jerusalem," for "I am gladdened in those who said to me, 'We will go into the house of the Lord.'" (13.9.10)

> ascendimus ascensiones in corde et cantamus canticum graduum. igne tuo, igne tuo bono inardescimus et imus, quoniam sursum imus ad pacem Hierusalem, quoniam iucundatus sum in his, qui dixerunt mihi: in domum domini ibimus. (13.9.10)

Augustine invokes Psalm 122, one of the psalms known variously as psalms of degree or psalms of ascent, which celebrates the pilgrimage of the greater community of Israel to worship in Jerusalem, probably on the occasions of the major temple feasts. He relies on inclusive language, a point we must not ignore as we consider how this recitation of orthodoxy positions Augustine's interpretive performance—one designed to engage a particular audience by applying eternal truth to their situation. He is conscious of the community to which he speaks.

Although limited in ability to understand the Trinity by his creaturely status, Augustine completes the basic tenets of doctrine in Genesis 1:1–3 by offering the self as analogous to the Trinity in the limited sense that by his certainty of his own being, knowing, and willing, he lives with distinctions that are inseparable in his experience, just as the three persons of the Trinity can be distinguished but never separated (13.11.12). What Augustine learns from this analogical exercise, though, is about the self, not about the mystery of the Trinity beyond its existence:

> Surely a man stands face to face with himself. Let him take heed of himself, and look there, and tell me. But when he has discovered any of these and is ready to speak, let him not think that he has found that immutable being which is above all these, which is immutably, and knows immutably, and wills immutably. (13.11.12)

> certe coram se est; adtendat in se et videat et dicat mihi. sed cum invenerit in his aliquid, et dixerit, non iam se putet invenisse illud, quod supra ista est incommutabile, quod est inconmutabiliter [sic] et scit inconmutabiliter [sic] et vult inconmutabiliter. (13.11.12)

The curious thing about Augustine at this point is that he cannot resist the dynamic juxtaposition of the self and community. No sooner does he introduce an analogy of the Trinity to the self than he turns around and equates the creation by Christ of heaven and earth with "the spiritual and the carnal parts of his Church," an interpretive move that will play out through the remainder of book 13 (13.13.13).

The distinction between the carnal and spiritual aspects of the church points to the practicality of what perhaps seems to us an effusion of abstract theology. However, for Augustine, his clerical correspondents, and interested listeners in or close to the church, this distinction resides at the heart of their experience. Peter Brown explains:

> "This is the door of the Lord," they wrote on the lintel of a church in Numidia, "the righteous shall enter in." "The man who enters," however, wrote Augustine, "is bound to see drunkards, misers, tricksters, gamblers, adulterers, fornicators, people wearing amulets, assiduous clients of sorcerers, astrologers. . . . He must be warned that the same crowds that press into the churches on Christian festivals, also fill the theatres on pagan holidays" (213).
>
> It was a disconcerting double image. The Africans' view of the church had depended on their being able to see in it a group different from the "world," an alternative to something "unclean" and hostile. The spread of Christianity in Africa, by indiscriminately filling the churches, had simply washed away the clear moral landmarks that separated the "church" from the "world." (*Augustine*, 213)

The orthodoxy of the church was everywhere being challenged, and the challenge was perhaps greater by volume in the lives of congregants served by the *servus Dei* than from the mouths and pens of skeptics, cults, or heretics attacking church doctrine. Augustine's confirmation of these basic tenets of orthodoxy—the doctrine of God, the Trinity, and the doctrine of Man—as inherent in the first three verses of Genesis resonates with contested issues of fourth-century thought and practice. In this light, we see Augustine's interpretation suited quite specifically to the needs of his anticipated hearers. It is far from a figurative flight of fancy.

Augustine will exhort from this foundation. He can now begin to teach us how to pursue and apply wisdom through interpretive performance. In this case, he presents a single interpretation of Genesis 1 to apply eternal principles to the temporal context—a practical guide to ministers for the redemption of the carnal church.

Rhetoric as a Semiotic Unity

We have been pursuing our inquiry into Augustine's interpretation as a continuing enactment or application of the interpretive conditions established in book 12, which he indicates at the end of that book (12.32.43). In book 13, having completed his recitation of orthodoxy directed to his listeners, Augustine considers belief in the authority of Scripture as his interpretation proceeds. The decisive move he makes is to rhetoric, a rhetoric which applies his semiotic sensibilities.

Consistent with the problem of epistemology—that is, the unverifiability of sensible things—Augustine has already acknowledged that the reliability and authority of Scripture cannot be proven but must be believed. He reiterates that position in transition from the realities of the carnal/spiritual dichotomy in the church, "Yet with us it is still by faith and not yet by sight," and quotes Romans 8:24 (13.13.14).

Reading the firmament of the sky in Genesis 1:6–8 allegorically as the Scripture, he can continue only on the basis of faith and hope grounded in belief (13.15.16). Were he an angel—above the firmament—he could "read" by direct and perfect sight in eternity. As it is, he and the rest of us under the firmament of Scripture, functioning within time, depend on the authority of its words (13.15.18). Augustine's discussion of faith and hope corresponds almost precisely to a passage in *De doctrina Christiana,* where he identifies the authority of Scripture as the engine of faith, hope, and love in the context of interpretation:

> In asserting rashly that which the author before him did not intend, he may find many other passages which he cannot reconcile with his interpretation. If he acknowledges these to be true and certain, his first interpretation cannot be true, and under these conditions it happens, I know not why, that, loving his own interpretation, he begins to become angrier with the Scriptures than he is with himself. And if he thirsts persistently for the error, he will be overcome by it. "For we walk by faith and not by sight," and faith will stagger if the authority of the Divine Scriptures wavers. Indeed, if faith staggers, charity itself languishes. And if anyone should fall from faith, it follows that he falls also from charity, for a man cannot love that which he does not believe to exist. On the other hand, a man who both believes and loves, by doing well and by obeying the rules of good customs, may bring it about that he may hope to arrive at that which he loves. Thus there are these three things for which all knowledge and prophecy struggle: faith, hope, and love.
>
> But the vision we shall see will replace faith, and that blessedness to which we are to come will replace hope; and when these things are falling away, charity will be increased even more. (1.37.41–38.42)

> Asserendo enim temere quod ille non sensit quem legit plerumque incurrit in alia quae illi sententiae contexere nequeat. Quae si vera et certa esse consentit, illud non possit verum esse quod senserat, fitque in eo nescio quo modo ut amando sententiam suam scripturae incipiat offensior esse quam sibi. Quod malum si serpere siverit, evertetur ex eo. "Per fidem enim ambulamus, non per speciem"; titubabit autem fides, si divinarum scripturarum vacillat auctoritas; porro fide titubante caritas etiam ipsa languescit. Nam si a fide quisque ceciderit, a caritate etiam necesse est cadat. Non enim potest diligere quod esse non credit. Porro si et credit et diligit, bene agendo et praeceptis morum bonorum obtemperando efficit ut etiam speret se ad id quod diligit esse venturum. Itaque tria haec sunt quibus et scientia omnis et prophetia militat: fides, spes, caritas. Sed fidei succedet species quam videbimus, et spei succedet beatitudo ipsa ad quam perventuri sumus, caritas autem etiam istis decedentibus augebitur potius. (2.37.41–38.42)

In other words, belief in the authority of Scripture is an exclusively temporal phenomenon and a necessary condition for faith and hope, particular modes of belief that produce charity. Skepticism and pride negate charity. Augustine's appeal to Psalm 42 and 43—where the writer is taunted by Skeptics who ask "Where is your God?"—reinforces our consciousness that we rely on belief alone to negotiate our way "in this still uncertain state of man's knowledge"—that is, our temporal experience (13.13.14–14.15). He follows the introduction of the Skeptics' question with a barrage of direct quotations from Scripture.

Augustine believes in the authority of Scripture because he has been persuaded by its effect—particularly on himself (13.15.17). He had reported that, "It gave joy to my pride to be above all guilt, and when I did an evil deed, not to confess that I myself had done it. . . . I loved to excuse myself, and to accuse I know not what other being that was present with me but yet was not I" [delectabat superbiam meam extra culpam esse, et cum aliquid mali fecissem, non confiteri me fecisse, ut sanares animam meam, quoniam peccabat tibi, sed excusare me amabam, et accusare nescio quid aliud, quod mecum esset et ego non essem] (5.10.18). So his explanation of the persuasive power of Scripture grows directly from personal experience:

> For we do not know any books which so destroy pride, which so destroy "the enemy and the defender," who resists your reconciliation by defending his own sins. I do not know, O Lord, I do not know any such pure words, which so persuade me to make confession and make my neck meek to your yoke, and invite me to serve you without complaint. (13.15.17)

> neque enim novimus alios libros ita destruentes superbiam, ita destruentes inimicum et defensorem resistentem reconciliationi tuae defendendo peccata sua. non novi, domine, non novi alia tam casta eloquia, quae sic mihi persuaderent confessionem, et lenirent cervicem meam iugo tuo, et invitarent colere te gratis. (13.15.17)

Therefore, we hear that for Augustine rhetoric dominates temporal human experience and knowledge, personally and socially. His interpretation rings of belief, faith, hope, and persuasion as the means to negotiate the uncertainty of knowledge in temporality. Temporality is also the condition that necessitates belief in the authority of Scripture, since no human soul can enlighten itself or is self-sufficient (13.16.19).

The exteriority of temporal church society in its carnal and spiritual divisions continues to drive Augustine's allegorical interpretation. Now in the third day of creation and having arrived at Genesis 1:9–13, Augustine's progress through the narrative quickens. He proceeds by contrasting God's gathering of the seas in one place—the society of carnal, embittered souls—to the appearance of the dry land in another—the society of spiritual, compassionate souls (13.17.20–21). Through faith and hope, the dry land is distinguished by its production of fruit (13.17.21–18.22).

At this point, Augustine makes two crucial moves simultaneously. One unmistakably directs the interpretation to those serving the mixed constituencies of carnal and spiritual souls within the church—explaining different rhetorical approaches to each. The other identifies a crucial epistemological role for Scripture.

> In it you hold discussion with us, so that we may distinguish between intelligible and sensible things, as between the day and night, or between certain souls dedicated to intelligible things and other souls given over to things of sense. (13.18.22)

> ibi enim nobiscum disputas, ut dividamus inter intellegibilia et sensibilia tamquam inter diem et noctem, vel inter animas alias intellegibilibus, alias sensibilibus deditas. (13.18.22)

We must pause momentarily to consider this brief statement, for it stands as a monument proclaiming Augustine's full application of semiotics in a rhetorical context. He seals the rhetoric-semiotic relationship, enacting explicitly his semiotic disposition toward interpretation. It is a disposition conditioned by belief rather than skepticism.

To distinguish between intelligible and sensible things demands some true knowledge of each, which Augustine says Scripture provides. What is at stake, as Mark D. Jordan indicates, is nothing less than "the ability to see an intelligible *res* behind a sensible *signum*" (189). Likewise, inherent in this straightforward commitment to scriptural authority lies Augustine's ability to hear words "as sensible signs of knowable realities" (Colish 54). His claim that Scripture serves the purpose of helping us distinguish the intelligible from the sensible instantiates his belief that the Incarnation stabilizes the sign function effectively enough to allow for genuine, if proximate, intelligibility. As Paul Henry has noted, temporal revelation for Augustine is a word relation (16). But it is not *only* a word relation. Augustine presumes it to be a relation sufficient to substantiate a comprehensive and fruitful epistemology; a semiotic mandate for interpretation and performance in temporality (Hanson-Smith 184).

Through his applied semiotic propensities, Augustine orders various rhetorical approaches that his audience might consider. First, he addresses the occurrence and limited usefulness of appeals through extraordinary, nonlinguistic signs. Then he introduces a more desirable linguistic approach, revealing his favorable predisposition to ordinary preaching. But Augustine insists on the coordination of words and deeds, the fully semiotic appeal he finally presents as superior.

We might simply view Augustine's interpretation as a figurative fanfare that gets him through the last three days of creation. If we took such a view, however, we would be simply mistaken. Through his rhetorical choreography he instructs the very ministers who have asked for his *Confessions* on how to conduct their rhetorical work in their own temporal age. The interpretation embarks on a comparison, based on the creation narrative, of the appropriate methods for engaging first the carnal and then the spiritual souls within their midst.

Discussing the fourth day of Creation—the creation of the heavenly lights—he correlates the greater light with "the word of wisdom" and the lesser light with "the word of knowledge" (13.18.23). These two "words" Augustine imports from a 1 Corinthians (chap. 12) taxonomy of the gifts of the Holy Spirit to the church, as distributed to its various members. The word of knowledge and other extraordinary gifts—for example, healing, miracles, prophecy, and tongues—apply to the carnal. "But the natural man . . . let him not hold his night to be bereft of all light, but let him be content with the light of the moon and stars" (13.18.23). The listeners of the *Confessions* are not carnal, for they must learn when and how to address such words of knowledge to the carnal:

> Follow the Lord, if you will be perfect, a comrade of those among whom he speaks wisdom, who knows what to distribute to the day and to the night, so that you also may know it and so that for you lights may be made in the firmament of heaven. But this will not be done unless your heart is in it, and again this latter will not be done, unless your treasure is there; as you have heard from the good Master. (13.19.24)

> et sequere dominum, si vis esse perfectus, eis sociatus, inter quos loquitur sapientiam ille, qui novit, quid distribuat diei et nocti, ut noris et tu, ut fiant et tibi luminaria in firmamento caeli: quod non fiet, nisi fuerit illic cor tuum; quod item non fiet, nisie fuerit illic thesaurus tuus, sicut audisti a magistro bono. (13.19.24)

The discernment needed by the audience can only grow from the heart, the residence for wisdom learned from the incarnate Word. Augustine spins an intricate web of Scripture to impress upon his listeners this dual role of ministry to the night and the day, the carnal and the spiritual. He employs unmistakable imagery from Psalm 19:2 to reinforce the point:

> Shine over the whole earth, and let the day, brightened by the sun, utter unto day speech of wisdom, and let the night, shining with the moon, declare to the night the word of knowledge. (13.19.25)

> lucete super omnem terram, et dies sole candens eructet diei verbum sapientiae, et nox, luna lucens, annuntiet nocti verbum scientiae. (13.19.25)

The intertextual move to Psalm 19 provides Augustine with a ready-made scriptural distinction between knowledge and wisdom. A word of knowledge—addressed in the night—is a sign rarely accompanied by words. By contrast, a word of wisdom—addressed in the day—is unique by its status as speech.

The fifth day of Creation offers new figures: the creation of sea creatures and birds and the creation of "the living soul" on dry land (13.20.26, 13.21.29). To the carnality of the sea, God sent messengers to perform wonders and present mysteries, albeit under the authority—the firmament—of Scripture (13.20.26). The carnal "people alienated from your eternal truth" need the Word administered in this fashion to be liberated from the Fall of Adam (13.20.27–28). If it were not for the Fall,

> [t]here would have been no need for your dispensers to work corporeally and sensibly amid many waters, and thus produce mystical deeds and words. For now the creeping things and the flying animals seem to me to be such. Men subject to corporeal rites, and instructed and initiated by such signs, would not make further progress unless the soul began to live spiritually upon another plane, and after words of admission would look forward to their consummation. (13.20.28)

> atque ita non opus esset, ut in aquis multis corporaliter et sensibiliter operarentur dispensatores tui mystica facta et dicta. sic enim mihi nunc occurrerunt reptilia et volatilia, quibus imbuti et initiati

> homines coproalibus sacramentis subditi non ultra proficerent, nisi spirataliter vivesceret anima gradu alio et post initii verbuum in consummationem respiceret. (13.20.28)

More could be said about this correlation between the Creation narrative and instruction to ministers addressing groups of their carnal parishioners or nonbelievers in general. But the basic interpretive point cannot be realized apart from Augustine's contrast between dispensation of a word of knowledge versus speaking a word of wisdom. The word of knowledge, addressed to the carnal, consists of a nonlinguistic sign: a rite, a wonder, a miracle. Augustine has defined its appropriate but limited place and efficacy. The word of wisdom, the word spoken to the spiritual, represents that "progress to another plane."

> Therefore, let your ministers now work upon the earth, not as upon the waters of infidelity by preaching and speaking through miracles and mysteries and mystic words, where ignorance, mother of wonder, is made attentive out of fear of these secret signs. Such is the entrance into faith for the sons of Adam, forgetful of you, while they hide themselves from your face and become a deep. But let them [ministers] work as upon the dry land, separated from the whirlpools of the great deep. Let them be a pattern to the faithful by living before them and by arousing them to imitation. For thus do men truly hear, not merely to hear, but also to do. (13.21.30)

> Operentur ergo iam in terra ministri tui, non sicut in aquis infidelitatis, annuntiando et loquendo per miracula et sacramenta et voces mysticas, ubi intenta fit ignorantia mater admirationis in timore occultorum signorum—talis enim est introitas ad fidem filiis Adam oblitis tui, dum se ascondunt a facie tua et fiunt abyssus—sed operentur etiam sicut in arida discreta a gurgitibus abyssi, et sint forma fidelibus vivendo coram eis et excitando ad imitationem. sic enim non tantum ad audiendum sed etiam ad faciendum audiunt. (13.21.30)

We sense that the bishop is hitting his oratorical stride; pushing the sermon toward its climax. Living spiritual souls have no need for wonders and miracles—they only need the Word via his messengers (12.21.29). Augustine reveals his zeal for preaching as the dominant "means of grace" to be applied in the church (Meer 345). Of course, Augustine has been practicing this very admonition throughout the entire *Confessions*, submitting himself and his interpretation to Scripture.

Augustine does not commend preaching alone. His pulpit rhetoric demands a high level of extrinsic ethos (Sutherland 146). He interprets human dominion over the creatures as self-control among clerics (13.

21.30). He exhorts self-control that his listeners might be worthy of imitation by others. But for their own imitation he recommends only the Trinity, as he summarizes late in the book, "After your own image and likeness, you renewed the mind, made subject to you alone and needful to imitate no human authority" (13.22.32, 13.34.49). The pinnacle of humanity in Augustine's interpretation of Genesis is to be restored to the image of God—not to become God but to retain His image in eternal perfection and to ascend to the assigned place for humanity in God's created order (13.22.32).

> Thus man, although now spiritual and "renewed unto knowledge of God according to the image of him who created him," ought to be "a doer of the law" and not a judge. Nor does he judge concerning that distinction, namely, of spiritual and carnal men, who are known to your eyes, O our god, but have not yet become apparent to us by their works so that we might know them by their fruits. (13.23.33)

> sic enim homo, licet iam spiritalis et renovatus in agnitione dei secundum imaginem eius, qui creavit eum, factor tamen legis debet esse, non iudex. neque de illa distinctione iudicat spiritalium videlicet atque canralium hominum, qui tuis, deus noster, oculis noti sunt, et nullis adhuc nobis apparuerunt operibus, ut ex fructibus corum cognoscamus eos. (13.23.33)

Knowing the general distinction between carnal and spiritual and the appropriate rhetorical mode to teach each—the extraordinary, nonlinguistic sign to one, the more ordinary and fruitful union of word and deed to the other—does not mean that even the spiritual man can make a right judgment about the eternal destiny of another's soul. No dominion belongs to one human soul over another (13.23.33; Markus 198). But there is appropriate dominion over the rest of material creation; a right role of judgment.

Understanding Augustine's distinction between carnal and spiritual is crucial, not only for the ministers he addresses but for people who would interpret him. Although not the central issue of this inquiry, we should see even from the passages under consideration that Augustine offers these as categories of embodied souls, not as a distinction between the body and the soul.[5] The minister must be prepared to instruct both carnal and spiritual people through mysteries, wonders, rites, preaching, and self-control.

From the general dominion, Augustine passes on to right ecclesiastical judgments regarding "sacramental administration," which corresponds to the word of knowledge "whereby those men are initiated whom your mercy searches out in many waters, and then to interpretation 'on the earth'" (13.23.34). It is right for the spiritual minister to judge

> [t]he signs and utterance of words, made subject to the authority of your book, like birds flying under the firmament, by interpreting, expounding, discoursing, disputing, blessing, or praying to you, with the signs thereof bursting from the mouth and sounding forth, to the end that the people may answer "Amen." (13.23.35)

> sive in ea sollemnitate sacramentorum, quibus initiantur quos pervestigat in aquis multis misericordia tua; sive in ea qua ille pscis exhibetur, quem levatum de progundo terra pia comedit; sive in verborum signis vocibusque sbiectis auctoritati libri tui, tamquam sub firmamento volitantibus, interpretando, exponendo, disserendo, disputando, benedicendo atque invocando te, ore erumpentibus atque sonantibus signis, ut repondeat populus: amen. (13.23.35)

Consistent with the union of words and deeds, the "spiritual man" may rightly judge the fruit produced "in the deeds and habits of the faithful," apparently an instructive, practical judgment limited to the interpretation of temporal actions (13.23.34).

The Literal and the Figurative

Genesis 1:28, "increase and multiply," fuels Augustine's explicit discussion of interpretation. He makes a proper disclaimer—"let my betters, that is, men more intelligent than I am make better use of it"—and then argues for his figurative interpretive approach (13.24.36–37). Ultimately, he renders from the verse the unique faculty of human signification as a positive good and posits the rational ability to produce multiple true interpretations as a blessing.

> I conclude that the power and the faculty has been granted to us to express in manifold ways what we understand in but one, and to understand in manifold ways what we read as obscurely uttered in but one way. Thus are the waters of the sea replenished, and they are moved by various significations. Thus by human offspring is the earth also replenished, the dryness of which appears in its longing for you, and over which reason rules. (13.24.37)

> in hac enim benedictione concessam nobis a te facultatem ac potestatem accipio et multis modis enuntiare, quod uno modo intellectum tnerimus, et multis modis intellegere, quod obscure uno modo enuntiatum legerimus. sic implentur aquae maris, quae non moventur nisi variis significatibus, sic et fetibus humanis impletur et terra, cuius aridtas apparet in studio, et dominantur ei ratio. (13.24.37)

The confirmation of wisdom, and the foundation of right interpretation and expression, Augustine finds in the fruit produced by the earth. "We were saying that by these fruits of the earth are signified and figured forth in an allegory the works of mercy" (12.25.38). He returns to the good deeds he admonished us to perform in concert with interpretive performance (13.21.30). In this case, however, the emphasis is not on the outward act to be imitated but on the inward motive. What makes a work of mercy merciful is not the act itself but the will from which it grows. "I have learned to distinguish between gift and fruit. The gift is the thing itself given by a man who bestows these necessities, such as, money, food, drink, clothing, lodging, and help. But the fruit is the good and right will of the giver" (13.26.41).

Although Augustine has not finally completed his consideration of Genesis in the *Confessions,* he does conclude his discussion of the Creation narrative by emphasizing that God's judgment of His work as "very good" should be seen in terms of the unity of Creation—the whole being superior to any of the parts (12.28.43). Augustine plays out no allegory here.

Much has been made of what scholars term "obscurantism" in Augustine's rhetoric, that is that he uses figurative interpretation to cloak doctrinal truth in such a way as to make it more pleasurable to the faithful and less vulnerable to the objections of hostile critics (Weithoff). I submit that in the process of Augustine's interpretive account of the Genesis Creation narrative, he presents us with an illustration of interpretation as a rhetorical performance based on semiotic invention. Augustine moves from literal to figurative interpretation as he proceeds through the Genesis text. As interpreter—from book 11 through book 13—he never loses sight of his goal: the provisional application of eternal truth within the flux of temporal human experience, to an audience situated historically, culturally, socially, and politically. He enacts this approach as a convergence of his semiotic insight, rhetorical/philosophical orientation, spiritual/theological convictions, and acknowledged status as a temporal human being. For Augustine, we may recall, finds wisdom in this unity.

The concluding chapters of book 13 document our suggestion as they retrace the *Confessions'* interpretation of Genesis in books 11–13. Augustine begins by asserting that Scripture is a temporal expression of the eternal Word, a reminder of his literal interpretation in the beginning of book 11 of Creation by the eternal God as the ground of our temporal existence (13.29.44). He then reinforces the literal interpretive response to Manichaean objectors from the second part of book 11, deriding their dualism and misdirected enjoyment of Creation instead of its Creator (13.30.45–31.46). From a synopsis of the literal interpretation of Genesis 1 (13.32.47), Augustine turns to reemphasize his insistence that Genesis 1:2 presents the unity of form and matter as inherent in Creation, the starting point and theme of the book 12 primer on interpretive practice in our temporal, semiotically mediated experience (13.32.48). Finally, the bishop provides a brief recap of the allegorical interpretation of Genesis 1:3–31.

These final chapters of the *Confessions* could position us to illustrate a commonplace, four-level summary of how Augustine's interpretive scheme moves from literal to topological to allegorical to anagogical interpretation. The latter might be rightly seen in Augustine's consideration of the eternal Sabbath as the *Confessions* ends (13.35–38).

From our consideration of Augustine's exemplar of interpretation in book 13, we must conclude that the typical allegorical approach associated with Augustinian interpretation would distract us from the heart of Augustine's purpose in interpretation, which is not the text alone or the proper execution of an interpretive formula but the adaptation of the truth in the text to the audience: an expression of wisdom. Augustine's employment of figurative interpretation—of allegorical reading for instance—does not function as an escape route from temporality to mystical contemplation of eternity. Neither does he practice any slavish devotion to an allegorical mode of interpretation. He utilizes it only selectively and in a limited way (Hamilton 110). Furthermore, scholars of Augustine generally agree that his practice shifts from more to less figurative interpretation by the time he writes the *Confessions,* and that he consistently gives priority in interpretation to literal meaning (Colish 46; Starnes, "Exegesis," 347; Meer 448).

When Augustine does employ figurative interpretation, it serves to intensify and direct that interpretation to a specific audience either as a public refutation—experienced by Manichaean objectors to the doctrine of Creation, or as a public exhortation—directed to the *servus Dei* and other ecclesiastical or lay ministers. Figurative interpretation for Augustine does not constitute the obscuring of clear doctrinal teaching for obscurity's sake, as has sometimes been implied. The figuration is perceived to be in the text, not in the interpretation. So, interpretation addresses figurative passages to bring them out of obscurity in such a way as to advocate sound doctrine from passages otherwise easily exploited to promote heresy.

Augustine provides an example of his thinking when presenting a figurative interpretation of "increase and multiply" (13.24.37). This passage confirms that the figurative interpretation does not contradict the literal meaning but extends it and applies it to his audience more concretely. In other words, the work of interpretation is to make figurative language relevant to the audience whenever necessary (Patton 100).

What Augustine advocates through the process of interpretation in books 11 through 13 is a redeemed rhetoric.[6] The rhetoric he enacts both in the final three books and throughout the balance of the *Confessions* bears little resemblance as a whole to the rhetorics that precede it. Undeniably there are significant traces. We will consider, however, how Augustine's interpretive inclinations compare with interpretive rhetorics developed more recently and similarly grounded in semiotic assumptions about language.

A fundamental similarity Augustine shares with the postmodern critical approaches to which we will compare him is that his rhetorical method, an integral part of the wisdom he has long pursued, is a means of negotiating an uncertain temporal experience rather than a technical manual for performance or criticism of public discourse. That is, Augustine is advocating rhetoric as a way of being.[7] Whether Augustine would agree with our nomenclature is irrelevant, since he has long since completed his own temporal tenure, but I believe he could be persuaded.

Chapter 5

The Wisdom of Incarnational Rhetoric

The entire *Confessions* is an interpretation (Brown, *Augustine*, 156; Colish 26). We have observed that Augustine's reflections on memory and time in the narrative of the first nine books are explicated in books 10 and 11. Now having heard Augustine develop his approach to interpretation as a rhetorical performance in books 12 and 13, we will conduct a retrospective examination of how his interpretive purview extends through the *Confessions* beneath the firmament of Scripture.

Our inquiry challenges the hasty dismissal of Augustine's current relevance on the charge that he attends only to Scripture. It also dispenses with the naively reductive notion that Augustine's interpretive strategy finally reads charity as the meaning of every text. The *Confessions* itself flatly contradicts such assertions, as well as other contemporary under-readings and misappropriations. No doubt, interpretation of Scripture commands much of the bishop's attention—it being his primary vocational task. But Augustine neither concerns himself with nor interprets Holy Writ exclusively. For him, the Holy is writ large throughout Creation *in harmony with* Scripture (6.5.7–8, 13.15.16–18, 13.23.34).

By considering Augustine's *Confessions* as an interpretive rhetorical performance we are attempting to recognize the complexities of the text and the interpretive rhetoric it enacts for the expressed purpose of making it accessible to contemporary readers (Welch 26). In the process, we suggest its relevance to recent discussions, particularly in the areas of interpretation and criticism. The inquiry proceeds decidedly from the perspective of the *Confessions,* showing how Augustine concurs with guiding themes that span the spectrum of postmodern interpretation and how he can be read as confronting problems within postmodernism from certain shared assumptions about language. We proceed to consider the *Confes-*

sions in relation to examples of postmodern discourse on autobiography and interpretation that illustrate the consonance and dissonance between Augustine and postmodernism.

Subjectivity in Autobiography

In an essay entitled "Being in the Text: Autobiography and the Problem of the Subject," Paul L. Jay uses the *Confessions* as a foil against which to compare the issue of discursive construction of self—or subjectivity—in the autobiographical projects of Paul Valery and Roland Barthes.[1]

Jay's consideration of subjectivity in autobiography is precipitated by the sense in recent literary studies that the autobiographical genre is paradigmatic of the "I" as a discursive construction—a process through which the self is "invented" (1045–46). He reads the *Confessions* as one of the first identifiable texts that addresses the "problematical status of the subject" (1046).

> Augustine performs an intricate deconstruction of the processes of perception, remembering, and representation, and he does so in a way which systematically calls into question the status of the "I" of his narrative, and the ability of its language to bridge the distance between the temporal self and the eternal God. (Jay 1047)

Reading the *Confessions* from this perspective helps us recognize the text as a comprehensive act of interpretation—the narrative interpreting Augustine's experience. From this perspective, Jay accurately identifies a main interpretive current as Augustine's interrogation of himself and the stability of discourse in relation to temporality and eternity. Furthermore, he points to Augustine's self-consciousness about writing as an epistemic process in the *Confessions* (1047; Colish 16–17). Augustine later commits himself to this perspective explicitly, as Campenhausen reports, quoting Epistle 143.2: "He knew he 'wrote by advancing in knowledge, and advanced by writing'" (268).

But Jay's initial clarity regarding the *Confessions*, even to the point of acknowledging the inquiry into subjectivity, becomes clouded in his reading of how Augustine resolves the attendant problems. Relying on Kenneth Burke's *Rhetoric of Religion*, Jay uncritically adopts a Neoplatonic interpretation of the *Confessions* (1048).[2] Robert J. O'Connell, foremost of recent proponents for a Neoplatonic reading, suggests that Augustine moves "*away* from the text, as it were, an inward and upward move to consult the light of eternal Truth still streaming downward into the soul" (*Art*, 104). We contend that—consistent with our earlier argument for the *Confessions* as a critique of Neoplatonism—the Neoplatonic reading itself moves *interpreters* away from the grounded text and context of the *Confessions* (Starnes, "Exegesis," 55). Despite passages in the text that directly contradict their assertions, Neoplatonic interpretations proceed by dismissing such passages as intended to occult the latent "actual" meaning of the *Confessions*. Therefore, interpreters explain Neoplatonic doctrine instead of Augustine's discourse.

By adopting the Neoplatonic interpretive paradigm, Jay places himself in the position of making certain remarkable claims about Augustine's view of subjectivity. First, he asserts that Augustine equates the Scripture and the incarnate Word, thus deploying scriptural quotations to transcend temporality:

> With the language of the Word woven thoroughly into his narrative, Augustine's past could be represented in a language he believed could literally transform (and authorize) its meaning. Recounting what had "passed away" into fallen images in the language of scripture Augustine sought to elevate the empirical events of his life to a level at which its meaning became "transcendent." In its role both as prodigal son and confessing writer, the subject in and of the *Confessions* is thus presented as a transcending being, elevated in part by the scriptural language of its text. (1048)

Were this the case, we might expect Augustine to conclude his personal remarks with some evidence of ascent to transcendence. But the discordance he reports in his preconversion narrative never transcends temporality into perfect eternal concord through the confessional discourse, whether by quoting Scripture or not. His scarce glimpses of eternity are ephemeral, and the most detailed postconversion ascent—the paraphrased account of his vision with Monica at Ostia—quotes Scripture sparsely when compared to many other points in the narrative (9.10.23–26). As Paul Ricoeur notes, Augustine's ascents are failures, and his few ecstatic moments never eliminate the temporal for him (1:29).

In the postconversion books, Augustine remains a cluster of scattered personas showing little expectation and less evidence of lasting ascent to transcendence in this life. Inquiring into his own memory, he finds himself incoherent (10.16.25). Later, he periodically qualifies his statements, recognizing the possibility of self-deceit (10.23.34, 10.32.48, 10.39.62). Augustine eschews the Neoplatonic notion that human subjectivity is ultimately joined without distinction to the One—a oneness without relation. The *Confessions* documents and promotes relations and the relational; personal relations are distinctive in Augustine's treatment and interaction with the Trinity and the incarnate Word (Henry 17–19). He confesses his anti-Platonic realization to God that, "I myself was not you. Not even when I did these things, that is, not even that power of mine by which I did them, not even that was you" [nec ego ipse, cum haec agerem, id est vis mea, qua id agebam, nec ipsa eras tu] (10.40.65). From this acknowledgment, he continues to discuss his temporal state:

> In all these things which I review as I consult you, I can find no safe place for my soul except in you. In you may my scattered longings be gathered together, and from you may no part of me ever depart. Sometimes you admit me in my innermost being into a most extraordinary affection, mounting within me to an indescribable sweetness. If this is perfected in me, it will be something, I know not what, that will not belong to this life. But under my burdens of misery I sink down to those other things. (10.40.65)

> neque in his omnibus, quae percurro consulens te, invenio tutum locum animae meae nisi in te, quo colligantur sparsa mea nec a te quicqaum recedat ex me. et aliquando intomittis me in affectum multum inusitatum introrsus ad nescio quam dulcendinem, quae si perficiatur in me, nescio quid erit, quod vita ista non erit. sed reccido in haec aerumnosis ponderibus et resorbeor solitis. (10.40.65)

Augustine maintains himself as distinct from God in all cases, and therefore can be "in" God while maintaining relations with God. He explains that this same relation obtains within the Trinity itself (13.5.6, 13.11.12). The ultimate ascent for Augustine occurs in a dimension completely other than the temporal, a place Augustine anticipates but never resides in through the *Confessions*. He expects to ascend with the community of the faithful to an appropriate place in God's created order—still subordinate to God and higher created beings (13.9.10, 13.23.33). To assert that Augustine uses extensive scriptural references as a means to personal transcendence ignores the unique role of Scripture in the *Confessions*. It is provisional revelation limited to temporality—imparting correction, instruction, and training to guide people into true thought and action in their temporal experience (13.15.17, 13.18.22, 13.23.33).

Jay next claims that "Augustine confines the critical examinations which call into question the efficacy of his project to the "exegetical" books which follow the narrative of his life" (1049). He assumes that the issue of subjectivity and Augustine's interrogation of that subjectivity begin exclusively in the book 10 discussion of memory, but a topical summary of Augustine's questions of himself or statements about the self throughout the *Confessions* suggest quite the opposite.

Augustine begins book 2 in shattered pieces and ends it as a wasteland (1.1.1, 2.10.18). From there he proceeds to explain the self-deceit of iniquity, that it lies to itself (3.8.16). In the preamble to book 4, Augustine declares himself the "leader of my own destruction" [dux in praeceps] (4.1.1) and becomes a riddle to himself, a refrain that will be repeated in his postconversion inquiry (4.4.9, 10.33.50). Despite his confusion, Augustine sees no escape from himself but cannot discern his own motives (4.7.12, 4.14.22). After excusing his sins as conveniently outside himself (5.10.18), he records that "my very vitals were torn by care" [cum ego curis eviscerarer] (6.6.10).

These pointing moments throughout the narrative section of the *Confessions* are not otherwise isolated comments but merely the most explicit evidence of Augustine's enduring critical preoccupation with subjectivity. The preoccupation comes to narrative fruition in books 7 and 8, culminating in Augustine's account of his struggles with self immediately prior to the scene at the Garden of Milan, which *is* an interrogation of the multiple minds, wills, and natures he perceives within himself. He demonstrates an acute sensitivity to aspects of his own persona that we might today term "multiple subjectivities" (8.7.16–11.25). He conducts this inquiry from much the same position as Valery claims for his "principal witness," one aspect of the self, which "is made up of many different persons and a principle witness who watches all these puppets bobbing" (Valery, in Jay, 1054).

Finally, Jay completes his argument on Augustine—the conclusion to which he must come if the *Confessions* is to serve its purpose as a contrast to Valery and Barthes: the *Confessions* uses its narrative "to recall, and in the process of recalling, to reanimate, what is posited as a previously unified—or more authentic—self" (1051). Jay comes to this conclusion, despite Augustine's manifold insistence throughout the *Confessions* that his own self is ultimately unsearchable, by exiting the text for Neoplatonic speculation that transcends Augustine's stated knowledge. This takes place in a footnote:

> In Augustine's case, of course, this "unity" is to come not in the return to a temporal and earthly, but a heavenly "past." Thus birth is a "fall" into "immoderation and unlikeness far distant" from God, and Augustine depends upon the Word in order that he be "recalled" to "unity" with Him. In the meantime, he writes, "we labor amid the remains of our obscurity." (1061)

The passages Jay quotes have nothing to do with subjectivity. Instead, they refer to the general nature of all spiritual and corporeal matter. When applied specifically to people, Augustine concludes that having once turned from being toward nonbeing, the entire race labors together in obscurity (13.2.2–3). The Fall Augustine acknowledges is not a Neoplatonic fall of the soul into the body, but the fall of human beings possessing bodies and souls at the same time. The curse that resulted from the Fall affects both body and soul.

The "birth is a 'fall'" motif is an extratextual Neoplatonic import. In the *Confessions*, Augustine speculates on his own origin in scriptural terms, answering an initial question on innocence in infancy with a simple statement of the doctrine of original sin: "Who will bring to my mind the sins of my infancy? For in your sight no man is clean of sin, not even the infant who has lived but a day on the earth" [quoniam nemo mundus a peccato coram te, nec infans, cuius est unius diei vita super terram] (1.7.11). Then he presses further back in his history, quoting from Psalm 51 to identify his being in the state of iniquity common to humanity from conception via a rhetorical question that denies any prevenient state of human innocence: "But 'if I was conceived in iniquity,' and if my mother nourished me within her womb in sins, where, I beseech you, O Lord my God, where or when was your servant innocent?" [quod si et in iniquitate conceptus sum, et in peccatis mater mea me in utero aluit, ubi oro te, deus meus, ubi, domine, ego, servus tuus, ubi aut quando innocens fui?] (1.7.12).

All this simply indicates the interpretive gymnastics required to consider the *Confessions* as "a totalizing kind of self-history which by its very nature posits the idea of a unified, historical, self" (Jay 1051). The foil the *Confessions* supposedly provides depends upon the claim that Augustine's text presents this unified self. Any such text would lack "the kind of radical critique of subjectivity" that "comes only with the 'crisis of subjectivity' which has had such an enormous influence on 20th century literature" (Jay 1051). Jay refers to the concept of the "decentered self." Lester Faigley summarizes this concept and its import in contemporary liberal studies:

> One of the most troubling ideas for the humanities and the social sciences in the last two decades is the "decentering" of the individual subject from the atomic, rational consciousness of Descartes to a socially-constructed self located in networks of discourses. (396)

Working from textual evidence in the *Confessions*, we notice that Augustine nowhere proposes the sort of Cartesian self that Jay attributes to him. For Augustine, the problem of the status of the subject is *not* resolvable in terms of temporal, human language—even when that language incorporates Scripture. Augustine not only criticizes human subjectivity in the *Confessions*, but also experiences the "crisis of subjectivity" personally and abides with the problems of subjectivity unresolved through the conclusion of the discourse.

Augustine rejects the Neoplatonic, individualistic ascension into transcendence and instead embraces the temporal, with all of its paradoxes and dilemmas, maintaining belief, faith, and hope in the eternal. In the temporal context, Augustine cannot conceive of a unified, coherent human subject other than the incarnate Word. Not surprisingly, many aspects in the autobiographical works of Valery and Barthes that Jay attempts to contrast with the *Confessions* actually resonate with Augustine's text. One question we might consider is: given the historical milieu of these men, whose text is more subversive?

Jay argues that "philosophical, psychological, and epistemological questions" take precedence in organizing the works of Valery and Barthes over biography (1052). These three areas of inquiry have all become associated with the *Confessions* as commonplaces for which Augustine's work has been valued, while biographers continue to be distressed by Augustine's omission of historical details they wish he would have incorporated in the text.[3]

Valery and Barthes allegedly work in contrast to Augustine by dismissing the chronology and biography associated with traditional narrative (1053, 1055). Ricoeur suggests that Augustine directs our view away from "rectilinear" time as well, but in such a way that narrative is enriched by its liberation from straight chronology (1:22). The liberty is gained through Augustine's insistence on the eternal, which intensifies the existential (Ricoeur 1:22). Ricoeur is working from Augustine's conclusion in book 11 that the past does not exist, the future does not exist, and the present has no extent.

A distinction does exist between the twentieth- and fifth-century writers on this point, one heightened by the fact that Barthes cannot genuinely "eschew" memory. Jay reports that "He treats of the distance between the biographical and the written self by affirming it, deconstructing "Barthes" into a group of fragments which are arranged under a series of names, topics, and concepts" (1055). To eschew memory it would seem that one would have to surrender speaking and writing to subvert the illusion it perpetuates of functional memory, for to classify under "names, topics, and concepts" demands memory of words over time. All three writers make some move away from the dominance of a chronological perspective. The twentieth-century autobiographers, denying any fixed or fixable substance, attempt to disrupt the confessional form. Augustine, at least according to conventional wisdom, founds it. The question is, given some of these similarities, how can he do it?

According to Jay, the *Confessions* is a nostalgic search for Augustine's lost "other," a more authentic past self (1055). Understanding Augustine's views on time and his self-reports of every past self recorded in the *Confessions*, the notion of such a nostalgic search holds no plausibility. Any past self no longer exists except in memory and the records of these selves are thoroughly undesirable. Even if we accepted the Neoplatonic interpretation, the authentic past can only mean ascent to reunion through the One, a goal one would hardly pursue through public discourse. What Augustine seeks is to become a more authentic self in the elusive present, and he seeks it through rhetoric—that is, through belief in a certainty produced through discourse. In this regard, Augustine conflicts most sharply with Barthes.

Jay finally alerts us to what will emerge as the fundamental distinction between Augustine and Barthes. "Barthes's text constitutes a denial of the 'fiction' of the subject as anything other than a creation of human consciousness and human language" (1056). He concludes his text with a self that "*is* shattered, scattered, decentered, and . . . always a 'fiction'" (1056). Ultimately, "There is for Barthes no language which might constitute the last, the redemptive, the incarnate Word" and no "grace" upon which to found autobiography ontologically (1056–57). Without the incarnate Word, without God, without grace (and therefore without charity), we postulate that this is exactly the place to which Augustine's understanding of language would take him: in full agreement with Barthes. To see this, we must digress for a moment to consider Augustine and Barthes in their shared semiotic perspective—the perspective on human discourse that energizes their work in self-interpretation.

The idea that has revolutionized contemporary criticism and philosophy is the reversal of the Cartesian view that language is primarily a vehicle for conveying nonlinguistic meaning produced by an autonomous, coherent individual (Rorty 123). Instead, language precedes the individual and itself produces meaning (Eagleton 60). Coward and Ellis explain:

> Saussure disposed of the problem of origin that had been the major preoccupation of nineteenth-century bourgeois linguistics, replacing it with a model that takes a priori the human semiological system. . . .
> Saussurean linguistics does not look for identity but for difference; each element is distinct from its own origin, different at each new instance of its repetition, and similar or identical only in its opposition to all other elements in the signifying chain. It is taken for granted that each individual enters into a pre-existent linguistic world. (96–97)

This sounds more than a little like Augustine's account of his entrance into his local discourse and "the stormy society of human life" [vitae humanae procellosam societatem] (1.8.13). He expresses and enacts a similar view in the *Confessions* as one instance of his applied semiotics, which surpasses Saussure's theory fifteen hundred years prior to its advent.[4] For Barthes, as for Augustine, this semiotic view of language appears to be totalizing:

> Language cannot be considered as a simple instrument, whether utilitarian or decorative, of thought. Man does not exist prior to lan-

guage, either as a species or as an individual. We never find a state where man is separated from language, which he then creates in order to "express" what is taking place within him: it is language which teaches the definition of man, not the reverse. (Barthes in Schilb 427)

Known as part of the "linguistic turn" in criticism, the idea of language as anterior to the individual subject is not uniquely Saussurean. Heidegger posited much the same a priori view of language in *Being and Time* (Eagleton 62). Saussure himself did not utilize the radical potential of his own system but emphasized the elements conducive to sustaining transcendentalism. As Catherine Belsey has said,

> Structuralism thus proclaimed Eternal Man and the suppression of history with a new and resounding authority. Ironically, Saussure's analysis of language as a system of differences was invoked to initiate the elimination of all difference. (Lodge 402)

But in the *Confessions,* Augustine opts out of the Neoplatonic transcendentalism of his day and instead remains in temporality to grapple with the paradoxical existence of temporal humanity in history. Critics like Barthes recognized the power of the Saussurean system to correct the notion of the individual as the autonomous producer of language. Therefore, no individual subject could claim to be the source of language, so in a single move the primacy of language was established with its source being other than any individual and by implication other than humanity in general (Coward and Ellis 2–4, 122–24ff).

Barthes explains the primacy, or sovereignty, of language in his discussion of semiology and its limitations:

> It is the responsibility of Semiology, and perhaps of Semiology alone of all the human sciences today, to question its own discourse: as a science of language, of languages, it cannot accept its own language as a datum, a transparency, a tool, in short as a metalanguage; strong with the powers of psychoanalysis, it interrogates itself as to *the place from which it speaks,* an interrogation without which any science and any ideological criticism are ridiculous: for Semiology, at least so I hope, there exists no *extraterritoriality* for the subject, even if he is a scientist, with regard to his discourse; in other words, finally, science knows no site of security, and in this it must acknowledge itself as *writing.* (Barthes, S/Z, 8)

To summarize, Barthes axiomatically posits language as preexistent to individual subjects and human society. As he has just claimed, the semiotician cannot retreat to a point outside of language from which to observe and report on language. Human discourse about human discourse necessarily implicates itself and negates any "objective" view.

Beyond the narrative on being born into a preexistent system of signs, including language, Augustine believes in the anteriority of language to all humanity and material things (11.5.7, 11.7.9, 11.9.11). No point, no thing—that is, absolutely nothing—exists outside of language. He is highly self-conscious of his subjective temporal situation, welcoming other perspectives in addition to his own. Obviously, the fundamental distinction between Augustine and Barthes manifests itself here in the sense that when Barthes claims that language is preexistent, he speaks exclusively of human language. Augustine's limit in terms of language is God's Word.

Returning briefly to Jay's comparison, Augustine and Barthes share basic assumptions about the structure and function of language, and that language precedes and constructs subjectivity in the context of human society. Augustine does not make the transcendental move Saussure did. Instead, he contradicts Jay's representation of the project in the *Confessions* as a two-dimensional, inherently contradictory linguistic attempt to return to a transcendent self (1051).[5] To do so, Jay must portray the Scripture and the incarnate Word as synonymous. But Augustine is insistently semiotic in the *Confessions*. He will not take the Scripture without the incarnate Word too (10.4.6, 11.8.10). They are distinct, and integral, but never synonymous.

On the other hand, Barthes does end up in a two-dimensional pose, preoccupied with literate textuality—that is, writing. This posture reduces him to the subversion of one illusory form with another illusory form, since Barthes's reality is a linguistically constructed, inescapable illusion. His discourse is consistent with this belief: language may construct many illusions but never authentic security.

Augustine finds security, stability, and substance not by abandoning the implications of his own semiotic inclinations but in the midst of the same semiotic field where Barthes, denying the incarnate Word, celebrates the shattered, scattered, disjointed subject (1056). Augustine cannot center himself by his own effort, discursive or otherwise. Whether before or after his conversion, when Augustine examines himself in his temporal experience he finds himself to be ultimately problematic (Markus 124; Brown, *Augustine*, 179). Never does he achieve temporal unity, coherence, or authentic subjectivity through transcendence or temporal discursive construction. He precludes any such possibility from the start of the *Confessions*: "Who has the art and power to make himself?" [an quisquam se faciendi erit artifex?] (1.6.10)

The incarnate Word Himself, by securing the present of the semiotic moment, stabilizes what Barthes refers to as the "infinite deferral of the signified" ("Work," 715). The Incarnation moves Augustine from the infinite play of linguistic signifiers in a two-dimensional linguistic field called a text (Barthes, "Work," 714–15), into a three-dimensional field that integrates language with flesh and blood temporal experience. Augustine participates in this field on the basis of rigorously reasoned belief. There is no leap of faith, no Platonic ascent, no dogmatic claim of objective reality immediately available through verifiable perceptions. Therefore, belief surfaces as a critical issue, a precursor to what sort of criticism (that is, interpretation) one might perform.

Rhetorical Interpretation in Postmodern Terms

Augustine is a critic. He relishes critical activity and values the critical faculties of others, as indicated by his praise of Nebridius, "an ardent seeker after a happy life and a subtle critic of the most difficult questions" [beatae vitae inquisitor ardens, et quaestionum difficillimarum scrutator acerrimus] (6.10.17). We have examined how Augustine utilizes narrative in the *Confessions* as an interpretive performance that, among other things, constitutes a critique of human subjectivity, resonating in many ways with certain postmodern critical themes. Now we turn to the critical process itself in textual studies. By considering the correspondence between Augustine's *Confessions* and the postmodern interpretive coordinates presented in Steven Mailloux's *Rhetorical Power*, we will examine how Augustine's perspective may stimulate a dialogue on pertinent issues in contemporary criticism.

Mailloux's approach to interpretation applies the shared assumption of Augustine and Barthes that nothing exists outside of the semiotic condition of language. On this basis, Mailloux questions all interpretive theory, which he argues can only be constructed on the assumption that meaning can be located apart from rhetorical action:

> All Theories believe that some pure vantage point can be established beyond and ruling over the messy realm of interpretive practices and persuasive acts. Only in this way, it is thought, can correct interpretation, privileged meaning, be accounted for. Hermeneutic realism, for example, assumes a stability of meaning before any rhetorical acts take place. Meaning is determinate, objective, and eternally fixed because of the constraints in the text itself which are independent of historically situated critical debates. In a strangely similar way, hermeneutic idealism also assumes stability of meaning outside situated practices. Meaning is determinate, intersubjective, and temporarily fixed because of constraints provided by the communal conventions in readers' and critics' minds. (16)

Once again we encounter the binary poles that assign mutual exclusivity to true interpretation as correspondence with an objective, eternal reality versus true interpretation as intersubjective, temporal coherence.[6] Mailloux finds both theoretical approaches to interpretation unsatisfactory in their shared willingness to isolate meaning from discursive practice. As an alternative, he proposes "rhetorical hermeneutics," an "anti-Theory theory" that challenges the need for any comprehensive theory of interpretation and offers flexible methodological coordinates for interpretive practice in exchange (15).

> Concepts such as "interpretive strategies" and "argument fields" are, we might say, simply descriptive tools for referring to the unformalizable context of interpretive work, work that always involves rhetorical action, attempts to convince others of the truth of explications and explanations. (15)

Mailloux situates himself and his rhetorical hermeneutics within a broader contemporary movement "to incorporate rhetoric at the level of interpretive theory and its analysis of literary and critical practice" (18). He identifies his own work with others who "place theory, criticism, and literature itself within a cultural conversation . . . which is the 'primal scene of rhetoric'" (18). The influence of critics like Mailloux should by now be evident in our own inquiry. For instance, we share his "attraction to narratives surrounding specific rhetorical acts and their particular sociopolitical contexts" (18).

The *Confessions* has provided a rich site for such a critical expedition. However, I am contending that juxtaposing Augustine and Mailloux can extend the contemporary dialogue in a fruitful way. I recognize the risks inherent in arguing for similarities across millennia, and disavow any claim of manifest or latent Augustinian influence on Mailloux or his contemporaries. I believe that Mailloux's interpretive commitments emerge independently from the *Confessions*, which makes the comparison more provocative—both as it enlightens the relationship between Wisdom and interpretation for Augustine, and as it helps us interrogate the wisdom of our own interpretive practice.

Interpretive Process

Part 3 of *Rhetorical Power,* a section entitled "Neo-pragmatism and the Politics of Interpretation," presents Mailloux's interpretive agenda. He initially argues for "a move from explaining interpretation in terms of isolated readers and isolated texts to discussing rhetorical exchanges among interpreters embedded in discursive and other social practices at specific historical moments" (133).

The method growing out of this move defines interpretation as a process that compounds three basic steps into an interpretive whole:

(1) situating the interpretation within current critical debates; (2) situating the interpretation "in the rhetorical traditions within relevant institutional discourses"; (3) situating the interpretation within its own historical context (134). The methodology seems to imply a double contextualization, both to the moment in which the interpretive performance takes place and the moment upon which the interpretive act focuses. Mailloux explains the goal of his interpretive methodology as the presentation of a rhetorical history that "does not claim absolute coverage for its narratives but does attempt to make a persuasive case for each of them" (134).

In the *Confessions* Augustine approximates Mailloux's steps. For example, in book 11 he defines the critical debate over the Genesis narrative in terms of Manichaean arguments against the doctrines of creation ex nihilo and the nature of God's work antecedent to Creation (11.10.12, 11.30.40, 13.30.45). Having situated himself within this set of arguments, he moves to book 12 attending to current ecclesiastical debates over the proper methods for interpreting Scripture—in particular, the relation between meaning and intentionality of the human writers and adaptation of the truths of Scripture to certain hearers.

The *Confessions*, from its title through its concluding chapters, addresses itself from and to the institution of the church. Even to those outside the church it serves as an institutional invitation to enter the ecclesiastical discourse. The text certainly stretches conventions and reforms them as it reinstantiates them, but in constructive rather than subversive ways. Augustine respects the well-defined institutional conventions of the church and Late Roman Africa, even as he violates or extends them. He relies on rhetorical traditions in the church, from orality to abundant scriptural quotations and allusions to doctrinal affirmations. The ministerial emphasis of books 11 through 13 sharpen the institutional focus markedly.

Furthermore, the *Confessions* attends to the historical context of the interpretive act. This is most evident in the narrative, and to a lesser extent in the interpretation of Genesis 1. The narrative of Augustine's experience, criticized for its imprecision on individual details, reads like an inventory of late-fourth-century social practices in North Africa and Italy. The suppression of specifics in many cases makes the *Confessions* richer in its descriptions of pedagogy, literary culture, the circus, the theater, the baths, marriage, schools of philosophy, the church, travel, friendship, and other aspects of social and cultural life. The interpretation of Scripture provides the conditions for Christian history, both in the discourse on time and in the interpretation of the Genesis account of Creation. As in the narrative portion of the *Confessions*, the final three books—especially book 13—are situated within the social/rhetorical practices relative to church leaders and the communities they serve, concentrating particularly on the spiritual diversity of parishioners.

We may safely infer that Augustine performs this final step quite consciously, for he prescribes just such attention to the details of social and cultural life in the *Confessions* (3.7.12–8.16) and *De doctrina Christiana* (2.28.42–43, 3.12.18–15.23) as essential to plausible interpretation. One commentator on the *Confessions* goes so far as to suggest that the entire work represents Augustine's pursuit of how historical events become signs (Crosson 159).

Finally, Augustine nowhere claims complete coverage either in interpreting his life or Scripture. He qualifies his own narrative as incomplete; for example, in book 9: "I omit many things, as I am making great haste. Accept my confessions and acts of thanksgiving, O my God, for countless things, even those I pass over in silence" (9.8.17). He also questions the veracity of his own memory, both in the volume and accuracy of its accounts. He leaves his own actions open to alternative interpretations, such as the way he chose to resign from teaching rhetoric in Milan or his tears at the death of Monica (9.2.4, 9.12.33). Augustine even prefaces book 13, his example of textual interpretation, by denying the completeness of its coverage while arguing for its merit as one true interpretation (12.32.43).

Interpretive Purpose

Mailloux interprets as a performance, not to confirm or falsify theory or move toward an "objective" account of interpretation. He resists theorizing aimed at making "ahistorical generalizations, statements of the form 'interpretation in general always does or should work this way'" (135). The transition from interpretation as theory producing to interpretation as performance results in a corresponding shift from "*confrontation* between knower and object" to "*conversation* between knowers" (144).

We assume that Mailloux is reacting against modernist forms of interpretation—that is, any approach "idealistically seeking to discover how a reader's mind determines a text's shape or realistically seeking to discover how a text causes a reader's certainty" (145). In this sense, a strict comparison to Augustine would be anachronistic. However, though he does not live through the modern era, Augustine may yet contribute to Mailloux's argument.

For instance, we might recall that the charge against Augustine from semiotic theorists is that he is too concerned with application and, therefore, probably does not understand what he is doing.[7] But as should be manifest by now, Augustine knows exactly what he is doing—he values the practice of interpretational rhetoric more than ahistorical, transcendent theorizing.

Augustine precedes book 10, his most specific consideration of epistemology, with the most direct and extensive appeal to listeners

(10.1.1–5.6). From this point on in the *Confessions* he dwells on memory, history (temporality and eternity), and interpretation through a performance whereby he interprets his experience thinking through these issues. He makes his intention clear from the beginning of book 10—to maintain dialogue with the members of the community defined through his discourse. It is finally this community to which he submits his *Confessions*, though many others may hear it. As Mailloux states:

> Interpretive practices are never idiosyncratic; that is, acts of making sense are always a function of shared beliefs of interpretive conventions. Every individual interpreter is a member of an interpretive community. (151)

Augustine's submission to the community, while implicit in the *Confessions*, is more immediately evident in the pre-*Confessions* books of *De doctrina Christiana*. In this regard, Mark D. Jordan speaks specifically to Augustine's practice of subordinating interpretation to the community:

> Such subordination prevents Augustine's remarks about historical and literary contexts from becoming merely a logician's doctrine of interpretation by consistency. Because he is relying on a lived grounding of all interpretations in the community, he says that rules are always less valuable than a keen memory. (185)

Mailloux indicates that much has been made of interpretive communities by Stanley Fish and other postmodern critics (151). But when Jordan notes, regarding Augustine's interpretive agenda, "that the needs of the community for whom the exegete expounds the Scriptures determines the validity of his interpreting," he seems to be looking exclusively at book 3 of *De doctrina Christiana*. There is not a postmodernist in sight.

Mailloux finally introduces an outworking of the interpretive implications of semiotic commitments like those of Barthes to which many who consider themselves postmodernists would subscribe: that belief precedes knowledge. In his discussion of the issue, Mailloux invokes "Against Theory," an essay by Steven Knapp and Walter Benn Michaels, who argue that there is no "condition of knowledge prior to and independent of belief" (738). Knapp and Michaels begin with a problem similar to Mailloux's concern about hermeneutic realism and idealism:

> Some theorists have sought to ground the reading of literary texts in methods designed to guarantee the objectivity and validity of interpretations. Others, impressed by the inability of such procedures to produce agreement among interpreters, have translated that failure into an alternative mode of theory that denies the possibility of correct interpretation. (723)

Although Mailloux questions some of their conclusions, he identifies the fundamental point of agreement between Knapp and Michaels and other interested parties in this discussion. From the position that no person can move outside of language, and the sociopolitical world it constructs, they conclude that there is no objective plane from which to theorize. Therefore, all discourse, even discourse which claims to be objectively valid, functions at the level of persuasion from a point of view that can never be validated objectively (156–59, 161). In other words, all discourse is rhetorical in that it proceeds from one person who already believes and is attempting to produce belief in another.

That Mailloux arrives at this antitheoretical point interests us on two counts. First, in the process he demonstrates that belief as the antecedent of knowledge is a shared concern among well-known Academics like Fish, Richard Rorty, and Edward Said, generally considered to be of the postmodern persuasion. Second, the statement that "belief precedes knowledge" is a most prominent commonplace among Augustine's interpretive and philosophical axioms.[8]

The *Confessions* introduces its initial and guiding assumption that belief precedes knowledge (1.1.1) and speech (1.5.6).[9] In the preconversion narrative, his recognition of belief as a precursor to action and knowledge marks a turning point in which he recognizes that belief is essential to his healing (6.4.6). Augustine also promotes belief while criticizing demonstration and pure reason as insufficient means for obtaining true knowledge (6.5.7–8). The same axiom occurs elsewhere in Augustine's works, including an early treatise *The Freedom of the Will* (2.2.6) and *The Literal Interpretation of Genesis* (book 11). In sermon 43.4, a discourse dedicated to scriptural exegesis, Augustine says:

> Every man desires to be understood, no one does not desire to understand, but not every one desires to believe. If someone says to me: "I would understand in order that I may believe," I answer: "Believe so that you may understand." (Mourant 41)

Augustine places priority on belief as a comprehensive interpretive issue. It is not an isolated item of ecclesiastical dogma limited to soteriology. His documented semiotic perspective, when combined with his commitment to life in a state of radical temporality, brings him to the same point as postmodern interpretive theorists (or antitheorists). It may surprise some to learn that, despite his willing submission to the authority of Scripture, the fact that his conviction grows out of belief leads to the admission that he cannot *prove* its truth by demonstration (6.5.7). Augustine says that he would like to ask Moses, as writer of Genesis, what he meant in Genesis 1:1, and that if Moses spoke in Latin, he could understand the words. Then Augustine asks, "Yet how would I know whether he spoke the truth?

Even if I knew this, would I know it from him?" [sed unde scirem, an verum diceret? quod si et hoc scirem num ab illo scirem?] (11.3.5).

Here the distinction between life in Barthes's semiotic universe and Augustine's becomes clear. Augustine can know that what Moses says is true, not because of Moses but because the truth of Moses's words is confirmed by the Truth that speaks to Augustine's interior ear. Ultimately, the Truth Augustine claims will divide him from postmodernism—although it is in no way equivalent to Platonic truth. The salient point for the moment, however, is that for Augustine, the best human semiotic efforts can produce is belief. This applies even, and especially in the *Confessions,* to Augustine's discourse itself:

> When they hear me speak about myself, how do they know I speak the truth. . . . But because "charity believes all things" among them whom it unites by binding them to itself, I too, O Lord, will confess to you in such manner that men may hear, although I cannot prove to them that I confess truly. But those men whose ears charity opens to me believe me. (10.3.3)
>
> et unde sciunt, cum a me ipso de me ipso audiunt, an verum dicam. . . . sed quia caritas omnia credit, (inter eos utique, quos conexos sibimet unim facit,) ego quoque, domine, etiam sic tibi confiteor, ut audiant homines, quibus demonstrare non possum, an vera confitear; sed credunt mihi, quorum mihi aures caritas aperit. (10.3.3)

Augustine recognizes that "objective" demonstration of truth is out of the question in human communication. Our temporality disrupts our ability to know ourselves and to communicate immediately with others. The mediation, through temporal signs, makes proof a practical impossibility. The only way we can interact truthfully is to employ rhetoric—that is, discourse intended to produce belief—within a sympathetic community marked by charity. And this is exactly where Mailloux ends up, with a diagnosis assessing just such a circumstance:

> Problems may arise with such rhetorical self-consciousness. One danger is that rhetorical candor will be read as narcissistic self-indulgence, that it will be seen not as a necessary theoretical move required by rhetorical theory but as another case of theory's fashionable rereading of itself—self-critique as self-display. There's no easy way that a consistent rhetorical theorist can avoid this complaint. He or she can only hope that a sympathetic reader understands that a rhetorical theory cannot pretend to be outside of its own rhetorical history by ignoring that history in its account of itself. A rhetorical hermeneutics can be truly rhetorical only if it locates itself within, not above, its own history. (167)

What Mailloux cites as dangers mark the commonplace criticisms of the *Confessions* lodged by hostile critics.[10] Self-indulgence and self-display are particularly easy claims to make against the *Confessions*. Numerous modern critics have reveled in making such charges. B. B. Warfield, aligning himself with Adolf Harnack and others, remarks:

> Even in such heart-throes as express themselves in this book, he could not away with the frivolous word-plays, affected assonances, elaborate balancing of clauses and the like that form the hallmark of the sophistic rhetoric of the times . . . . Unfortunately, he also had a curious facility of dropping into offensive rhetorical tricks in the midst of the most serious discussions, or the most moving revelations of feeling. Apart from such occasional lapses—if lapses so frequent can be called occasional—the very form given this book as a sustained address to God is wearisome to many. (248)

The point of all this is not to certify that the *Confessions* is a case of rhetorical hermeneutics or that Mailloux has actually composed a confession. We have simply aimed to present in a limited way the evidence that Mailloux and Augustine work with interpretive coordinates that correspond at crucial points. I recognize that such correspondences may be entirely coincidental, or an accident of proximity in the mind of one listener. Stranger things have happened.

At the very least, I hope to have shown that in the *Confessions*, Augustine grapples with interpretive questions that we find pertinent today. Of particular import, we have seen his concerns with the limitations of human communication in semiotic terms, his insistence on the radical temporality of the human condition, and our reliance on rhetoric to negotiate our discursive and temporal lives through interpretation. From this space, we are poised to explore Augustine's value in questioning our contemporary assumptions about interpretation.

The Intuitive Problem of Relativism

Contemporary interpreters have managed to make a strong case for dispensing with theories either tied to realism or to idealism, both of which ultimately claim to have a vantage point outside of their own situatedness; their own perspective. However, these same interpreters have not so effectively dispensed with concerns that their assumptions finally devolve into chaos, anarchy, solipsism, and relativism.

For some postmodern writers inquiring into philosophical and theoretical issues, acknowledging the radical implications of the decentered self and disruptions in language causes celebration and suggests a strategy for liberation, not a concern. Barthes makes this apparent through the discursive play in his anticonfessional autobiography—the allegedly "more creative moments in which he is composing it" (Jay 1056–57). In it he tries to actualize his beliefs about the infinite deferral of the signified (in this case himself), the infinitude and play of the signifier, and the text as a movement of dislocations, overlappings, and variations (Barthes, "Work," 715).

Others recognize strategies for resistance and subversion of established sociopolitical institutions in postmodern assumptions about language and subjectivity. Chris Weedon, a feminist critic, notes that "poststructuralism theorizes subjectivity as a site of disunity and conflict, central to the process of political change and preserving the status quo" (21). She shares the belief, taken from Saussurean linguistics, that no meaning is fixed, translatable, or generalizable to a universal level (22). Weedon recognizes and embraces the relativism inherent in her beliefs:

> A poststructuralist position on subjectivity and consciousness relativizes the individual's sense of herself by making it an effect of discourse which is open to continuous redefinition and which is constantly slipping. The reassurance and certainty of humanism, with its essence of subjectivity disappears, but so does the inevitability of particular forms of subjectivity with their attendant modes of consciousness. However, to see subjectivity as a process, open to change, is not to deny the importance of particular forms of individual subjective investment which have all the force of apparently full subjectivity for the individual and which are necessary for our participation in social processes and practices. (106)

One sort of conflict envisioned by Weedon has been articulated in various ways by Michel Foucault. In one of his later essays, "The Subject and Power," Foucault describes anti-authority struggles as immediate, localized attempts to subvert power effects which claim privilege of knowledge, especially such effects which operate from appeals to totalizing abstractions (780). He affirms that these struggles, which deploy the situational, perspectival, and relative, aim toward anarchy and are part of the solution to endemic authoritarianism, not part of the problem. But Foucault also questions the dominance of a Barthesian poststructural view on the basis that it constitutes a disconnect from experience. In *Power/Knowledge*, Foucault asserts that "History has no 'meaning,'" then immediately qualifies this statement with, "though this is not to say that it is absurd or incoherent" (114). He claims that, despite the meaninglessness of history, it is still intelligible, but not through the gaze of an exclusively linguistic semiotics:

> Neither the dialectic, as logic of contradictions, nor semiotics, as the structure of communication, can account for the intrinsic intelligibility of conflicts. . . . "Semiology" is a way of avoiding its violent,

bloody and lethal character by reducing it to the calm Platonic form or language and dialogue. (114)

We consider Foucault precisely because he believes that there *is* some position outside of discourse from which to find intelligibility. Richard Rorty finds himself in the same position. When he is contesting a representationalist theory of objective reality, Rorty acknowledges the inherent solipsism of his own beliefs:

> You had better admit that all your conception of inquiry allows you to do is to recontextualize your beliefs and desires. You don't find out anything about objects at all—you just find out about how your web of beliefs and desires can be rewoven so as to accommodate new beliefs and desires. You never get outside your own head.
> What I have been saying amounts to accepting this gambit. (101)

Yet he immediately retrenches to a position from which to argue that people who hold his view are immune from living, believing, and behaving arbitrarily because they have a complex of "central, difficult-to-imagine-revising beliefs" precipitated by "external pressures" (101). Rorty concludes that for the antirepresentationalist, "At worst, the community of inquirers to which she belongs, the one which shares most of her beliefs, is stuck, for the time being, within its own vocabulary" (101).

For postmodernist practitioners of interpretation, relativism presents a greater challenge and poses a recurrent problem. Frank Lentricchia identifies the conditions we have been considering as "two errors that lead to the unacceptable dead ends of anarchic subjectivism and vicious relativism" (261). He assumes these are to be avoided.

Postmodern critics have become skilled at responding to direct, hypothetical, and/or intuitive charges of relativism in its many forms when discussing interpretation. They commonly employ the sort of communitarian appeal Rorty offers as a check against radical relativism. Fish, suspecting the charge of solipsism and relativism, dismisses it on the basis that "when interpreters act as extensions of an institutional community, solipsism and relativism are removed as fears because they are not possible modes of being" (321). Mailloux similarly recognizes his vulnerability to claims that his interpretive agenda is finally relativistic:

> Putting aside realist and idealist foundationalism, however, does not mean that just anything goes. Arguments are always embedded in historical circumstances, rhetorical traditions, episodes of cultural conversations—all of which make certain arguments appropriate and others inappropriate at certain moments. (145–46)

Because Mailloux's "anti-Theory theory" rhetorically dismantles foundationalist theory, he attempts to evade charges of nihilism by denying the foundationalist terms of argument that appeal to transhistorical theories of "the good, the true, and the beautiful" (168). In exchange for such transhistorical theories, Mailloux substitutes what sounds like an alternative transhistorical theory:

> Every attempt to appeal to some general, transhistorical set of herme-neutical principles is automatically involved in a specific context of rhetorical politics, and such appeals do not end debate but provide new grounds for potential disagreement. (168)

Were Mailloux actually charged with promoting a neofoundationalist theory, we would expect him to reply that, like Edward Said in *Orientalism*, he too admits elsewhere in his work that it presents nothing beyond a perspective, but that this in no way precludes distancing his admission from the conclusion of his argument—allowing for its objectivist appearance and *practical impact* (Mailloux 156–57).

Recognizing that the roster of critics and theorists just named diverge in some significant ways, we should also note that they are often considered as species of the genus postmodern and/or poststructural. In our inquiry, they serve as representatives of a postmodern impulse to establish, assert, or explain a sense of existential stability. With the exception of Barthes, we have seen that in practical terms, the representative postmoderns we have hailed in some way echo this concern expressed by Robert Scholes: "Are we nothing but our codes? I think we are more, though it is not easy to say exactly what this 'more' may be" (26). Weedon suggests that our subjectivity "feels full," even though it is not. Foucault disparages linguistic semiology as naive textualization for evading flesh and blood violence—the sheer physicality of human conflict. Rorty acknowledges that the solipsistic web of beliefs that constitutes his self must somehow account for "external pressures." Fish finds stability in his interpretive community, a community that, according to Mailloux, everyone experiences as an inevitable historical, rhetorical context.

I believe that Scholes captures a common ethic at the heart of what drives many of these postmodern interpretive projects and their commonplace linkage of subjectivity and interpretation:

> We must respect the Other in the text, because, as human beings, we have a dimension that is irreducibly social. We have been constructed as human subjects by interacting with other people, learning their language and their ways of behaving. Having come to consciousness in this way, we have an absolute need for communication. As human subjects we must exchange meanings with others

> whom we recognize as subjects like ourselves, whose desire to communicate we need to respect, in order to confirm our own right to be treated as subjects rather than objects. (50)

Scholes, however, submits himself to the following contradiction: he claims that the human need for communication in the construction of the self is absolute. But when he turns to discuss ethics, he asserts that we have no access to the absolute, that our ethics are always temporary and provisional (154). This places Scholes in the excruciating double bind of trying to talk himself out of the practical futility theoretical Truthlessness presents to the critical project:

> [Provisional ethics] does not mean, however, that we inevitably fall into some pathos of unhappy consciousness. It only means that we must build our protocols even as we build our readings, our interpretations, and our criticisms. If we have no Truth with a capital T, we must stop using the notion of such Truth—in whatever guise—to measure what we then take to be our failure to attain it. But we must not give up distinguishing between truth and lies within whatever frameworks we can construct to make such determinations. (154)

Augustine's claim that, if nothing else, people universally pursue happiness seems to have some staying power. We want to escape the "pathos of unhappy consciousness," even if it demands a postmodern blind leap of faith. In practice, postmoderns cannot finally accept the radical discontinuity, incoherence, and deferral as presented by poststructuralist linguistics, despite the fact that we rely on such views of language to convince ourselves that we can literally talk ourselves out of unhappiness and undesirable subjectivities. Therefore, postmodern critics not only react against foundationalism in both its realist and idealist forms, arguing that no essentials exist (Weedon 167; Foucault, *Power/Knowledge,* 83; Mailloux 160). They also must deny the radical relativism of their guiding assumptions about language.

Besides the fact that radical relativism contradicts intuition and experience, any sustained charge of such relativism constitutes a withering argument against the relevance of interpretation or criticism in the postmodern frame. Unless some sense of community can be maintained, the value of the critical voice can be summarily dismissed as merely a personal opinion.

At the beginning of this discussion, I suggested that postmodern interpreters do not dispense with the charge of relativism effectively. The persistent force of the charge, even against postmodern counterarguments, rests in the fact that once we fully embrace our temporality—the contextualizing appeal to the local, the historical, the situational, the rhetorical—our selves, communities, and interpretations become subject to the same infinite regression that Augustine applies with such precision to time in the *Confessions,* book 11.

First we posit that all are mistaken who do not perceive themselves as decentered, incoherent, and disunified subjectivities—maintaining the self as a "cultural artifact," a "fiction," and an "illusion" (Greenblatt 256–57). Then we argue that such disappropriated subjectivities can be collected into a stable community which assures temporal belief, truth, coherence and therefore provides a safe haven against radical relativism, chaos, and anarchy.

But the temporal community too closely resembles our temporal subjectivity to provide the coherence we ask of it. For instance, given the limits of our temporal perspective, how do we *locate* a community in time, space, and discourse? Can we sustain the assertion that interpretive communities are *less* arbitrary—because intersubjective—than the arbitrary connections between signifiers and signifieds which render temporal communication enigmatic and individual subjects incoherent? We cannot. Collectivity we can no more escape the implications of temporality and semiotics than subjectivity. As Julia Kristeva indicates, such concepts of truth that rely exclusively on the coherence of communities cannot evade the void of meaninglessness (219, 226, 236). The best we can hope for in this case is company along the way . . . perhaps.

However, if we allow that collectivities are the synergistic product of the postmodern subjectivities we are, then the decenteredness of the collective disperses by geometric proportions. Even if we assume that an utterly homogenous, hegemonic community precedes an individual subject, the tyranny of temporality still prevails. The community is never for a moment in the same location or situation. Its perspective remains in constant flux. Within the community no subject ever experiences the community as the same, for no two subjects can ever inhabit the same perspective in the same moment, from the same entry point in space or time, in the community. Augustine comes quite close to this position in the *Confessions* according to Peter Brown:

> The sombre preoccupation of Augustine with the manner in which a man could imprison himself in a "second nature" by his past actions makes the *Confessions* a very modern book. In so many ancient and medieval biographies, for instance, we meet heroes described in terms of their essential, ideal qualities. It is almost as if they had no past: even their childhood is described only in terms of omens of the future "peak" of their life—S. Ambrose plays at being a bishop, S. Cuthbert refused to turn cartwheels. We meet them full face: it is as if they had sloughed off, in their past, all that did not point directly to the image of perfection to which they conformed.

> By contrast, we twice meet Augustine firmly held in his past: in the Garden of Milan, and in the terrible day that followed the death of his mother. For Augustine regarded a man's past as very much alive in his present: men were different from each other precisely because their wills were made different by the sum total of unique, past experiences. (*Augustine,* 173–74)

Augustine's self, like the postmodern self, is not autonomous in the Cartesian sense. But neither the Augustinian self nor the postmodern subject is less unique. If we contextualize our subjectivities with precision, we acknowledge that no two temporal subjects can be identical, and therefore every claim to the existence of a community or culture—with its implied claim of a temporal center or coherence—is a hasty generalization. Subjectivity and community become one. Both are fictions. Just as the postmodern self disintegrates into an ultimately incoherent collection of subject positions, the postmodern community disintegrates to such a degree that our selves and our communities become difficult to distinguish: we can share neither with an "other." Temporality and the inevitable change that attends it renders the postmodern community as illusory as postmodern subjectivity. The community we depend upon to legitimate our interpretive activity appears to be there ... until we look for it.

I purposely push my argument to this extent to illustrate how postmodern assumptions invite us to accept a semiotics of exclusive temporality. Even a moderate voice like Robert Scholes submits to exclusive temporality in practice. Identifying Knapp and Michaels as interpretive "fundamentalists" he argues:

> The fundamentalist view of interpretation requires two things: that meaning be fixed eternally, outside of time, and that texts in time-bound languages convey meaning so directly that it can be discerned without interpretation. Fundamentalist attempts to fix the meaning of texts all—without exception—can be shown to require some timeless zone in which true meanings are said to reside. (53)

Scholes attributes such approaches to a "nostalgia for eternity" that ultimately drives them to an unquenchable desire to discover a one right reading (53, 151). Whether or not Scholes has fairly interpreted Knapp and Michaels's project, he makes plain the postmodern connection between interpretation, subjectivity, and time:

> Texts and people do not abide in some timeless moment but in time. They are both thoroughly impregnated with time; they are constructed and deconstructed in time and by time. They are made of time. And nothing made of time and functioning in time can be complete or perfect. (151)

Through his commentary on eternity and time, Scholes rehearses for us a fundamental doctrinal point of postmodern orthodoxy that has its roots at least as far back as Martin Heidegger: the abandonment of eternity (Ricoeur 3:81).

A number of factors make this belief in exclusive temporality problematic. For instance, the same argument that says since language precedes and constructs us we cannot find a point outside of our discursive context from which to generate or discover foundational theories or essentials about interpretation, applies equally to our ability to get outside of time to discover its essence. We cannot assume that a community changes at a consistent or manageable rate rather than arbitrarily or predictably instead of at random. What seems to be a steady evolution from one perspective may be viewed as a sudden disruption from another *and nothing can be generated on the temporal plane to commend one perspective over another, they are merely different and utterly relativistic.*

But Scholes's views of eternity and time represent a more penetrating problem for postmodern interpretation. In terms of interpretive practice, Scholes assumes that belief in eternity demands that meaning is fixed, that meaning is singular, and finally, that interpretation is unnecessary, because meaning can be discerned without interpretation. In other words, he equates belief in eternity with foundationalist interpretation. He also belies a broader assumption about eternity by suggesting that one could be nostalgic for it—as if eternity could possibly be in the past. These views are not unusual, they are commonplaces of postmodern interpretation. We may recall that Jay wielded the same "nostalgia" assumption prima facie against Augustine's work on eternity in the *Confessions* (1055, 1057). This problem—the one Augustine addresses and to which the Wisdom of the incarnate Word responds in the *Confessions*—is the temporal fallacy of postmodern interpretation.

The Postmodern Critique of Western Philosophy

Postmodern philosophers, theorists, and critics may vary on particulars, offer competing theories, and contest each other's work, but they identify critique of "the Western philosophical tradition" as a common project. Literary critic Terry Eagleton, describing poststructuralism, says that it "cast grave doubt upon the classical notions of truth, reality, meaning, and knowledge, all of which could be exposed as resting on a naively representational theory of language" (143). Weedon appropriates certain aspects of the work of Jacques Lacan and Jacques Derrida, identifying with their common aim to dismantle "rationalist theories of language, consciousness and the *logocentric* tradition of Western metaphysics, which presuppose that the meaning of concepts is fixed prior to their articulation in language" (52–53). Eagleton also points to logocentrism as a definitive concept of Western philosophy:

> It has been in a broader sense "logocentric," committed to a belief in some ultimate "word," presence, essence, truth or reality which will act as the foundation of all our thought, language, and experience. It has yearned for the sign which will give meaning to all others—the "transcendental signifier"—and for the anchoring, unquestionable meaning to which all our signs can be seen to point (the "transcendental signified"). A great number of candidates for this role—God, the Idea, the World Spirit, the Self, substance, matter, and so on—have thrust themselves forward from time to time. (131)

Eagleton's concise characterization of a postmodern view of logocentrism captures the tendency to amalgamate *all* Christian theology and *all* Platonic, Neoplatonic, and semi-Platonic philosophy under this single linguistic or discursive classification.

Using a slightly different emphasis and terminology, Richard Rorty also equates Christianity and Platonism as *the* representative streams of a monolithic Western "ontotheological" tradition. Rorty identifies belief in the existence of a "True Self" and an "Eternal Reality" as indicators of the ontotheological tradition (117–18). The true self of which Rorty speaks is perfected in the Cartesian self: centered, coherent, and ahistorical. He refers to Augustine as representative of the Christian theological side of the equation (106). For Rorty, Heidegger represents an early attempt to overcome this ontotheological tradition (71–72).

The inclusion of Heidegger as a progenitor of the assault on classical Western philosophy touches our inquiry particularly as it relates to the temporal fallacy. Paul Ricoeur, in *Time and Narrative*, provides an in-depth comparison between Augustine's discussion of time in the *Confessions* and Heidegger's *Being and Time*. In his study, Ricoeur identifies Heidegger's abandonment of eternity as a defining contrast to Augustine (3:135). As we have seen, Scholes echoes Heidegger's assumptions about time, clearly connecting the philosophical discussion of time and the postmodern critical focus on language (151, 154).

The postmodern synthesis of exclusive temporality and semiotics—the assumption that nothing exists apart from human language in temporality—emerges in criticism and interpretation as attention fixed on the localized, social function of historically situated discourse.[11] Mailloux epitomizes the synthesis when he concludes that his version of antitheoretical theorizing at its best is to produce rhetorical histories of discourse self-conscious of their own situated discursiveness (135). These fundamental coordinates have been incorporated as axioms in the mainstream of postmodern theories and critical practices.

Augustine's *Unconventional* Confessions

Many Augustinian commentators assume that in one respect or another the *Confessions* is about a Neoplatonic Augustine (Starnes, *Conversion*,

277ff). Taking this view, the text necessarily becomes a deceit to some degree and Augustine maintains his commonplace label as "the Christian Plato." These interpretations correlate neatly with most historians of semiotics, who have minimized Augustine's semiotic relevance, and the rare contemporary mentions of Augustine—like those of Fish, Jay, and Rorty in our study—which cast him, with Plato and Plotinus, in the classical Western ontotheological tradition.

But the text of the *Confessions* explodes the presumption capsulized in the equation of the Western ontotheological tradition and Augustine. Augustine is not susceptible to charges of logocentrism or ontotheologism in the postmodern construction of those terms. He enacts a perspective in the *Confessions* unanticipated by postmodern critiques, one against which conventional postmodern attacks on classical philosophy and rhetoric are rendered impotent.

First, as we have seen, Augustine relies on no "naively representationalist theory of language." He consistently employs a semiotic perspective that closely approximates contemporary poststructuralist theory. Second, Augustine is nowhere logocentric. He acknowledges no meaning prior to language. In fact, he agrees fully with Barthes's contention that language preexists humanity and all material reality. Finally, Augustine speaks primarily as a critic of the fundamentals of the classical philosophy of his day, not as a propagator of Western ontotheological tradition. He denies the coherence of temporal human subjectivity—even in redeemed humanity prior to the resurrection. And, as we observed when comparing him to Mailloux, Augustine's project in the *Confessions* is at least atheoretical if not decidedly antitheoretical. His prescriptions are as direct as Mailloux's statements on methods and the bulk of the work presents a rhetorical history.

We have cataloged myriad correspondences between the *Confessions* and postmodern theory and practice. In addition to the issues of language, subjectivity, and temporality, Augustine's approach to interpretation yields numerous similarities: belief as anterior to knowledge, interpretive communities as checks on interpretive validity, multiple meanings, the dilemma of intentionality, criticism as performance, the temporal constraints of interpretation, admission of extratextual material as germane to interpretation, and interpretation as an act of persuasive argument.

However, Augustine is not a proto-postmodernist. An eternity of charity, wisdom, and truth separates Augustine from his postmodern colleagues, even in the fully temporal discourse of the *Confessions*. He is anchored, but in a unique way—a way without resemblance to the autonomous, ahistorical essentialism of the Western ontotheological self.

Augustine embodies the distinction in his consistent self-presentation as an incoherent, temporally situated, locally conscious but dynamically centered person. He never assumes a centered self as essential to his or anyone else's humanity. But neither does he accept the decentered self as a linguistic inevitability, an illusion produced by temporal language. From his acquisition of language through the completion of temporality, Augustine assumes a fully semiotic posture toward communication in the *Confessions*—not limiting his accounts to the linguistic but demanding the full integration of verbal and nonverbal discourse—even in the incarnate Word. The disintegration of verbal and nonverbal discourse parallels divisions between form and content, style and substance, and philosophy and rhetoric to name a few.

Augustine's critique of the disruption of form and content begins long before his encounter with Cicero's *Hortensius*. Acting as cultural critic, he decries societal neglect of substance in exchange for attention to style alone at school and at play. When he does encounter the *Hortensius*, it provides an alternative grammar, method, and paradigm to his own sophism. From the point of this encounter, Augustine knows that no closed system—whether religious or philosophical—can ever satisfy the demands he charts for himself. Yet he finds such systems alluring. Tracing his wanderings, he abandons the materialistic dualism of the Manichaeans, the skepticism of the Academics, and the transcendentalism of the Platonists. From these experiences Augustine gained much knowledge but no wisdom.

The Radical Alternative of Wisdom

In our journey through the *Confessions* we have observed how in many cases Augustine asks our questions, works from familiar frameworks on language, interpretation, and meaning, and puzzles over himself and human beings in general, presenting us with common ground for dialogue (Meagher 10). He finds the temporal realities of communication in the semiotic realm uncomfortable and unconvincing (Manetti 160). He recognizes that from his inescapably human perspective, the world and human thought and action are provisional and contingent (Meagher 23, 25; Patton 100).

For example, given his temporal constraints, Augustine decisively opts for belief over relativism and skepticism (Gilson 9). As Knapp and Michaels have more recently proposed, Augustine views skepticism quite simply as reason lacking belief (Knapp and Michaels 738; Gilson 33). Belief does not precede the ability to reason, but it always precedes understanding.

In brief, Augustine consciously works within the same dynamic field, the same semiotic structure that postmodernism recognizes. However, these conditions do not lead him to abandon his semiotic inclinations or his temporal situation. To grasp the alternative he presents to us in the *Confessions* we must return to develop the distinction between Augustine and Barthes that was mentioned earlier.

We hear Barthes's claim that no position exists outside of human language from which we can observe it—that is, we cannot get outside of human language. He sounds like a foundationalist while making the argument—a linguistic essentialist. But more important still, Barthes argues for a closed semiotic system. On one hand, certain perspectives—any which claim to be outside the semiotic system—are inadmissible, because human language constructs and constrains our selves and our attendant realities. On the other hand, the constant deferral of meaning is assured by the temporality of human language. Barthes concludes that apart from human language there can be no reality. But within human language discourse can present us with illusions at best—fictions that masquerade as realities external to human language.

Likewise, Augustine claims that no position exists outside of human language from which we can observe it. But by contrast with Barthes and postmodernism in general, he argues from an open, nonsystematic view of language and reality. Augustine posits a view which admits, expects, and proclaims radical creativity and initiative in this semiotic world. The language that preexists human subjects and secures their being is the Word incarnate, which literally speaks all things into existence ex nihilo. Such speech creates the very conditions of temporality and human language upon which Barthes reflects.

As such a creature of discourse, grounded in time, Augustine recognizes that he cannot escape human language to encounter the eternal Word of the Neoplatonists or discover any other "transcendental signifier." He knows his temporal and linguistic constraints by experience and reflection. Yet through the initiative of the incarnate Word—the semiotic mediator and eternal Wisdom inhabiting the temporal world of human language—Augustine learns that even his temporal experience can be made stable and meaningful. The incarnate Word re-creates the integrity of the world as experienced by people of diverse times, places, cultures, and communities. Instead of sacrificing temporality's historical, social, situational character, the presence of eternal, radical otherness intensifies it (Ricoeur 1:22).

The openness of Augustine's view sees human language as a created derivative, universally imputed to humanity as part of the image of God. Selves and meanings are not fragmented because of the essential nature of human semiotic systems. Our current faculties and experiences with human language are not representative of human potential, but symptomatic of the corruption that attended the Fall (Vance 27; Warfield 158). Therefore, although an uncertain and provisional proposition in the temporal context, we can learn to know ourselves and others. Fashioned by human language as a secondary cause, our selves are secured by the Word upon which our existence ultimately depends. Augustine's subjectivity, though not coherent or autonomous, is centered and can be experienced as such through belief—a temporal fact, not an illusion.

The distinctions between the postmodern view of subjectivity and discourse and Augustine's perspective are evident as well in applied interpretation. Put simply, Augustine believes that interpreters can discern truth and meaning that is both coherent within the community and which corresponds to eternal truth in the temporal, critical act. Whereas the current impulse in interpretation may destroy the text for the sake of the subtext (Sontag 98), see its project as the exposure of incoherence, or simply highlight the disintegration of a discourse (Newton 58), Augustine pursues integrational interpretation (Guitton 34–35). He does so conscious of the varying coherence and incoherence of language in time. As Paul Ricoeur states:

> Our experience of temporality cannot be reduced to simple discordance. As we saw with Augustine, distentio and intentio mutually confront each other at the heart of our most authentic experience. We must preserve the paradox of time from the leveling out brought about by reducing it to simple discordance. We ought to ask instead whether the plea for a radically unformed temporal experience is not itself the product of a fascination for the unformed that is one of the features of modernity. In short, when thinkers or literary critics seem to yield to a nostalgia for order or, worse, to the horror of chaos, what really moves them, in the final analysis, may be a genuine recognition of the paradoxes of time beyond the loss of meaning of one particular culture—our own. (1:72)

The "leveling of time" Ricoeur mentions is consonant with what we have termed the "temporal fallacy." Augustine preempts the temporal fallacy by preserving and embracing the paradox of time and eternity, thereby applying Truth within varying historical situations rather than producing ahistorical theory, and stabilizing semiotic meaning without reduction to a single authoritative interpretation.

Interpretive practice in the *Confessions* demolishes relativism through the dynamic, temporal activity of the incarnate Word. That Word unifies the temporal and the eternal, time and eternity (Starnes, *Conversion,* 100; Meer 557). But the absolutely radical distinction we must observe about the Incarnation is direction. It initiates the relation between God and His people by abiding in temporality (Colish 34). R. A. Markus calls this directional move "the fundamental change in the soul's itinerary" from man's ascent to God's descent (82).

We cannot overestimate the implications of the full temporal participation of the incarnate Word. Not only does it invest temporality with eternal significance, but it also negates the error of equating Augustine's discussions of future participation in eternity with his present immersion in the experience of temporality. Augustine is grounded. Radical relativism ends, but relevance remains.

The same Incarnational move debunks the commonplace notion that eternal truth necessarily means foundationalist theory or uniform, universal practice. Augustine addresses the foolishness of equating the eternal existence of Justice, Truth, and Beauty with an insistence that such ideals be observed in exactly the same way from time to time and place to place (3.7.12–9.17). A careful reading of Augustine's directives on these matters demonstrates an unusual sensitivity to local custom combined with great respect for the plain moral teaching of the Bible. He mentions only the "commands of God" as cause for contravention of the diversity of cultural codes, without listing pious platitudes.[12]

The community plays a crucial, though not exclusive, role in validating the temporal aptness of a particular interpretation, evaluating its relation to Truth and relevance to the situation. As practiced in interpretation, eternal truths are applied variously according to temporal circumstances. In this sense, time approximates eternity, but only on the initiative of the Eternal (Ricoeur 1:29).

Neither the Eternal move to participate in the temporal, nor the temporal, diverse application of eternal truth sufficiently explains how the incarnate Word enables Augustine to practice interpretation that presents truth and meaning from and in human discourse. To do so, we must briefly recall his progression from book 10 through 13. As Augustine engages us in his present, he first explains how the incarnate Word stabilizes his memory and mental faculties. The presence of the incarnate Word does not negate Augustine's temporal condition, but enables him to have a measure of certain knowledge there (Colish ix). Initially, book 11 develops the discursive construction of all Creation, including time. Time does not create us, speech does. Time is a discursive construct for Augustine. In the remainder of the book he develops the means by which the incarnate Word stabilizes humanity in time. Again, temporality remains, but the Incarnation has secured his existence and the existence of the universe in Augustine's experience. Meaning becomes believable, and signs—though not transparent—point to discernible truths. On this basis, Augustine can judge learning via signs to be possible and worthwhile (Sebeok 63).

Because the incarnate Word first invests temporality with eternity, eternity and truth can arrest the regression of temporality toward the void—that is, absolute nothing. Interpretation then becomes the process of discerning semiotically the truths to be applied rhetorically to local hearers in their particular historical circumstances. The Incarnation thereby creates space for interpretation by enabling us to talk about truth in temporality—without pretense of personal transcendence—despite our incomplete knowledge of Truth. The condition of temporality also necessitates critical debate, since no one interpreter or interpretation can hope to exhaust the meaning of a given text over time.

Therefore, to summarize Augustine's preemption of the temporal fallacy, from the human perspective, eternity does not demand an exit from temporal circumstances into transcendence, an abdication of the historical for the ahistorical, or an exclusive, unitary meaning that ends interpretive dialogue. Temporality demands interpretation. Interpretive dialogue ends at the limit of human faculties or the end of time. Neither can one long for a past eternity, since the closest approximation we have for eternity is the temporal present, which is still other than the eternal. There is "no place for a derivation, in any conceivable sense of the word, of eternity from time. What is posited, confessed, thought, is in one stroke the contrast of eternity with time" in the *Confessions* (Ricoeur 1:22).

The Incarnational Paradigm: Charity in Interpretive Rhetoric

Augustine concludes the *Confessions* as a reformed rhetorician: fully temporal, believing in the eternal, experiencing interaction with the incarnate Word in his own context—both individually and collectively. His discourse invites us to join him on his quest for Wisdom, to travel with him through time on his own terms. It is a fair request. He presents a rhetorical performance, and a charitable one. For Augustine, interpretation derives from the Incarnation—a mimetic and creative act simultaneously.

The incarnate Word provides full semiotic integration for Augustine—not theoretical but applied and dynamic. Without the words *and the deeds* in the temporal context he would not have been convinced; he would not have first believed (10.4.6, 10.42.69, 11.8.10). The semiotic fullness makes Augustine more than a linguist; he aims his interpretations —including these *Confessions*—at the hearts of flesh and blood people living real lives constructed by language. But the language that creates— eternal language—is that same Word eternal. Certainly human language fashions us too—*imago Dei*—but only provisionally (Meagher 25). Without the Incarnation nothing holds together for Augustine (Starnes, *Conversion*, 117).

Augustine offers no foundationalist interpretive theory. To argue for a singular, comprehensive interpretation rankles him (12.25.34). He values ordinary language as a check against skepticism, as long as we understand our occasional imprecisions (Ricoeur 1:7–9, 13, 11.20.26). He follows the incarnate Word as his interpretive paradigm: the ultimate act of sacrificial love. Therefore, the prerequisite he demands for every interpretive performance is charity. The positive value of interpretation, whether as performance or dialogue, depends on the charity of the speaker and the listener.

Granted, Augustine presents an unusual interpretive scheme to our sensibilities, but I commend this scheme as one worth our consideration today. From the Incarnation it takes its cue to embrace the temporal while pursuing and practicing truth in present moments. In effect, Augustine proceeds to benefit his listeners via integration, rather than to see the interpretive act as dialectic, conflict, or subversion. Augustine aims to construct rather than deconstruct, to use criticism in pursuit of integrity, not to foster fragmentation.

Following the development of the *Confessions*, to practice wisdom Augustine interprets. He interprets as a rhetorical act, directed toward people, not texts. The contingency of temporal existence concerns the bishop of Hippo less than the contingency of human beings (Gilson 21). His critical rhetoric reflects an abiding preoccupation with true and false lives versus true and false words. What Jordan states about *De doctrina Christiana* applies equally well to the *Confessions* as interpretation, "Augustine is not providing a method by which one can discover the hidden core of a text. He is after a method by which the obscure passages of Scripture can be made fruitful" (189).

Augustine completes his *Confessions* speaking from his own historical context with faith, hope, and charity—still searching, questioning, and reforming. He is centered, but not fully coherent to himself; a former Sophist who finds temporal integrity in the incarnate Word (Hartle 124–25). His practice remains fully rhetorical, but it is a redeemed rhetoric—reasoned, substantial, stylized, and charged with manifest moral motives (Sutherland 152).

It is a rhetoric of the people, of community, of society—to believers and potential believers (W. R. Johnson 221–22; Marrou 34; Meer 417–18). But Augustine, being so thoroughly temporal for the moment, has no time for theory—whether interpretive or rhetorical. We might reconstruct an implied theory for the *Confessions*, but then it would be *our* theory. Augustine's only explicit guide is Wisdom.

The incarnate Word provides for Augustine what Cicero could only point to—the moral component to pursue wisdom by the integration of philosophy and rhetoric. Augustine is enabled to pursue the practice of temporal wisdom, including a full-fledged rhetoric that applies to all of life, not only the interpretation of Scripture. James J. Murphy rightly notes that Augustine avoids two characteristic rhetorical vices in the process: the "sophistic heresy" that "denies the necessity of subject matter and believes that *forma* alone is desirable," and the "Platonic heresy" that "depends on the belief that the man possessed of truth will *ipso facto* be able to communicate the truth to others" (*Rhetoric*, 60). He counters these routine heresies by an integration made possible by the Incarnation, not by moderating between them.

The potency of the Word incarnate constructs a temporal space for integrational interpretation, gives access to truth through belief rather than demonstration, and directs rhetoric toward listeners whose selves can be secured within a semiotic system still fully temporal but stabilized. The Word stands in our temporal present in the flesh, not in the past or future, which do not exist. As we enter each moment, eternal Being, Wisdom, Power, Justice, Holiness, Goodness, and Truth—all are embodied in the singular incarnate Word, who is already in the moment when we get there. As J. G. Kristo puts it, "Augustine's thinking rarely wanders too far from his principal dichotomy between God's eternity and stability and the world's temporality and precariousness" (138). Our temporal circumstances shift and change. Time is fleeting. But the Word never changes, although the applications do.

However, as Colin Starnes has noted, Augustine's is a hard teaching (*Conversion*, 101). Few today will submit themselves to the moral rigor associated with the Incarnation, let alone that rigor in combination with the comprehensive intellectual knowledge and performative skills that Augustine calls wisdom. The comfort for any who would attempt such a program in earnest is that there would be help, and that Augustine nowhere claims to achieve wisdom, only to pursue it.

In ages when "power" and "eros" dominate critical minds, and when charity seems almost entirely absent—ages like Augustine's and ages like ours—Wisdom still speaks. He has also set eternity in their hearts; yet they cannot fathom what God has done from beginning to end.

Notes

Introduction

1. I refer here to Kenneth Burke's *Rhetoric of Religion* and Robert McMahon's *Augustine's Prayerful Ascent*. Also of note in this vein, Joanne McWilliam has also edited an otherwise fine collection of essays entitled *Augustine: From Rhetor to Theologian*.

2. Among Latin texts, only Virgil's *Aeneid* has been translated into more languages than the *Confessions* (Ryan 1).

3. Some key figures in the history of this debate include: Alfaric, Vossier, Boyer, Courcelle, Gilson, and Harnack. A more complete discussion appears in chapter 1. Colin Starnes presents an excellent historical summary with commentary in an appendix to *Augustine's Conversion* (277ff).

4. I treat Augustine and the Second Sophistic in depth in chapter 1, from the beginning through the section entitled "Rejecting the Second Sophistic."

5. Bakhtin characterizes the *Confessions* as a precursor to the modern novel, his primary study (*Dialogic*, 135–46).

Chapter 1: The Integrity of Philosophy and Rhetoric

1. The label "Second Sophistic" has been credited to Philostratus and first appeared in his *Lives of the Sophists,* which chronicles the movement through A.D. 200. Philostratus identifies Gorgias as the founder of sophism. While Baldwin and Kennedy vary greatly in their judgment of the Second Sophistic, they agree that it (a) dominated Greek and Roman rhetoric from roughly the first through the fifth or sixth century; (b) is a rhetoric of themes concerned with virtuosity of performance; and (c) influenced early Christian rhetoric. See Baldwin 2–50 and Kennedy 38–40.

2. Dioscorus, a Greek who had come to Carthage to study, inquired of Augustine the bishop regarding Cicero's philosophy. Augustine sent a detailed reply correcting Dioscorus for dabbling in the pride and vanity of pagan learning (Flood 69–71).

Chapter 2: *Protocols for Reading* the Confessions

1. The irony of reducing to propositions a text that practices and advocates a theory of interpretation promoting a geometric explosion of interpretative discourse from even the smallest segments of text should not be missed.

2. John J. O'Meara has strictly warned against this temptation in Augustinian scholarship, saying, "If you find yourself coming to the conclusion that your author didn't know what he was saying—but you do—stop" ("Research," 284).

3. Because this book is intended for an educated audience most likely to encounter the *Confessions* in translation, all references are taken from John K. Ryan's 1960 English translation, *The Confessions of Saint Augustine*, unless otherwise noted.

4. The explicit identification of the audience and their motives for wanting Augustine's confessions in book 10 probably serves more as a natural transition for Augustine to discuss his immediate present than as any indication that the listeners had asked only for book 10 and following.

5. John J. O'Meara speculates, based on a triangle of correspondence not fully extant, that Augustine wrote a biography of his close friend and bishop of Thagaste, Alypius, for Paulinus of Nola:

> Courcelle supposes that Alypius asked Augustine to fill Paulinus's request. Augustine wrote to Paulinus in the summer of 396 saying that he was completing the requested life of Alypius. . . . The life of Alypius would appear to have been completed—some of it, as we have already indicated, is incorporated in the *Confessions* (6.7–10, 11–16). Courcelle supposes that Paulinus received it and, impressed by it, requested Augustine to do in relation to his own life what he had done for Alypius. ("Fiction," 83)

However, it seems more likely that Paulinus, if indeed he did make a specific request, was one of many inquisitors and an audience wider than the *servus Dei* alone (Keenan 81; Meer 349).

6. In the *Confessions* one can hear Augustine the bishop identifying with Ambrose, his model bishop, in a report on Ambrose's day-to-day existence. Augustine says:

> I was unable to ask him what I wanted and in the way I wanted, for crowds of busy men, to whose trouble he was a slave, shut me away from both his ear and his mouth. When he was with them, and this was but a little while, he either refreshed his body with needed food or his mind with reading. (6.3.3)

> Non enim quaerere ab eo poteram quod volebam, sicut volebam, secludentibus me ab eius aure atque ore catervis negotiosorum hominum, quorum infirmitatibus serviebat: cum quibus quando non erat, quod perexiguum temporis erat, ut corpus reficiebat necessariis sustentaculus aut lectione animum. (6.3.3)

7. The foregoing is but a drop in the bucket compared to the fine biographical and historical work available on Augustine and his situation during the composition of the *Confessions*. For a few particularly strong biographies of Augustine, I suggest Brown, Meer, Marrou, and O'Donnell.

8. The popularity of "books on tape" presents a contemporary exception to our assumption about the ordinary reading of books aloud to adults.

9. Contrary to the conventional wisdom, which assumes that Augustine composed the *Confessions* in a piecemeal fashion from 397–400, James J. O'Donnell has recently proposed that the discourse's power to carry the reader along with it suggests it was a consuming passion for Augustine that he completed in a much shorter amount of time (5.1.41 42).

10. Using Brown's conservative dating, these works, in chronological order, include: *Quaestiones evangeliorum; Contra Faustum Manichaeum; Confessiones; Contra Felicem Manichaeum; De natura boni contra Manichaeos; Contra Secundinum Manichaeum; Adnotationes in Job; De catechizandis rudibus; De Trinitate; De consensu evangelistarum; Contra epistolam Parmeniani; De baptismo contra Donatistas; Ad inquisitiones Januarii; De opere monachorum. De bono conjugali. De sancta virginitate. Contra litteras Petiliani;* and *De Genesi ad litteram* (*Augustine*, 184–85).

11. Cf. Isaiah 57:15; Isaiah 66:2; Psalm 51:17.

12. Colin Starnes breaks the *Confessions* into three sections—books 1–9, 10, and 11–13—and identifies three respective audiences. He argues that the first audience is humanity in general, the second audience is Christians in general, and the third audience is Christian philosophers. (*Conversion*, xiv–xv).

13. The professor is Dr. Joseph Kockelmans, distinguished professor of philosophy, Pennsylvania State University. I am indebted to him for introducing me to the study of medieval rhetoric.

14. Commentators often speculate on the reasons why Augustine neglects to name the woman he lived with for about fourteen years—the mother of his son, Adeodatus—as well as his brother and sister.

15. The pear-stealing episode has attracted much attention from commentators. See for example Ferrari, "Pear," and Mann.

16. Brown 147; Meer 457; O'Meara 82–83; Matthews 253; Adam 93; Kristo 126–27; Markus 7.

17. Clearly, the interpreter of the *Confessions* as Neoplatonic would hail the naming of Cicero as confirmation of that reading. This interpreter would say that Cicero is a "safe" philosopher to mention among more conservative Christians of Augustine's day, but Augustine would never dare to mention Plotinus or Porphyry by name. The logic of this reading is unassailable: Assuming that Augustine is a Neoplatonist, his ecclesiastical position forces him to mask his Neoplatonism. The cases where Augustine is evidently speaking of some other system allegedly offer cues that point to the latent or hidden Neoplatonism of the text. Starnes comments (in this case referring to Courcelle) that regarding such esoteric approaches, "so long as the text itself is not supposed to have any inner integrity that is accessible to us, it becomes impossible to prevent its meaning from being forced to accord with the meaning of the external sources and parallels that are supposed to explain it" (*Conversion*, 289). We are led into the realm of the textual unconscious, where no reading can be falsified.

18. See Hagendahl 588. Also, Augustine includes fragments of the *Hortensius* in *contra academicos III, De beata vita, Soliloques, De civitate Dei, Contra Julianum,* and *De Trinitate* (Outler 65n 4).

19. This religious impulse is treated in more detail in the first chapter of this book.

20. See, for example, Baldwin, *Medieval,* 51–73 and Murphy, *Rhetoric,* 56–63.

21. I choose the term *share* here to indicate that Cicero and Augustine in fact use the same terms but invest them with different shades of meaning and place different emphases upon them. For further reading on the similarities and differences between their rhetorics, see Baldwin, Clarke, Press ("Doctrina" and "Structure"), Fortin, and Milovanovic-Barham.

22. While not central to the project at hand, it is interesting to note that the notion of the wife as slave under contract to her husband as lord, the common status of wives under Roman law, is subverted by Monica, who treats this state of affairs as a joke.

Chapter 3: *The Significance of Incarnational Wisdom in Time*

1. The prefiguration of books 10–13 reveals the richness of Augustine's discourse, paralleling the biblical narrative of the Creation, the founding of Israel, and attendant prophetic foreshadowing that is fulfilled via the Incarnation, which is followed by the fuller exposition of the incarnate Word through the Scriptures of the New Testament.

2. Other passages that anticipate book 10's discussion of memory include: 2.7.15, 3.11.20, 3.12.21, 4.3.6, 4.6.11, 4.8.13, 4.13.20, 5.3.3, 8.7.16, and numerous other places where Augustine comments on the clarity or obscurity of his memory in particular cases.

3. The passage resonates with his comments about Ambrose as bishop of Milan (6.3.3).

4. The basic script of testimony from Creation never changes. It is always "He (God) made me/us!" See 10.6.9–10.

5. Paul Ricoeur finds it ironic that Augustine raises an ontological question from which to pursue a phenomenological answer (5.1.7). However, Augustine's project, in the midst of its depth and precision of thought, is integrational and practical rather than analytical. Ricoeur's point seems entirely consistent with Augustine's view of time; that is, by nature it can provide only phenomenological answers, since all created things in time are tending toward nonbeing. Etienne Gilson also sees that Augustine favors the ontological over the existential and attributes this to Platonic influence (21).

6. A more thorough discussion of Welch's phrase "the lure of the informational" appears in chapter 2.

7. Vance 20; Manetti 168; Kelly 45; Eco, *Semiotics,* 33; Todorov, *Theories,* 1, 24, 33; Deely 33.

8. Deely 17; Manetti 157; Todorov 33.

9. Ryan translates two distinct verbs, *tenere* and *colligere,* both as "infer" and "inferred," respectively. A simpler translation that reflects Augustine's choice of different verbs in the progression of the passage seems more appropriate. Thus we have referred to the first as Augustine's "grasping" and then "gathering" or collecting.

Chapter 4: Rhetorical Interpretation

1. Conventional wisdom on Augustine's rhetoric as dealing exclusively with the interpretation and explication of Scripture can be found in widely used textbooks like George Kennedy's (153–55, 158), and Thomas M. Conley's (76). Kelly provides another example of how Augustine's work is frequently viewed as limited to Scripture alone (46).

2. In addition to Fish's own *Is There a Text in This Class?*, "Interpreting the Variorum" can also be found in Davis and Finke, and Lodge.

3. Augustine in no way approves of such misinterpretations, even when they produce an ultimately good effect. As he notes in *De doctrina Christiana*:

> However, as I began to explain, if he is deceived in an interpretation which builds up charity, which is the end of the commandments, he is deceived in the same way as a man who leaves a road by mistake but passes through a field to the same place toward which the road itself leads. But he is to be corrected and shown that it is more useful not to leave the road, lest the habit of deviating force him to take a crossroad or perverse way. (1.36.41)

4. Augustine scholars have carefully documented his request for a "sabbatical" of intensive scriptural research, including Adam (37), Brown (*Augustine*, 206; *Religion and Society*, 276), and Meer (7).

5. In a passage of *De doctrina Christiana* written prior to the *Confessions*, Augustine distinguishes "flesh" from any negative association with the body:

> "The flesh lusteth against the spirit: and the spirit against the flesh; for these are contrary to one another." For this was said on account of the unconquered habit of the flesh against which the spirit has a concupiscence of its own, not that the body should be destroyed, but that its concupiscence, which is its evil habit, should be conquered so that it is rendered subject to the spirit as natural order demands. . . . However, not even those who, depraved by a false opinion, detest their bodies would be prepared to lose one eye without pain. (1.24.25)

6. See Sutherland 148; Colish 2, 17, 29.

7. The phrase "rhetoric as a way of being" is borrowed from Thomas W. Benson.

Chapter 5: The Wisdom of Incarnational Rhetoric

1. Jay also includes *The Prelude*, by Wordsworth, in his study, but this aspect of the essay does not figure in our current discussion (1049ff).

2. Burke uses the *Confessions* as a springboard for his speculations on "logology" (vi). He seems content to exploit it for its power to illustrate his thesis: "In sum, what we say about *words*, in the empirical realm, will bear a notable like-

ness to what is said about *God* in theology" (13–14). He relies on the Neoplatonic paradigm for interpretation of the *Confessions,* and wastes no time situating the work historically or himself within the discourse surrounding the *Confessions.* For Burke the text is data; a case study.

3. See chapter 2. John J. O'Meara, among others, finds Augustine's lack of historical detail in the *Confessions* disturbing.

4. See chapter 3.

5. Augustine's view of subjectivity in the *Confessions* also reveals the fallacy in Richard Rorty's assertion that there is a "picture of the self common to Greek metaphysics, Christian theology, and Enlightenment rationalism: the picture of an ahistorical natural center, the locus of human dignity, surrounded by an adventitious and inessential periphery" (176).

6. For a full discussion of coherence versus correspondence theories of truth, see chapter 3.

7. See the comments of Deely, Kelly, and Todorov in chapter 3.

8. The following writers could serve as starting points for tracing the literature on the "belief precedes understanding" motif: Portalie (117–18), Crosson (158), Gilson (33), Henry (15).

9. A full analysis of 1.1.1 appears in chapter 2.

10. For example see Harnack or McCabe.

11. For examples see: Bakhtin (30); Fish (321); Foucault, *Power/Knowledge* (81–85); Mailloux (15–18); Newton (71); Weedon (24).

12. We might recall that the commands Augustine most frequently cites are the summary commands offered by Christ of the entire law—namely, love of God and neighbor.

Bibliography

Adam, Karl. *Saint Augustine: The Odyssey of His Soul.* Trans. Dom Justin McCann. New York: Macmillan, 1932.
Augustine. *Augustine: Confessions and Enchiridion.* Trans. Albert C. Outler. Philadelphia: Westminster, 1955.
———. *The Basic Writings of Saint Augustine.* 2 vols. Ed. Whitney J. Oates. New York: Random House, 1948.
———. *The City of God.* Trans. Marcus Dods. New York: Random House, 1950.
———. *The Confessions of Augustine.* Ed. John Gibb and William Montgomery. London: Cambridge, 1927. Reprint, New York: Garland, 1980
———. *The Confessions of Saint Augustine.* Trans. John K. Ryan. New York: Doubleday, 1960.
———. *The Confessions of Saint Augustine.* Trans. R. Warner. New York: NAL Penguin, 1963.
———. *De magistro.* Trans. G. C. Leckie. Vol. 1 of *Basic Writings of Augustine.* Ed. Whitney J. Oates. New York: Random House, 1948.
———. *On Christian Doctrine.* Trans. D. W. Robertson Jr. New York: Macmillan, 1958.
Bailey, F. G. *The Prevalence of Deceit.* Ithaca: Cornell University Press, 1991.
Bakhtin, Mikhail. *The Dialogic Imagination: Four Essays.* Ed. Michael Holquist. Trans. Caryl Emerson and Michael Holquist. Austin: University of Texas Press, 1981.
———. *Speech Genres and Other Late Essays.* Ed. Caryl Emerson and Michael Holquist. Trans. Vern W. McGee. Austin: University of Texas Press, 1986.
Baldwin, C. S. *Medieval Rhetoric and Poetic.* Gloucester, Mass.: Peter Smith, 1959.
Barthes, Roland. "From Work to Text." In *Literary Criticism and Theory: The Greeks to the Present,* ed. Robert Con Davis and Laurie Finke, 713–18. New York: Longman, 1989.
———. *The Semiotic Challenge.* Trans. Richard Howard. New York: Hill and Wang, 1988.
———. *S/Z.* Trans. Richard Miller. New York: Hill and Wang, 1974.
Benson, Thomas W. "Rhetoric as a Way of Being." In *American Rhetoric: Context and Criticism,* 293–322. Carbondale: Southern Illinois University Press, 1989.

Bonner, Gerald. *St. Augustine of Hippo: Life and Controversies.* Philadelphia: Westminster Press, 1963.
Bourke, Vernon J. *Augustine's Love of Wisdom: An Introspective Philosophy.* West Lafayette, Ind.: Purdue University Press, 1993.
Brinton, Alan. "Cicero's Use of Historical Examples in Moral Argument." *Philosophy & Rhetoric* 22 (1988): 169–84.
Brown, Peter. *Augustine of Hippo.* Berkeley: University of California Press, 1967.
———. *Religion and Society in the Age of Saint of Augustine.* New York: Harper & Row, 1972.
Bubacz, Bruce Stephen. "Augustine's Account of Factual Memory." *Augustinian Studies* 6 (1975): 181–92.
———. "Augustine's Illumination Theory and Epistemic Structuring." *Augustinian Studies* 11 (1980): 35–48.
Burke, Kenneth. *The Rhetoric of Religion: Studies in Logology.* Berkeley: University of California Press, 1970.
Burnaby, John. *Amor Dei, A Study of the Religion of St. Augustine.* London: Hodder & Stoughton, 1960.
Campenhausen, Hans von. *The Fathers of the Latin Church.* Trans. Manfred Hoffman. London: Adam & Charles Black, 1964.
Chadwick, Henry, ed. Introduction. *Confessions.* By Augustine. Oxford: Oxford University Press, 1991.
Clark, Mary T. "Book Review: *St. Augustine's Early Theory of Man,* A.D. 386–391 and *St. Augustine's Confessions: The Odyssey of Soul* by Robert J. O'Connell." *International Philosophy Quarterly* 11 (1971): 427–39.
Clarke, M. L. *Rhetoric at Rome.* New York: Barnes & Noble, 1963.
Colish, Marcia. *The Mirror of Language: A Study in the Medieval Theory of Language.* Lincoln: University of Nebraska Press, 1983.
Conley, Thomas M. *Rhetoric in the European Tradition.* New York: Longman, 1990.
Courcelle, Pierre Paul. *Recherches sur les Confessions de saint Augustin.* Paris: E. de Boccard, 1950.
Coward, Rosalind, and John Ellis. *Language and Materialism: Developments in Semiology and the Theory of the Subject.* Boston: Routledge & Kegan Paul, 1980.
Crombie, A. C. *Augustine to Galileo.* Cambridge, Mass.: Harvard University Press, 1979.
Crosson, Frederick. "Religion and Faith in St. Augustine's *Confessions.*" In *Rationality and Religious Belief,* ed. C. F. Delaney. Notre Dame, Ind.: University of Notre Dame Press, 1979.
Davis, Robert Con, and Laurie Finke. *Literary Criticism and Theory: The Greeks to the Present.* New York: Longman, 1989.
Deely, John. *Introducing Semiotic: Its History and Doctrine.* Bloomington: Indiana University Press, 1982.
DiLorenzo, Raymond. "The Critique of Socrates in Cicero's *De Oratore:* Ornatus and the Nature of Wisdom." *Philosophy & Rhetoric* 11 (1978): 247–61.
Eagleton, Terry. *Literary Theory: An Introduction.* Minneapolis: University of Minnesota Press, 1983.

Eco, Umberto. *Semiotics and the Philosophy of Language*. Bloomington: Indiana University Press, 1984.
Faigley, Lester. "Judging Writing, Judging Selves." *College Composition and Communication* 40, no. 4 (1989): 395–412.
Ferrari, Leo C. "Beyond Augustine's Conversion Scene." In *Augustine: From Rhetor to Theologian*, 97–108. Waterloo, Ontario: Wilfrid Laurier University Press, 1992.
———. "The Pear-Theft in Augustine's 'Confessions.'" *Revue des Etudes Augustiniennes* 25 (1979): 35–46.
Fish, Stanley. "Interpreting the *Variorum*." In *Is There a Text in this Class?*, 147–73. Cambridge, Mass.: Harvard University Press.
Flores, Ralph. "Reading and Speech in St. Augustine's Confessions." *Augustinian Studies* 6 (1975): 1–13.
Fortin, Ernest L. "Augustine and the Problem of Christian Rhetoric." *Augustinian Studies* 5 (1974): 85–100.
Foucault, Michel. *Power/Knowledge: Selected Interviews & Other Writings*. New York: Pantheon, 1980.
———. "The Subject and Power." *Critical Inquiry* 8 (1982): 777–95.
Gilson, Etienne. *The Christian Philosophy of Saint Augustine*. Trans. L. E. M. Lynch. New York: Random House, 1960.
Grant, Patrick. "Redeeming the Time: The *Confessions* of St. Augustine." In *By Things Seen: Reference and Recognition in Medieval Thought*, ed. David L. Jeffrey, 21–32. Ottawa: University of Ottawa Press, 1979.
Greenblatt, Stephen Jay. *Renaissance Self-Fashioning, From More to Shakespeare*. Chicago: University of Chicago Press, 1980.
Guitton, Jean. *The Modernity of Saint Augustine*. Trans. A. V. Littledale. Baltimore: Helicon Press, 1959.
Hagendahl, Harald. *Augustine and the Latin Classics*. Stockholm: Almqvist & Wiksell, 1967.
Hamilton, Gordon J. "Augustine's Methods of Biblical Interpretation." In *Grace, Politics & Desire: Essays on Augustine*, ed. Hugo A. Meynell, 103–22. Calgary: University of Calgary Press, 1990.
Hanson-Smith, Elizabeth. "Augustine's *Confessions*: The Concrete Referent." *Philosophy* 2 (1978): 176–89.
Harnack, Adolf. *Monasticism: Its Ideals and History and the Confessions of St. Augustine*. Trans. E. E. Kellett and F. H. Morseille. London: Williams, 1901.
Hartle, Ann. *Death and the Disinterested Spectator: An Inquiry into the Nature of Philosophy*. Albany: State University of New York Press, 1986.
Henry, Paul. *Saint Augustine on Personality*. New York: Macmillan, 1960.
Jay, Paul L. "Being in the Text: Autobiography and the Problem of the Subject." *MLN* 97 (1982): 1045–63.
Johnson, Douglas W. "*Verbum* in the early Augustine (386–397)." *Recherches Augustiniennes* 8 (1965): 25–53.
Johnson, W. R. "Isocrates Flowering: The Rhetoric of Augustine." *Philosophy & Rhetoric* 9 (1976): 217–31.
Jordan, Mark D. "Words and Word: Incarnation and Signification in Augustine's *De Doctrina Christiana*." *Augustinian Studies* 11 (1980): 177–96.

Keenan, Mary Emily. *The Life and Times of Saint Augustine as Revealed in His Letters.* Washington, D.C.: Catholic University Press, 1935.

Kelly, Louis G. "Saint Augustine and Saussurean Linguistics." *Augustinian Studies* 6 (1975): 45.

Kennedy, George A. *Classical Rhetoric and Its Christian and Secular Tradition from Ancient to Modern Times.* Chapel Hill: University of North Carolina Press, 1980.

Kevane, Eugene. "Paideia and Anti-Paideia: The *Prooemium* of St. Augustine's *De Doctrina Christiana.*" *Augustinian Studies* 1 (1970): 154–80.

Knapp, Steven, and Walter Benn Michaels. "Against Theory." *Critical Inquiry* 8 (1982): 723–42.

Kristeva, Julia. *The Kristeva Reader.* Ed. Toril Moi. New York: Columbia University Press, 1986.

Kristo, J. G. *Looking for God in Time and Memory: Psychology, Theology, and Spirituality in Augustine's Confessions.* Lanham, Md.: University Press of America, 1991.

Kuhns, Richard Francis. *Literature and Philosophy, Structures of Experience.* London: Routledge and Kegan Paul, 1971.

Lentricchia, Frank. *After the New Criticism.* Chicago: University of Chicago Press, 1980.

Lewis, C. S. *God in the Dock.* Grand Rapids, Mich.: Eerdmans, 1970.

Lodge, David. *Modern Criticism and Theory: A Reader.* New York: Longmans, 1988.

Mailloux, Steven. *Rhetorical Power.* Ithaca: Cornell University Press, 1989.

Mallard, William. *Language and Love.* University Park: Pennsylvania State University Press, 1994.

Manetti, Giovanni. *Theories of the Sign.* Trans. Christine Richardson. Bloomington: Indiana University Press, 1993.

Mann, William. "The Theft of the Pears." *Aperion* 12 (1978): 51–58.

Markus, R. A. *Saeculum: History and Society in the Theology of Saint Augustine.* Cambridge: Cambridge University Press, 1970.

Marrevee, William H. *The Ascension of Christ in the Works of St. Augustine.* Ottawa: University of Ottawa Press, 1967.

Marrou, Henri Irenee. *St. Augustine and His Influence Through the Ages.* Trans. Patrick Hepburne-Scott. New York: Harper Torchbooks, 1957.

Matthews, Alfred Warren. *The Development of St. Augustine from Neoplatonism to Christianity, 386–391 A.D.* Washington: University Press of America, 1980.

McCabe, Joseph. *St. Augustine and His Age.* New York: Putnam's Sons, 1903.

McMahon, Robert. *Augustine's Prayerful Ascent: An Essay on the Literary Form of the Confessions.* Athens: University of Georgia Press, 1989.

McWilliam, Joanne, ed. *Augustine: From Rhetor to Theologian.* Waterloo, Ontario: Wilfrid Laurier University Press, 1992.

Meagher, Robert. *Augustine: An Introduction.* New York: Harper and Row, 1978.

Meer, Frederik van der. *Augustine the Bishop, the Life and Work of a Father of the Church.* New York: Sheed and Ward, 1962.

Miethe, Terry L. *Augustinian Bibliography, 1970–1980: With Essays on the Fundamentals of Augustinian Scholarship.* Westport, Conn.: Greenwood Press, 1982.

Milovanovic-Barham, Celica. "Three Levels of Style in Augustine of Hippo and Gregory of Nazianzus." *Rhetorica* 11, no. 1 (1993): 1–26.

Mourant, John A. *Introduction to the Philosophy of Saint Augustine: Selected Readings and Commentaries.* University Park: Pennsylvania State University Press, 1964.

Murphy, James J. *Rhetoric in the Middle Ages: A History of Rhetorical Theory from Saint Augustine to the Renaissance.* Berkeley: University of California Press, 1974.

———. "The Metarhetorics of Plato, Augustine, and McLuhan: A Pointing Essay." *Philosophy & Rhetoric* 4 (1971): 201–14.

———. "Saint Augustine and the Christianization of Rhetoric." *Western Journal of Speech* 22 (1958): 24–29.

Newton, K. M. *Interpreting the Text.* New York: St. Martin's, 1990.

Oates, Whitney J. Introduction. *The Basic Writings of Saint Augustine.* By Augustine. 2 vols. New York: Random House, 1948.

O'Connell, Robert J. *Art and the Christian Intelligence in St. Augustine.* Cambridge, Mass.: Harvard University Press, 1978.

———. "Augustine and Plotinus: A Reply to Sr. Mary Clark." *International Philosophical Quarterly* 12 (1972): 604–8.

———. *St. Augustine's Confessions: The Odyssey of Soul.* Cambridge: Belknap Press, 1969.

———. *St. Augustine's Early Theory of Man,* A.D. 386–391. Cambridge: Belknap Press, 1968.

O'Donnell, James J. *Augustine.* Boston: Twayne Press, 1985.

———. *Augustine: Confessions.* 3 vols. Oxford: Clarendon Press, 1992.

O'Meara, Dominic J., ed. *Neoplatonism and Christian Thought.* Albany: State University of New York Press, 1982.

O'Meara, John J. "Augustine's *Confessions:* Elements of Fiction." In *Augustine: From Rhetor to Theologian,* ed. Joanne McWilliam. Waterloo, Ontario: Wilfrid Laurier University Press, 1992.

———. "The Neoplatonism of Saint Augustine." In *Neoplatonism and Christian Thought,* ed. Dominic J. O'Meara. Albany: State University of New York Press, 1982.

———. "Research Techniques in Augustinian Studies." *Augustinian Studies* 1 (1970): 277–84.

———. *Studies in Augustine and Eriugena.* Ed. Thomas Halton. Washington, D.C.: Catholic University of America Press, 1992.

———. *The Young Augustine: The Growth of St. Augustine's Mind up to His Conversion.* New York: Longmans, Green, 1954.

Ong, Walter J. *Orality and Literacy: The Technologizing of the Word.* 1982. New York: Routledge, 1991.

Patton, John H. "Wisdom and Eloquence: The Alliance of Exegesis and Rhetoric in Augustine." *Central States Speech Journal* 28 (1977): 96–105.

Portalie, Eugene. *A Guide to the Thought of Saint Augustine.* Trans. Ralph J. Bastian. Chicago: H. Regnery, 1960.

Press, Gerald A. "*Doctrina* in Augustine's *De Doctrina Christiana.*" *Philosophy and Rhetoric* 17 (1984): 98–120.

―――. "The Subject and Structure of Augustine's *De Doctrina Christiana.*" *Augustinian Studies* 2 (1980): 99–124.
Reeves, John-Baptist. "St. Augustine and Humanism." In *Saint Augustine,* ed. M. C. D'arcy et al., 121–52. New York: Meridian, 1957.
Ricoeur, Paul. *Time and Narrative.* 3 vols. Trans. Kathleen McLaughlin and David Pellauer. Chicago: University of Chicago Press, 1984.
Riley, Floyd K. "St. Augustine, Public Speaker and Rhetorician." *The Quarterly Journal of Speech* 22 (1936): 572–78.
Riley, George F. *The Role of Marcus Tullius Cicero in the Educational Formation of Saint Augustine of Hippo.* Ann Arbor: UMI, 1980.
Rorty, Richard. *Objectivity, Relativism, and Truth.* New York: Cambridge University Press, 1991.
Sattler, William M. "Some Platonic Influences in the Rhetorical Works of Cicero." *The Quarterly Journal of Speech* 35 (1949): 164–69.
Schilb, John. "Composition and Poststructuralism: A Tale of Two Conferences." *College Composition and Communication* 40, no. 4 (1989): 422–43.
Scholes, Robert. *Protocols of Reading.* New Haven, Conn.: Yale University Press, 1989.
Scott, Jamie. "From Literal Self-Sacrifice to Literary Self-Sacrifice: Augustine's *Confesssions* and the Rhetoric of Testimony." In *Augustine: From Rhetor to Theologian,* ed. Joanne McWilliam, 31–50. Waterloo, Ontario: Wilfrid Laurier University Press, 1992.
Sebeok, Thomas A. *The Sign and Its Masters.* Lanham, Md.: University Press of America, 1989.
Shiel, James. *Greek Thought and the Rise of Christianity.* London: Longmans, 1968.
Sirridge, Mary. "Augustine: Every Word Is a Name." *New Scholasticism* 50 (1976): 183–92.
Sontag, Susan. *Against Interpretation and Other Essays.* New York: Farrar, Straus & Giroux, 1966.
Starnes, Colin. *Augustine's Conversion: A Guide to the Argument of Confessions I–IX.* Waterloo, Ontario: Wilfrid Laurier University Press, 1990.
―――. "Augustinian Biblical Exegesis and the Origins of Modern Science." In *Collectanea Augustiniana,* ed. Joseph C. Schnaubelt and Frederick Van Fleteren, 345–56. New York: Peter Lang, 1990.
Steinhauser, Kenneth B. "The Literary Unity of the *Confessions.*" In *Augustine: From Rhetor to Theologian,* ed. Joanne McWilliam, 15–30. Waterloo, Ontario: Wilfrid Laurier Press, 1992.
Sutherland, Christine Mason. "Love as Rhetorical Principle: The Relationship Between Content and Style in the Rhetoric of Saint Augustine." *Grace, Politics, and Desire: Essays on Augustine,* ed. Hugo A. Meynall, 139–56. Calgary: University of Calgary Press, 1990.
Testard, Maurice. *Saint Augustin et Ciceron.* Paris: Etudes augustiniiennes, 1958.
Todorov, Tzvetan. *Theories of the Symbol.* Trans. D. Swabey and J. Mullen. Ithaca: Cornell University Press, 1977.
Vance, Eugene. "Saint Augustine: Language as Temporality." In *Mimesis: From*

Mirror to Method, Augustine to Descartes, ed. John D. Lyons and Stephen G. Nichols, 20–35. Hanover, N.H.: University Press of New England, 1982.

Warfield, Benjamin Breckinridge. *Studies in Tertullian and Augustine.* 1930. Westport, Conn.: Greenwood, 1970.

Weedon, Chris. *Feminist Practice and Poststructuralist Theory.* New York: Basil Blackwell, 1987.

Weithoff, William E. "The Merits of *De Doctrina Christiana* 4.11.26." *Rhetoric Society Quarterly* 15 (1985): 116–18.

Welch, Kathleen E. *The Contemporary Reception of Classical Rhetoric: Appropriations of Ancient Discourse.* Hillsdale, N.J.: Lawrence Erlbaum Associates, 1990.

Index

academic tourism, 83
Academics, 70, 160, 172; failure of, 64–66
Alfaric, Prosper, 34
Alypius, 78
ambiguity, 115–16, 119, 122
Ambrose, 12, 25, 34, 52, 167; his eloquence, 30–31, 75–77, silent reading, 47–48, 105
Anthony, Saint, 70
argument, 79, 94
Aristotle, 15, 17, 18, 20, 24, 25, 51–52, 111
art, speech as work of, 14
ascent, 74, 76–77, 147–48, 151, 155, 174
audience, 56, 58, 81, 129–30, 137–38, 142–43
Augustine the Orator, 27
autobiography, 82, 94, 146–55, 162

Bailey, F. G., 110–12
Bakhtin, Mikhail, 8–9, 47
Baldwin, Charles Sears, 14
Barthes, Roland, 146, 149, 151–55, 159–60, 162–63, 165, 171–73
being, 73, 132, 146, 149, 178
belief, 116, 119, 134–36, 151, 155, 161, 167, 169, 172, 177; "precedes understanding," 42, 159–60
Belsey, Catherine, 153
bibliolatry, 110
biography, 151
body, 6, 22

Boissier, Gaston, 33
Bonner, Gerald, 65, 82
Bourke, Vernon J., 64, 83
Boyer, Charles, 34
Brown, Peter, 15, 22, 25, 34, 38, 40, 58, 61–62, 133, 167
Bubacz, Bruce Stephen, 88–89
Burke, Kenneth, 28, 146

c. iulian. op. imperf., 21
calling, 42, 46
Campenhausen, Hans von, 25, 76, 130, 146
canons of rhetoric, 14
caritas, 115–16, 122, 124
catechizing, 46
Cato the Younger, 16
certainty, 109; uncertainty, 136
Chadwick, Henry, 34
"chair of lies," 1, 4, 12
"chair of truth," 4–5
charitable: listener, 58; reader, 129
charity, 10, 86, 116, 122, 125, 131, 135, 145, 152, 161, 171, 176–78
Christ, 2–3, 5, 64–66, 70, 74–75, 69, 86, 102, 116, 133; embodiment of wisdom, 73; incarnate, 69, 73; mediator, 93, 95, 98; name of, 68, 71, 73
Christianity: Catholic, 46, 117; era of, 22; Europe, 32; history, 157; orthodoxy of, 67, 117, 129–33; Protestants, 117; rhetoric of, 26–28
church, 33, 46, 84, 109, 157; Fa-

thers, 23, 25, 94; spiritual and carnal, 133–34, 136–37, 139–40
Cicero, Marcus Tullius, 2, 4–5, 9, 11–35, 52, 63, 65, 70–71, 73, 78, 118, 172, 177; and Augustine, 18–23; on rhetoric and philosophy, 16–20, 26; his shortcomings, 75
City of God, 21–22
civil, 14; rhetoric, 15; Roman courts, 46
Civitas, 32
Clark, Mary T., 34
Clarke, M. L., 14
cognition, 89
coherence, 110–13
Colish, Marcia, 89
common consent, 107
commonsense, 110
community, 101, 119, 125–27, 129–30, 133, 148, 161, 166–69, 174–74, 177; interpretive, 122, 124, 159; of Israel, 132
confessional, 135, 147, 162; form, 82, 151; quest, 105
construct, 177; deconstruct, 117, 146, 177
contemplation, 5
content, 12, 38, 53, 71, 76, 80, 117, 122, 172
context, 8, 36, 38, 103, 105–7, 129, 165; contextualization, 166, 168; decontextualize, 37; oral, 47
Contra academicos III, 21, 65
Contra Julianum, 21
conversion, 5, 9, 13, 33, 61, 69, 71, 74, 103, 128, 130, 154; postconversion, 147, 149, preconversion, 147, 160
corporate, 77, 130
correspondence, 111–14
Courcelle, Pierre Paul, 34
Coward, Rosalind, 152
creation, 9, 83, 91, 95–96, 130–31, 136–39, 142, 145, 157, 175
criticism, 9, 23, 80, 87–88, 117, 155–56, 177; author's approach, 39; feminist, 163; literary, 1, 7,
169; postmodern, 117; space, 25; textual, 36–39, 66
cults, 130, 133
Cuthbert, 167

Darius, 50
De beata vita, 21
De civitate Dei, 21, 66
De Doctrina Christiana, 7, 21, 25–28, 32–33, 50, 77–78, 106–8, 109, 117–18, 134, 158–89, 177
De Genesi ad litteram liber imperfectus, 128
De Genesi contra Manichaeos, 128–29
De magistro, 7, 97, 106–7
De republica, 22
De trinitate, 21, 44
declamation, 14
Deely, John, 109, 118–19
deliberative, 4
delivery, 4, 14
Derrida, Jacques, 169
dialectic, 23, 177
dialogue, 80, 172, 176; of Cicero and Augustine, 22
Dialogues, 33
DiLorenzo, Raymond, 17
discourse, 104, 108–9; artistic, 112; lived social, 110; religious, 112–13
disembodiment, 3; disembodied, 6
Divination, 22
doctrina, use of term, 26
doctrine, 33, 157; of Man, 130–31, 133
dogma, 128, 155, 160

Eagleton, Terry, 169–70
eclectic philosophy, 16–17, 19, 20, 24, 34
Eco, Umberto, 105, 109
education: Augustine's with Cicero, 18–19; Dioscurus's school, 24; rhetorical training, 12, 24, 31, 97; Roman, 11, 13, 14, 16, 18, 73
Ellis, John, 152
eloquence, 12, 13, 17, 25, 27, 31,

52–53, 64, 72, 75–78, 92, 104, 115, 125; Greek, 30; neutrality of, 30
emotion, 62–63, 71
epistemology, 3, 9, 85, 88, 92, 108, 115–16, 118, 134, 137, 146, 151, 158
eternity, 3, 5, 9, 10, 93–95, 97–102, 169–70, 174
ethics, 29, 165–66
ethos, 139
Evodius of Uzalis, 50
exegesis, 128, 130, 148, 159
experience, lived, 110

Faigley, Lester, 150
faith, 2, 22, 27, 34, 40, 42, 75, 84, 103, 112, 134–36, 151, 155, 177
Fall, the, 138, 149–50, 173
Faustus, 52, 65–66
Ferrari, Leo C., 48
Fish, Stanley, 118, 122–23, 159–60, 164–65, 171
flesh, 15, 66, 69, 102–3, 115, 178
foreknowledge, 22
forensic, 4; invention, 26
form, 11, 38, 53, 68, 71, 76, 80, 83, 117, 120, 122, 126–27, 131, 142, 172; formlessness, 119–20, 127, 130–31
Fortin, Ernest L., 18
Foucault, Michel, 163–66
Freedom of the Will, The, 160
friendship, 80, 157
future, 99–101, 178

Galileo, 109
Garden in Milan, 5, 64, 69, 74, 75, 149, 168
Gilson, Etienne, 34
God: descent of, 174; distinct from Creation, 130–31; dwelling place of, 91; in flesh, 66, 69; gift of speaking given by, 29; image of, 130, 140, 173, 176; immaterial nature of, 22, 66; interpretive helper, 100; radical otherness of, 93, 130, 173

"Gold from the Egyptians," 25, 69, 76
Gospel, the, 98, 103, 115, 128
guilt, 135
Guitton, Jean, 60

Hagendahl, Harald, 11, 16, 20, 21, 23, 24, 69, 72
happiness, 26, 74, 81, 166; happy life, 28, 90
Harnack, Adolf, 20, 33, 162
Hartle, Ann, 35
Heidegger, Martin, 153, 169–70
Henry, Paul, 24, 137
heresies, 130, 133, 177
Hierius, 30–31, 52
historical, 36–37, 61, 129, 156–57, 159, 163, 175
hope, 134–36, 151, 177
Hortensius, 15, 18, 19–22, 24, 29, 32, 61, 63–66, 68, 70–74
human condition, 93, 109
humanism, 26, 163; humanist rhetoricians, 32
humility, 10, 68, 70

ideal orator, 16, 28, 64, 71–75; Cicero as, 21
ideal, Platonic, 89
idealism, 159, 162, 166
illumination, 89
illusions, 154
imagination, 120
Incarnation, 2–7, 10, 42, 69, 71–77, 102–5, 109, 114–16, 154, 174–78; in language, 113–15; as sign, 113; stabilizes, 137
incarnational rhetoric, 116, 145–75
inference, 106–7
integrity, 5, 74, 92, 102, 177
intelligence, 52, 63
intelligibles, 88–90, 93, 97, 103, 108, 136–37
intentionality, 123–24, 127, 157
interior, 31; truth, 97–98; "interior ear," 120–21, 124, 161
interpretation, 3, 85, 115–16, 117–144, 156–58, 162, 177; allegorical, 136; disagreement,

124; embedded, 156; figurative, 141–44; literal, 142–44; practice of, 9; purpose, 158–62; as rhetorical performance, 125, 145; of Scripture, 95, 117; textual, 26, 118, 158

Jay, Paul L., 146–52, 154, 169, 171
Jerome, 23
Johnson, W. R., 4, 26, 32–24, 56, 50, 83
Jordan, Mark D., 136, 159, 177
joy, 90, 135
judgment, 86–88, 140–41
justice, 11, 175, 178; Roman ideals of, 22

Kelly, Louis G., 106
Kennedy, George A., 14
Knapp, Steven, 159–60, 168–72
knowledge, 41, 68, 70, 92, 95, 108, 115, 119, 132, 136, 138, 169, 172; word of, 137, 139
Kristeva, Julia, 110–14, 167
Kristo, J. G., 178

Lacan, Jacques, 169
language, 88–90, 99–100, 108, 145, 152–55, 169; acquistion, 105–7; inclusive, 132; ordinary, 176; semiotic assumptions, 144; stabilization of, 115
law, 12–14
learning, 88–89
Lentricchia, Frank, 164
liberal arts, 31, 51, 72
libraii, 49
lies, 12, 78, 86; rhetoric of the lie, 13
linguistic turn, 153
literacy, 9
Literal Interpretation of Genesis, The, 160
logocentrism, 169–71
Logos, 2, 5–6, 75
love, 58, 87, 116, 118, 122, 125, 127, 176
"lure of the informational," 37–38, 99

Mailloux, Richard, 7
Mailloux, Steven, 155–62, 164–65, 170–71
Manetti, Giovanni, 106
Manichaeans, 2, 19, 57, 63, 70, 128–29, 131, 142, 157, 172; errors, 75; failure of, 64–66
Marius, 70
Markus, R. A., 92
Marrou, Henri, 25
matter, 71, 126–27, 142
McCabe, Joseph, 15, 57
McMahon, Robert, 42, 49, 53–54, 67
Meagher, Robert, 83
meaning, 107, 155, 157, 163, 168–89, 173–76; comes from God, 127; construction of, 38–39; mulitplicity of, 123–24, 128
medieval, 104; middle ages, 103
Meer, Frederik van der, 27, 44–45, 48, 50, 78
memory, 3, 9, 19, 31, 51, 85–93, 116, 145, 148, 151, 158–59, 175
Michaels, Walter Benn, 159–60, 168, 172
mimesis, 176
mind, 91–92, 101
Monica, 54, 57, 79, 147, 158, 168
morality, 11, 22, 83
Moses, 94–96, 121–22, 124–25, 127, 160–61
motive, 62–63, 142
Murphy, James J., 13, 16, 97, 116–17, 177
mysticism, 5, 26, 77

naming, 85, 89, 119
narrative, 79–80, 83, 94, 102, 105, 131, 136–39, 142, 145–47, 149, 151, 154, 157, 160; metanarrative, 95, 117
Nebridus, 155
negative, the, 119–20
Neoplatonism, 1, 3, 5–7, 19–20, 23, 25, 33–35, 39, 42, 66–69, 71, 75–76, 131, 146–47, 149–50,

170, 173; Christian, 38; the One, 147, 152
notarii, 48–50, 54

Oates, Whitney J., 27, 34
O'Connell, Robert J., 6, 34, 75, 146
O'Donnell, James J., 35, 60, 71
O'Meara, John J., 18, 34, 67, 71
"On the Beautiful and the Fitting," 113
Ong, Walter, 9, 52
oral: analogy, 126; culture, 52, 126; discourse, 98; interpretation, 49; thought, 52
orality: 9, 157; and literacy, 47–48
oratio, 103
ordinary language, 115
ornamentation, 4; ornament, 14; ornatus, 17
other, the, 165, 168

participation, 60–61, 83
past, 99–101, 178
Patricius, 57
"pear-stealing episode," 56, 161–62
persuasion, 136, 160
philosophy: Augustine's pursuit of, 16, 64; Greek, 2, 15, 20, 25, 76; not equal to wisdom, 71; private, 15; Western, 32
Plato, 20, 32, 34, 37, 111; "Christian Plato," 171; recollection, 88
Platonism, 2, 17, 25, 32, 35, 53–54, 63, 70, 74–75, 105, 131, 155, 161, 170, 172, 177; anti-Platonism, 147, failure of, 66–69; sign theory of, 106
Plotinus, 171
poetry: Plato's view, 22
Ponticianus, 70
Portalie, Eugene, 128
postmodernism, 9, 117, 144–78, 169; orthodoxy, 169
power, 40, 178
praise, 40–43, 83
praxis, 23
prayer, 36, 58, 62, 103

preaching, 4, 5, 24, 28, 42, 46, 50, 70, 75–76, 78, 94, 137, 139–40
present, 58, 83, 99–101, 152, 178
pride, 12, 40–41, 65, 68, 70, 125, 127, 135
"process stories," 79
prudence, 17
psychology, 83, 90, 101, 151
public, 5, 15, 46, 118–19, 143–44; prayer, 36, 62

Quintilian, 4, 14

ratio, 103
reading, 51, 82
realism, 159, 162, 166
reason, 27, 34, 62, 71, 86–87, 103, 104, 160, 172
redemption, 133
referent, 105–6
relativism, 9, 162, 164, 166–67, 172, 174–75
religion, 15, 68, 93, 118
res, 136
resting heart, 42
restlessness, 41–42
resurrection, 22, 113–14, 171
Retractiones, 50
revelation, 22, 27, 34
rhetoric: art of, 12, 37; Augustine chair of, 13; condemnation of, 11, 13, 16, 32; interpretive, 176–78; of the lie, 16; and philosophy, dichotomization, 15, 34; and philosophy, integration, 16–17, 24, 65; redeemed, 177; Roman, 4, 9, 23; synthesis of wisdom and eloquence, 26; as way of being, 144
Ricoeur, Paul, 93–94, 100, 147, 151, 170, 174
Riley, George F., 13, 17, 23
Rome, lost morality of, 22
Rorty, Richard, 160, 164–65, 170–71
Ryan, John K., 42, 72

Sabbath, eternal, 143

Said, Edward, 160, 165
Sattler, William M., 17
Saussure, 106, 152–54, 163
Scholes, Robert, 165–66, 168–70
Scott, Jamie, 55
Scripture: authority of, 59, 134–36, 138, 160; enemies of, 121; epistemological role, 136; firmament of, 134, 145; inspired by God, 124; as rhetoric, 119
Second Sophistic, 3–5, 9, 13, 17, 24, 27–28, 30, 32–33, 72, 78, 115, 172, 177
self, 133, 148–51, 154, 165–66, 168, 171, 173, 178; authentic, 152, 170; Cartesian, 150, 170; decentered, 150, 152, 162, 167, 172; discursive construction of, 146; unstable, 108
self-control, 10, 92, 139–40; deceit, 147–48; indulgence, 162
semiotic, 4–5, 7, 9, 83, 85, 105–16, 120, 122, 134, 136–37, 142–44, 152–54, 158, 160–63, 165, 167–68, 170–73, 176
senses, 86–91
sensibility, 93, 96, 103, 134, 136–37
servus Dei, 44–46, 49–51, 59, 129, 133, 143
Shiel, James, 15
sign theory, 105–9, 110, 116
signification, 86, 89, 113, 116, 141–42, 163, 170
signifier, death of, 113
signum, 136
silence, 97
Simplicianus, 69–70, 75
sin, 40–41, 56–57, 68, 82, 96, 115, 149; "original sin," 115, 150; threefold character of, 92
Skepticism 2, 15, 17, 63, 75, 131, 133, 135–36, 172, 176
society, 85, 89, 107–8, 154, 177; social practices, 156–57
Solignac, A., 34
Soloiloques, 21
speech, 47, 89–90, 94, 96–97, 100, 175

Spirit, 131–32, 137
stability, 122, 137, 146, 154, 175, 178
Starnes, Colin, 7, 35–39, 43, 53, 59, 61, 66, 69, 72, 84, 102, 178
Stoic, 17, 105; sign theory of, 106
structuralism, 8, 153; poststructuralism, 163, 166, 169
style, 4, 14, 28, 71, 127, 172
subjectivity, 9, 146–55, 163–65, 167–68, 171, 173–74; crisis, 150, intersubjectivity, 156, 167, multiple subjectivity, 149
substance, 4, 11, 26, 28, 31, 68, 71, 75, 78, 83, 103, 120, 127, 154, 172
supernaturalism, 84
systematic philosophy, 27

teaching, 70, 78, 79, 106–7, 157
temporality, 5, 9–10, 97, 102, 116, 160
temptation, 92
Teresa of Avila, St., 60
Teselle, 75
text, 8, 28, 38, 119, 126, 155, 174; primary, 35; subtext, 174; textual studies, 155; textuality, 154, 165
theology, 1, 4, 6, 22, 25–26, 33–34, 83, 170; abstract, 133, ontotheology, 170–71; speculative, 129
thought, 62, 89–90
time, 3, 5, 9, 10, 85, 93–95, 98–99, 101–105, 115–16, 145, 168, 174–75
Todorov, Tzvetan, 109, 118–19
transcendence, 6, 147–48, 150, 170, 173, 175–76; transcendentalism, 153–54, 172
Trinity, 75, 130–33, 140, 147
truth, 9, 11, 15, 59, 69, 74, 88, 90, 95–98, 102, 109–16, 119–25, 127, 160–61, 167, 169, 171, 174–78; Christian, 25; eternal, 146; intelligible, 90; listener's responsibility, 86–87; truthlessness, 166

Valerius, 50, 129

Valery, Paul, 146, 149, 151
Vance, Eugene, 106
vanity, 12
Victorinus, 70
virtue, 52, 64

Warfield, B. B., 20, 84, 162
Warner, R., 72
wasteland, 148
Weedon, Chris, 163, 165, 169
Welch, Kathleen E., 37, 51, 105
will, 70, 73, 84, 86, 89–90, 92–93, 108, 115, 119, 132, 142, 149
wisdom, 5, 9–10, 15–17, 25–29, 31, 40, 53, 61, 64–66, 70–71, 76, 84–86, 92, 105, 110, 117, 119, 133, 138, 141–43, 151, 169, 171–78; of Cicero, 22; Cicero's definition of, 71, 73; eternal, 75, goal of happy life/*beata vita*, 24; in *Hortensius*, 30; of Jesus, 69; object of rhetoric and philosophy, 27; pursuit or quest for, 67, 74, 81, 83, 93, 95, 104, 109, 116, 118, 144; temporal, 103; word of, 137, 139
word and deed, 81, 86, 103, 113–14, 137, 141, 176